Keep Walking

Keep Walking

ONE MAN'S JOURNEY

TO FEED THE WORLD

ONE CHILD AT A TIME

LARRY JONES

DOUBLEDAY

NEW YORK LONDON TORONTO SYDNEY AUCKLAND

PUBLISHED BY DOUBLEDAY

Copyright © 2007 by Feed The Children
All Rights Reserved

Published in the United States by Doubleday, an imprint
of The Doubleday Broadway Publishing Group, a division of
Random House, Inc., New York.
www.doubleday.com

DOUBLEDAY and the portrayal of an anchor with a dolphin are
registered trademarks of Random House, Inc.

Feed The Children is a registered trademark of Feed The Children.

LIBRARY OF CONGRESS CATALOGING-IN-PUBLICATION DATA
Jones, Larry.
    Keep walking / Larry Jones. — 1st ed.
        p. cm.
    1. Jones, Larry. 2. Feed The Children (Organization) 3. Church
work with children. I. Title.
    BV2616.J66 2007
    363.8'83092—dc22
    [B]
                                                    2007023380

ISBN-13: 978-0-385-52136-9

PRINTED IN THE UNITED STATES OF AMERICA

10 9 8 7 6 5 4 3 2 1

FIRST EDITION

Dedicated to the hungry children
who have no idea if they will be fed tomorrow.

Larry Jones has a heart as big as the world. While others have debated and felt that little or nothing could be done to reduce poverty and hunger among vulnerable children, Larry just went out and did it! He is a man of action. Larry has more creativity and resourcefulness than any *Fortune* business innovator, more stamina than any pro athlete, and more guts than any fighter I've ever met.

Larry Jones is a mountain mover. He doesn't know how to quit, because his motivation is *pure love*—for Jesus, and for everyone else, especially children. Love keeps Larry going in spite of the enormity of the task. With more than 140 million orphaned children in our world today, Larry is passionate about an "endangered species" that most of the world ignores—children starving unnecessarily due to our apathy.

You've probably seen a Feed The Children television special as you've clicked past channels, looking for entertainment. Do not make the mistake of clicking past this book. It is in your hands for a reason.

In the grand scheme of things, Larry's legacy of saving countless lives will matter far more for eternity than any accomplishment you'll read about in the entertainment, sports, or financial pages. This man has made his life count, and I pray his story will motivate you to do the same. I am proud to call him my friend.

Dr. Rick Warren
The Purpose-Driven® Life
Global P.E.A.C.E. Coalition

Acknowledgments

This is essentially a story about a ministry that would not have unfolded, and could not be sustained, without the tireless efforts of my loving wife, Frances Jones.

Additionally, I thank my son and daughter, Allen and Larri Sue Jones, for participating in and praying for this outreach. Each was reared in Feed The Children, an organization in which they're now pivotal.

My exaggerated work ethic is invaluable when the hour is late, the distance far and fatigue pronounced. Since childhood, I've been conditioned to perform with stress, be it physical, mental, or emotional. I thank my late parents, Floyd and Lera Jones, for that.

My life story was given published birth and sculpted shape by Bill Barry and Andrew Corbin, ranking editors at Doubleday, and by B. G. Dilworth, the esteemed literary agent who paired me with them.

Rex Carney, my executive assistant, saw no job as too small, no hour as too late when it came to helping assemble this tome.

Don Richardson, former overseas administrator for FTC, forwent the publishing of his life story to provide information for mine.

Tony Sellars had been my public relations spokesperson for only a year when he dove into the dissemination of any information sought for this work.

Steve Whetstone's memory is beyond reproach, and he applied it generously to these pages.

Jana Brusa-Nette was a utility infielder, helping to gather information while attending to executive duties inside FTC's administrative offices.

All of the above, and others too numerous to mention, are official associates and unofficial co-laborers in an outreach that remains at the ready for natural disasters or hostile aggression. All the while, it supplements the feeding of more than 1.5 million people a day. The figure will be increased by the time this book is published.

The aforementioned men and women, along with my staff, employees, and intermediaries around the world, do integral parts to put food on tables and hope into hearts where there otherwise would be none.

May you be blessed by what you read. May you follow your heart as to how you'll respond.

Chapter One

*E*XACTLY 211 PEOPLE worked in the Oklahoma City headquarters of Feed The Children on January 20, 2006, when most attended a weekly chapel service to hear my story about someone they'd never met. Many, in fact, didn't know her name.

Essentially, I just repeated the words I'd spoken thirteen days earlier when I preached the funeral of Lera Maybell Jones.

She was my mom.

Close friends, including some at Feed The Children, wondered why Mom had asked me to undertake the painful act of delivering her eulogy.

"Isn't that asking too much of Larry?" was the recurring query. "How could she ask her own flesh and blood to *speak* about her?"

But it wasn't asking too much. I didn't think so—not for the person who had shaped my formative years more profoundly than any other. And mine weren't the last words ever spoken about her. I, along with many others, will talk about Mom's exemplary life for as long as God gives me breath.

Psychologists say that 90 percent of a human's personality is formed by age seven. Think about that. Ninety percent of the decisions that people make for the rest of their lives are based on behaviors they've learned by the time they enter second grade. Mom must have known this, and she worked the good right into me as a pup.

She wanted me to be "good for goodness' sake," as the Christmas song goes, believing that God had given my childhood to her and she'd better do right by Him.

"Train a child in the way he should go, and when he is old he will not turn from it" (Proverbs 22:6). That scripture was Mom's words to live by, and if I'm any proof, that principle holds true.

When I was attending elementary school and throwing two paper routes, neither Mom nor I had any idea I'd enter the ministry. The thought may never have crossed her mind until I brought it up when I was eleven. After that, she probably prayed more than I know that someday I would become a preacher.

Mom and my dad, Floyd, were barbers who charged sixty-five cents for a basic haircut during the 1950s. I did my share with my paper routes, and I earned twenty-four cents for every dozen soda pop bottles I found and returned to the grocery store.

Mom and Dad were tithers—they gave 6.5 cents (10 percent) of every haircut to the church. I followed their example, paying 2.4 cents, rounded off to three pennies, for each dozen returned and refillable bottles. I also paid 10 percent of my paper route earnings. The tithe was honored as much in my household as each of the Ten Commandments.

It may sound corny, but the word "wholesome" only begins to describe my boyhood. Our family was as innocent as an *Andy Griffith* rerun, and Bowling Green, Kentucky, was our Mayberry.

My small childhood home is situated within six hundred miles of three-fourths of the population of the United States, but we were as country as it gets.

Bowling Green is one of the nation's few places where, in the time of my boyhood, a child could get lost on concrete or inside piney woods in less time than it takes to warm a car on a frosty morning, and no one had to worry about it.

We came to Bowling Green when I was eight, leaving Indianapolis because my dad wanted to return to Kentucky, where he'd once lived in Allen County. My mom consented to go—on the condition that we live in town.

My parents owned separate barbershops. Each had gone to barber school. Mom did advanced-styling study. Her teacher was "Hollywood Joe" of New York City. She was Bowling Green's first lady barber, and possibly its first barber ever to use a blow-dryer. Today, almost anyone who works with hair is called a stylist. But a woman who opened her own "styling shop" in 1949? In rural Kentucky? Mom was a pioneer!

Mom cut men's and women's hair when most of the former were accustomed to a once-over with electric clippers. My dad knew how to give only one kind of haircut—the kind that started with a buzz and ended with all of your hair on the floor. And he gave it to every customer that came in the door.

People regularly stopped by the shop to shoot the breeze and exchange town gossip, even when they didn't need a haircut. My parents came to be the people in whom much of the town seemed to confide. I've never been a drinking man, but I'm told that people who drink frequently tell just about anything to their favorite bartender. In Bowling Green you told the barber. Mom and Dad never ceased to be amazed at the personal things people told them about themselves while sitting in the shop.

Barbershops in those days also offered shoe shines, and my parents' shine man was a likable fellow who was sometimes drunk on the job. He used to say that God always appointed someone to take care of fools, drunks, and babies. My mom scolded his philosophy, but willingly played into his hand by taking care of him. Besides signing his paychecks, she frequently did his laundry and fed him homemade meals.

The day after I played my first basketball game for Oklahoma City University, Mom and Dad were reciting a play-by-play of my performance for neighbors, who wondered how they knew so much about my game, played perhaps seven hundred miles away. There were no e-mails or fax machines in those days, and the regular-season game wasn't covered by Kentucky television.

I'd eventually learn that my parents heard all of my games in Oklahoma as they nestled in Bowling Green. How?

They drove to the highest hill outside of Bowling Green, parked, and absorbed the static-filled contest over an AM car receiver.

During one of those vigils, my parents encountered a police officer who later became a friend. He had mistakenly thought he'd spotted a teenage boy and girl locked in love's embrace inside their parked and darkened car. By moonlight, he sneaked to their vehicle, where he intended to startle them and then issue a citation for public display of affection. As the cop approached the car, Mom scared him. She noisily cranked down a window.

"We're not 'parking'!" she told the officer. "We're listening to our boy play basketball in Oklahoma City!"

He recognized my name from my high school days.

He asked Mom if the Larry Jones discussed on the radio was really me. She said it was and asked the lawman if he'd like to get into the car to listen to the game. Then she asked if he'd like some popcorn.

The cop joined my folks inside their car to follow the faraway contest. When the game ended, he said good-bye and so did Mom and Dad. But the evening wasn't over. It seems the car battery had been drained of power while the suspected lovebirds and their unexpected chaperone had been cheering. The officer then left my parents alone on that remote hill, promising to return with jumper cables. And he did. Mom and Dad, parked outside the city limits, had persuaded a city policeman to run their personal errand and revive their illegally parked car.

Having connected the cables to receive "juice" from the squad car, the cop asked Dad to turn the ignition. The car still wouldn't start. Drained by the radio and the cold weather, the battery wouldn't hold a charge. The hour was getting late, the November temperature was falling.

The car had a manual transmission. Perhaps the engine could be started by "popping the clutch"—pushing the car while the driver depressed the clutch, then releasing it when the vehicle gained momentum. Behind the driver's wheel, Dad did just that as Mom and the policeman pushed the car to a downhill grade. Success! The engine fired. The car went forward under its own power while Mom and the cop stood in its wake, cheering victory in the isolated wilderness. Years later, Mom said she and the cop had yelled as loudly for this victory as they had earlier for me and the game.

When Mom was sixty-seven and I'd been gone from Bowling Green for more than a quarter century, her penchant for economizing was thriving. I still chuckle at the following example.

The city was experiencing one of its intermittent periods of growth and construction. One building had been torn down after a fire, and Mom had a mind to use some of the bricks that would otherwise be discarded. Now, she didn't want to buy the bricks, and she didn't want to pay laborers to haul them. So this delicate, aging woman went to the sheriff, whose jail she regularly graced to hold Sunday night meetings for prisoners. Everyone at the jailhouse—sheriff, jailer, even the inmates—affectionately called her Lera. Can you say that your mom was on a first-name basis with bank robbers, extortionists, burglars, vagrants, gamblers, hot-check artists, flim-flam men, public drunks, and chicken thieves? My mom got Christmas cards from every sort. Our mail carrier claimed ours was the only house in town receiving scores of cards sharing the same return address: County Jail.

"Sheriff," Mom began her request, "these prisoners aren't doing you or themselves any good by lying around this jailhouse. I know a way they could improve themselves and the community."

Presenting her case, she persuaded the sheriff to release his inmates—including repeat offenders—to her custody. Then my mom (weighing all of a hundred pounds) led these men, by herself, to the messy lot where the bricks lay strewn. She instructed the inmates to pick up the bricks, clean them with chisels—and not run away. Then she took off their handcuffs.

Not one man fled.

Can you imagine? A bunch of criminals obeying the command of an old woman, "uniformed" in a flower print dress, instructing them to chip cement from piles of fallen bricks? Passersby did double takes at these motley wards of the county, overseen by a "warden" wearing an apron.

Those men respected and honored my mom because they sensed her love for them. She was a bright spot in their lives. They looked forward to her shuffling into the jail every Sunday night, singing the Lord's praises and preaching His Gospel. My mom ministered to a congregation separated from her by vertical bars—bars that kept the bodies of inmates inside but couldn't keep out her spirit.

IF NORMAN ROCKWELL had made movies, he would have filmed in Bowling Green.

I can imagine his lens focusing on fearful faces of schoolchildren perched before a darkened steel tunnel that served as an exterior fire escape. Weekly fire drills had us plunging down the tunnel while sitting on gunnysacks. Burlap pressed against slick metal gave a rapid ride.

For me, the pass through the tubular contraption was thrilling. It began in darkness and ended with a bolt into blinding sunlight. Nevertheless, it was all some of the kids could do to muster enough courage to climb inside the claustrophobic pipe.

When I watch present-day television, with its surplus of sex and violence, I'm reminded of Thursday nights during summers, when townsfolk gathered on grass to watch celluloid classics. Dr Pepper Bottling Company sponsored this community viewing of black-and-white films directed by Frank Capra or Cecil B. DeMille. Their endings were always predictable but never boring. Good always triumphed over evil. The old, brittle filmstrips broke frequently. But the crowd—mostly work-weary parents holding sleepy youngsters—waited patiently while a projectionist fumbled by flashlight to re-thread the reel. To my wide, expectant eyes, heroes never failed. A larger-than-life John Wayne or Randolph Scott overwhelmed the flimsy screen that quivered in the breeze. The aroma of popcorn mingled with the fragrance of newly cut grass. The smell of alcohol or smoldering marijuana, taken for granted at many of today's community functions, was unimaginable in 1940s Bowling Green.

There were folks in Bowling Green whom I didn't know. But there were no strangers. People weren't wary of each other back then.

I was a senior in high school and still eating regularly at Mrs. Spivey's. She owned a boardinghouse where she fed anyone as many staples as he or she could eat, plus pie, for sixty cents. She had two tables surrounded by sixteen chairs that were never vacant during the noon and evening meals. Diners had to eat in a rush. Hungry folks stood in line behind their chairs, waiting to take their places when they finished. The chain of diners seemed endless—workingmen and homemakers eating side by side, passing the "vittles" family style.

Everyone in 1940s and 1950s Bowling Green seemed like family. It's just that not all were related.

Probably no song has expressed the American spirit of that era more meaningfully than Tom T. Hall's "Engineers Don't Wave from the Trains Anymore." Its lyrics describe the friendliness that America's blue-collar folks expected from the men who ran the railroads in that time.

Air travel was still a luxury, something portrayed on television commercials as velvet excursions among the clouds that were available only to the rich. For the common people, though, glistening rails tied the familiar to the unknown—a conduit to a brightly imagined new world.

My favorite train was the Hummingbird, the passenger service that rumbled through town without stopping at 7:00 p.m. daily. A fluttering hummingbird was painted on the caboose. In wintertime, when darkness fell early, I could see the passengers inside the cozy, lit cars.

I was hypnotized by trains that rolled past the railroad gates. The horizontal restraints, with their stripes, blinking lights, and clanging bell, prevented motorists from crossing the path of thundering steel that shook the ground.

My young buddies and I enjoyed putting pennies on the track. After the train passed, they were flat enough to cut, hot enough to burn. One cent's worth of smashed copper made for a priceless treasure to little boys whose dreams went even further than a passing locomotive could take them.

The boxcars that stopped at the Bowling Green crossing were sometimes open. Sliding doors leaked sunlight into their mysterious darkness. To a nine-year-old, their ebony interiors held the secrets of everywhere they'd been.

And they held hoboes.

Many a fearful lad sneaked forward on tiptoes to peek at the sleeping, grizzled wanderers inside their makeshift mobile homes. More recently I've read of youths being arrested for dousing sleeping vagrants with gasoline and then setting them on fire. How times have changed. My buddies and I pitied the destitution but admired the tenacity of these grimy men, filled with wanderlust, whose freedom took them wherever rails could roll.

Another vivid memory: Bowling Green's chewing-tobacco-processing plants, where workers took cured leaves and twisted them by hand into braided rolls from which customers would eventually cut plugs with pocketknives. The laborers handled tobacco stalks with the precision of surgeons. We pressed our noses against the plant's windows in astonishment, marveling at what workers could do with what nature had grown.

I was personally so awestruck that at age fifteen I underwent a Bowling Green rite of passage. I chewed my first tobacco and did it the way I was told a man would. I swallowed my plug.

I don't remember ingesting the bitter leaves as clearly as I remember throwing up—for hours, it seemed. Had I told Mom about that incident, she would have imposed a punishment intended to deter future chewing. This would have been unnecessary, of course. Just the thought makes me ill ever since.

In addition to my errant recreational experiments, I also honed my entrepreneurial skills in Bowling Green. Beverage bottling was a big local industry. The bottling plants discarded heaps of slightly damaged bottles with barely visible flaws.

So my buddies and I raided a stockpile of rejects behind a bottling company one day. We loaded twenty-four into an old-fashioned wooden case, and then took our bounty to a grocer, who dutifully paid us two cents a bottle—forty-eight cents. I thought I had hit upon a scheme that was pure profit. I'd make a career, I thought, out of selling bottlers their own bottles. Talk about a low-overhead business!

It worked.

This career, however, was short-lived. My mom's morality went beyond biblical admonitions to avoid evil. She insisted that I avoid the appearance of evil as well. Thus, she put an end to my intended recycling empire. I don't remember if she made me return the money. If she did, it was probably after making me tithe on the ill-gotten gains.

Besides work and Christianity, sports played an important role in my childhood. I was consumed with baseball and basketball. As a teenager, I attended Oklahoma City University on a full athletic scholarship. But higher education was not among my foremost thoughts. My mind was purely in the games.

I played basketball year-round. When winter came and the weather got cold, my buddies and I broke into what was then the second-largest high school gymnasium in the state. Knowing that the doors would be locked on weekends, I simply unlocked a window on Friday nights.

My cronies and I would enter through the window most Saturday and Sunday afternoons and play basketball for hours. And then there were other weekends when I was the only one on the gym floor inside the cavernous hall that seated fifty-five hundred.

Mom knew where I was. What she didn't know was how I got in there. And she certainly would have deflated my basketball if she'd known that the law would call my method "breaking and entering."

The echo of my solitary dribbling inside the hollow room sounded as big as my sports ambitions. My dreams of someday playing on that court in a real game rose higher than the dome ceiling. So I continued, running and shooting solo, a one-man team against an imaginary squad that I always beat.

I did that for years and never once got caught. Not even by Mom.

ON JANUARY 3, 1996, I took Feed The Children's television crew to a remote part of Kentucky, far removed from the shadow of modern Bowling Green's office towers and chain hotels. The shade in this place came instead from towering oaks that concealed a dilapidated cabin to which no road led. The interior was more run-down than the decaying boxcars of my youth. It lacked plumbing, central heat, carpet, wallpaper, paint, running water, and the minimal dignities that separate man from the animals.

The house, when I first saw it, was no more than a pasteboard lean-to surrounded by rusting junk. A malnourished woman, a man of broken spirit, and three sickly children had lived inside the hovel. The outside air reeked of urine and feces.

On the day we came with the camera, children with teeth rotting from nutritional deficiencies played in a rusty, discarded washing machine. Dead insects floated in the water well. Flies swarmed around the children, who, on one day when I visited, had not eaten a bite—and probably wouldn't for the rest of the day.

The five-member family earned less than ten thousand dollars a year. There was frequently too much month remaining at the end of the money. In other words, they could underwrite their bleak existence for only three weeks of each month. They often went without food for the final week. On the day of my initial visit, the five possessed three potatoes. That was all the food they had until a check arrived in seven days.

I had to keep reminding myself that I wasn't in a foreign country. I was in my home state, rich in my sentimental memories and opportunity for all—or so I had always thought.

Twelve million children are hungry at any given time in America's suburbs, inner cities, and countryside. I know. I've seen them. I've bathed them. I've medicated them. I've clothed them. I've seen their eyes close in death while looking into my own. That doesn't happen when I do what I love to do most.

I feed them.

Having seen what I have seen, I'm always amazed at the number of Americans who think hunger is impossible in our land of plenty. America does have an abundance of food. I don't stump to raise more. I campaign to distribute what we have. Feed The Children is about getting food out of silos, grocery stores, and warehouses and into empty stomachs.

By the year 2010 I hope to be putting food into three million hungry mouths each day throughout the United States and around the globe.

I won't rest until I do.

The Bible advises us to pray without ceasing. My staff and I endeavor to pray—and work—without ceasing.

Why shouldn't we? Hunger never takes a holiday. Not even in

Kentucky, where engineers who ride the rails through the Appalachian countryside have long since stopped joyfully waving from the trains.

If they've seen what I've seen, I can understand why.

I DIDN'T REVEAL all of this the day I shared my recollections of Mom at her funeral. Instead, I said Mom had a different kind of hunger, a twofold nagging hunger for answers that only God could provide.

Until she died, Mom yearned to know why God let my brother, Mike, die at thirty-nine and why God didn't let Dad and her die together.

I told those at the service that I also have unanswered questions. I didn't disclose my secret queries there. But I'll share one here.

I used to wonder why the Lord selected me, a working-class kid of modest means from America's heartland, to interact with foreign governments, negotiate war zones, wade through the aftermath of hurricanes, speak before Congress, dodge bullets in war-torn countries, and more—all in the interest of feeding starving children.

But many years ago, after a series of humbling events, the nature of my question changed. I stopped asking God why I'm the one who *has* to do it. My overriding question for Him today is simply this: "Why, blessed Lord, am I *privileged* to do it?"

Until I learn the answer in heaven, I'll continue feeding on earth.

Chapter Two

A TRAIN MOVING SIXTY-FIVE MILES PER HOUR travels eighty-eight feet per second, and the rails beneath it make a pronounced clacking as cars career over connecting tracks. The steady pulse is like a metronome, affectionately called the "rhythm of the rails." My life moved forward with the beat of that rhythm for the first time in September 1958, when I rode the L&N Railroad from Bowling Green to Memphis, and the Rock Island Lines from Memphis to Oklahoma City. I was seventeen and leaving home.

That sound echoes in my reminiscence even today, almost half a century after the cadence was first mixed with the memories I left behind but never abandoned.

Recollections of childhood are often no more than impressions colored by emotion. Memories of adolescence often serve as moral instruction. During that train ride into the future, I took inventory of my teenage years. Time had already begun to convert my experience into lessons I would use.

"The closer I get to my home, Lord, the more I wanna be there," wrote Willie Nelson. For me, it was the opposite. The farther I got from home, the more I wanted to go back. My homesick crisis passed gradually, though, with travel across three states, during which I dined on boxed chicken salted with tears.

I STILL FOCUS ON GOD'S TIMELESS TEACHINGS that I was privileged to receive in my youth. I returned to their meanings as recently as the fall of 2005, when Feed The Children became the third-largest private charity in the United States (as determined by the previous year's contributions, which exceeded $800,500,000 in cash and gifts-in-kind). The staff and I treated more hungry and deprived people than ever in the ministry's twenty-six-year history. There was a downside, though: the figurative target on my back was bigger in the sights of my critics. As we thanked God for blessing our efforts, outsiders were firing verbal potshots at our deeds, many publicly.

Criticism is inherent to one who becomes a public figure through the solicitation of charitable funds. It's particularly pronounced for those who raise funds through the mass media. In 2005, our televised presentations were seen on all three commercial network affiliates, as well as seventeen cable channels.

I look like the guy next door because I am. I live in a regular neighborhood and drive a Ford. My salary is half of what others earn overseeing smaller, national charitable outreaches. The scope of Feed The Children is international, serving five continents.

When I'm asked how I withstand criticism, I respond that God gives me grace, that I pray for my enemies, and that I simply keep walking—with great and constant determination. I also draw instruction and comfort from situations in my past that prepared me for those in my present. Those precedents were often dire. Some were outright funny. God has a sense of humor. If you think He doesn't, look at the person sitting next to you. Better yet, look at my critics.

I was fifteen when first held up to public ridicule. (Actually, I held myself up to it.) Teenagers have a penchant for cutting up for the entertainment of their friends. I was no exception.

My friends and I had been taken by our American Legion baseball coach to my first major-league game in Cincinnati. We watched the Philadelphia Phillies play the Cincinnati Redlegs. I was an avid baseball fan who kept waiting for the drama! The action! The big play that I thought was a part of every major-league game.

I listened to NBC's *Game of the Week* on the radio every Saturday, when the play-by-play was given by the former St. Louis Cardinal great Dizzy Dean. I was under the impression that major-league games offered nonstop excitement—at least that's the way it sounded through the passionate voices of these legendary commentators.

But major-league play, during my first excursion to a big-time ballpark, paled in comparison to the broadcast version of the weekly games. At the top of the ninth inning, the score was three to two. No grand slams—not even so much as a home run. No tie-breaking runs had been thrown out at the plate. No player had staged a furious battle with an umpire. Fans remained nonchalantly slumped in their seats. The highly anticipated seventh-inning stretch was . . . a yawner.

I decided to change that.

I had long admired the Redlegs right fielder, Wally Post, so I resolved to get his autograph—while the game was in play.

I challenged my cronies to join me in leaping from the grandstands onto the grass, then sprinting across the foul line into right field. There were plenty of takers.

Or so they said.

My feet hit the dirt between the dugout and the right field fence. I was accompanied by my teammate Jackie Webb. Other guys perched for the leap—but didn't take it. So there we were: just Webb and I destined for right field, for the autograph of Wally Post—and for what I'd someday call my fifteen minutes of fame.

Or so I thought. Webb failed to run with me. He was stopped by fear—or better sense. I was stopped by sirens.

A crowd that had been bored suddenly roared to life. Cops who'd been passively looking at the ground were instantly encircling me. I'd never known anyone to stand simply because of my entrance. Here there were several thousand cheering and applauding—and booing—a solitary youth from Kentucky. For me it was sensory overload. I later wondered how the radio announcers described me.

Thus, I got everything mass attention could afford: both cheers and boos—but not Wally Post's autograph. I don't know if he signed after the game. I was ousted from the stadium.

I was sure my mom wouldn't hear about the hoopla back in Bowling Green. But I was wrong. She got the news before I got home, and I was grounded.

In 1955 nothing was harsher punishment for a teenage boy than being grounded—not getting to go anywhere except to school or work. It meant no hanging out with buddies whose admiration I'd sought. It meant no tuning in to broadcast baseball—not even when Wally Post was playing.

Being grounded also meant seeing no one socially except Mom and Dad, the two people I least wanted to see, as Mom continually reminded me of the reason for my confinement.

She'd remind me of what she'd always said: that I'm accountable for my own actions. My mischievous run to right field had been about pleasing my pals and myself. I hadn't thought about the ticket holders who were waiting to see the boring pitchers' duel broken, those on schedules who needed to return to work or home. In a crowd that large, there had to be thousands who were inconvenienced by my selfish stunt. My antic had caused no "official" harm—no injuries or arrests. But I'd taken away people's time for my own amusement.

I vowed never to do that again, and in fact my cheap thrill birthed a priceless personal axiom that I live by to this day: I count time and the consideration of others' needs among my primary concerns on earth. Always consider other people's time before you waste your own.

REMINISCING ABOUT THIS brings to mind another of my most formative lessons. It had come three years earlier when I was a patrol boy, an honorary position reserved for trustworthy and academically sound students, who ushered youngsters safely across busy intersections. What's more, patrol boys were occasionally dismissed from school to run errands for a teacher. (To me, this was the most significant award that could be bestowed on a sixth grader.)

F. W. Woolworth was America's largest chain of retail dime stores during the 1950s. It was a child's idea of heaven: it sold toys. But I was too old for such childish stuff. My desires turned to other Woolworth items more befitting someone as mature and responsible as a patrol boy. I had my eye on a pen.

Ballpoints were fast becoming adults' writing instruments of choice. The older boys carried pens in their shirt pockets. I reasoned that I, a man in my mind, should have one, too. I could have bought one for ten cents, just as I'd responsibly bought other things with my earnings. But a guy a grade shy of junior high school shouldn't buy a pen, I reasoned further. He should be man enough to steal one. With this erroneous thinking, I fell prey to Satan's oldest weapon—making something attractive to lure one into a sin that prompts another sin: postponed repentance.

Thus, at age twelve, I stole for the one and only time in my life. By age twenty, I still had not repented and carried God's conviction for eight years for having broken one of His Ten Commandments. The thrill of theft was heightened because Woolworth's was situated directly next door to guess where? My parents' barbershops! If I'd been caught, the store manager would have told my mom. But not getting caught meant I could escape her watchful eye and non-stop authority, just for a moment. What a thrill in my immature mind.

That thrill became my lament. Each time I saw my parents, even during visits from college, I had to walk through a cloud of guilt past the place where I'd committed an illegal act. According to the law of man, my petty theft was a misdemeanor. But according to God's law, it was a sin.

Sin, not the disposable pen, was the source of my conscious guilt, my spiritual conviction. I'd been taught to take God's law at face value. I therefore couldn't show myself in the store I'd violated. After I'd long since confessed my little larceny to God, I'd still done nothing to make amends with Woolworth's.

Finally I made my peace. I anonymously sent a dollar bill to that store (one within Woolworth's multimillion-dollar conglomerate). The currency was accompanied by a letter saying, "This is a debt I owe."

Did I sign my name? No. God knew the identity of the transgressor and I was no longer that person. When I, as a man, made restitution for something I'd done as a child, I experienced the full reward of repentance.

If I transgress against someone today, it's through my ignorance, not an agenda. I get letters from people saying that they approached me in an airport and that I ignored them. I answer those letters, apologize, and pray to be more considerate. This may seem like a small thing in the eyes of men—like my theft of a ten-cent pen. But I don't live to be evaluated by the eyes of men.

I believe God meant for man to obey His law to the letter and that He issued the Ten Commandments not as man's boss but as his protector. If I'm splitting hairs or adhering to legalism, so be it. So did Jesus.

In Matthew 19:18–19, Christ addresses a man asking how he can inherit eternal life. Jesus answers that to enter heaven he must obey God's commandments. When the inquirer asks which ones, Christ itemizes them. "Do not steal," Jesus says, right after He says, "Do not murder, do not commit adultery." Jesus doesn't say, "Do not steal, unless you're young and adventurous," or "Do not steal unless the theft is small." He clearly means that one should not steal, not anything, not even if you're a child.

In the thirteenth verse of the same chapter, the disciples think it trite to instill obedience in children. They rebuke adults who have brought youngsters to Christ for Him to share God's laws with.

Jesus then chastises the disciples for trying to interfere with his shaping of impressionable young minds.

"Let the little children come to me, and do not hinder them, for the kingdom of heaven belongs to such as these," Christ says.

Had I not stolen the pen, I would have been protected from years of heartache stemming from my childish act. My parents and the store proprietor might have forgotten, but I never could. But because of my repentance, God gave me an exercise in how He forgives and forgets. Where Satan had used sin against me, God had used His forgiveness to overrule the evil one and to bolster me.

Christians should constantly ask themselves, "Who am I?"

The question pertains to who we are when compared with whom God would have us be. We should ask ourselves this: Am I someone who hides my sins, knowing that God doesn't care if man thinks they're big or small? Or am I someone who believes that all have sinned and fall short of the glory of God?

I'm someone who wants all God has for me, at any age, at any time. I thank God for loving me enough to shower me with a strong conviction that passing years couldn't erase—and for His grace in offering me restitution through repentance.

I've heard it said that Abraham Lincoln once walked several miles to return to someone an ill-gotten penny. Some might say that such faithfulness to one's moral and spiritual beliefs is extreme. But I expect that those people have never felt the unspeakable joy, the peace that passes understanding, from acting in voluntary obedience to God's law. I have.

That's how my theft of a ten-cent pen eventually translated into another life lesson that has provided measureless rewards.

MY PARENTS TAUGHT ME that God is protective. This was proven in my experience with all the injuries inherent to active youth. For instance, I suffered a groin injury while simultaneously riding a bicycle and throwing newspapers. The wound enlisted prayer from my grandmother, and sutures from my doctor. That afternoon my paper route nonetheless went forward. Another time, I was hit in the head with a baseball bat, which called for stitches (that I didn't get). Instead, I went on to play nine innings. The blood that otherwise might have flowed freely did not, because I tucked torn skin under my cap. But more important, my parents kept me under a blanket of protective prayer, ensuring my welfare in spite of my boyish passion for sports, fast bicycles, and thrill-seeking adventure.

By the time I was seventeen, I was throwing three paper routes daily—one in the morning, two in the afternoon. In between, I mowed yards. My work ethic was etched even more deeply during my junior high and high school years. My paper routes had become too expansive to handle on a bicycle, so I got a Cushman motor scooter. I threw folded newsprint at twenty miles per hour. My accuracy was such that I could fire the parcels onto a porch adorned with empty milk bottles and surrounded with delicate flowers without hitting either. Occasionally, I did miss my mark, destroying one of the fragile obstructions. I'm glad that none of my customers were chicken farmers. A few might have eaten more poultry than they intended. My rarely errant hurl of one-pound newspapers could have decapitated a laying hen.

I once was speeding with my bag of papers along one of Bowling Green's first highway bypasses, four lanes of concrete surrounding the city. The speedometer on my Cushman showed twenty-five miles per hour. Given the tiny size of the scooter (much smaller than a twenty-six-inch bicycle), I felt like I was flying.

Earlier I'd lost the gasoline cap, which had sat on a tank immediately above the engine. I'd improvised a fix with an aluminum can that fit exactly into the fuel container's opening. Thus, I succeeded in preventing leakage that could have dripped on the engine below, igniting a fire.

Suddenly I heard friends calling to me from a Dairy Queen beside the highway. For a moment I took my eyes off the road. A moment was too long. Virtually at full speed, my 150-pound machine and I collided with two tons of stationary steel—a stalled car. The motor scooter slid instantly underneath the massive, unforgiving bulk of the automobile. There was no room between the car, the pavement, and the motor scooter for anything—especially a passenger of flesh and blood.

During the 1950s a prominent, retired pastor accidentally drove a bulldozer over a cliff in Moline, Illinois. Having lived to tell about it, he wrote a pamphlet titled *God Rode My Bulldozer*. A former parishioner in his congregation asked me if I thought God had been riding with me on my Cushman.

I'm sure He was. But more important, at the fateful moment, He took me airborne into the sky.

The motor scooter twisted on impact and contorted beneath the car. I went flying—sailing above and beyond the immovable automobile. I believe I was miraculously thrown free from the scooter.

I came back to earth, skidding seat first on concrete. The seat of my blue jeans was shredded, leaving my exposed buttocks unprotected against the friction. I was a bloody mess. Semiconscious, I began stumbling across an adjacent field where my buddies ran to me, yelling, "Are you all right?"

"I'm fine, I'm fine," I muttered.

In fact, I was treated at and released from a hospital. I suffered no serious physical injuries. However, I wasn't "fine." I kept imagining and reimagining what *could* have happened.

If I hadn't been thrown clear, no doubt my leg would have been lost to cement and cast metal. Best-case scenario, I would have been an amputee. Worst case, I might have bled to death, as the right leg includes one of the body's largest arteries.

I saw all of this in blessed hindsight. Thank God I lived to look back.

FROM AGE ELEVEN UNTIL SEVENTEEN, I had one predominant factor shaping my life.

At eleven, I acknowledged the "call" from God for me to preach the Gospel of Jesus Christ, as defined in the King James Bible's Matthew 28:19–20. "Go ye therefore, and teach all nations, baptizing them in the name of the Father, and of the Son, and of the Holy Ghost: Teaching them to observe all things whatsoever I have commanded you: and, lo, I am with you always, even unto the end of the world."

Most biblical scholars refer to this edict as the Great Commission. At the end of childhood, I felt the urge to act on that commandment. My call from God had come during a service at a summer camp sponsored by the Methodist Church. A minister invited those of us who wanted to become ministers to walk forward. I approached an altar, a gesture of commitment to life as a clergyman. Camp sponsors asked that I sign a paper pledging to spend my adult life as a preacher—which I did.

The next morning I went to my camp counselor and asked him to remove my name from the affidavit.

My mom heard that I had executed the "contract with God," and she was elated. She never knew until years later that I withdrew my signed proclamation twelve hours after making it.

I did, however, retain my *inclinations*, if not my signed commitment.

From the day I deleted my name until I was seventeen, I lived with a sense of pressing guilt for having reneged on my signatory vow to God. I felt my shame compounded by my mom's continual boasts about how her son had responded to the call of God, about how I was destined to become a full-time preacher.

I still read my Bible, prayed, and talked the talk. I wasn't really walking the walk, however. I continued to let Mom live with my deceit.

At seventeen, I regularly entered another public building secretly—just as earlier I'd sneaked into the school gymnasium. By dark of night, I quietly eased through the door of the Episcopal church at Twelfth and State streets in Bowling Green (which, unlike the school gym, was never locked).

Most always I was alone inside the small church, enjoying no company other than the presence of God. Assuming my position behind a pulpit situated above empty pews, I preached to anyone who'd listen—the occasional cricket, God, and me.

The Reverend Billy Graham has often recalled learning to preach on a tree stump surrounded by ducks. At least he had feedback—quacking.

My early forays behind the podium were accompanied by sheets of notes intended to prompt full-blown sermons. Alas, my topics were exhausted in two or three minutes, when I ran out of words. Nevertheless, I kept on talking—introducing topic after topic intended for future sermons.

Soon, in this one practice behind the pulpit, I found that I'd unintentionally sermonized a full four-week revival.

And so night after night, I preached within the invisible presence of the One whose spirit had sent me. Over time, I learned to collect my thoughts, and my words finally began to flow. Some ministers call this free association of thoughts an anointing of the Holy Spirit. It was then, and continues to be, an intensely warm and safe sensation like no other. Words eventually came faster than I could express them. Though insecure and still inexperienced, I let them flow.

I couldn't wait to hear what I'd say next.

WITH MY SENIOR YEAR OF HIGH SCHOOL under way, our first conference basketball game was scheduled in one week. I was hustling through a practice game when I darted for a fast break. I got the ball as I approached the lane and sprinted for a layup. As I leaped toward the basket, the stocky hulk guarding me bolted beneath me like a fire hydrant in motion. We tangled and I fell, catching all of my weight on my left hand. The bones in my hand crunched like a sack of glass.

Soon I was wearing a cast from my hand to my bicep and being sent to a hospital room for overnight observation. At 3:30 on the morning after the injury, I awakened in a hospital bed, still wearing my basketball uniform, feeling helpless, vulnerable, and alone.

Lying there, I worried about missing the rest of the basketball season of my senior year, the time when I'd likely be scouted for a college athletic scholarship. I also flashed on the appointment I'd scheduled the following week with an air force recruiter. I was supposed to take a physical examination—the final step before qualifying for a full scholarship to the United States Air Force Academy. The military schooling was to include my graduating as a commissioned officer. All this had been arranged by the U.S. congressman William Natcher of Kentucky. (My dad had cut his hair for years, and he'd been a family friend.) I was also being actively recruited by Oklahoma City University, which offered the opportunity to play for a nationally ranked team. I had the wonderful problem of deciding whether I'd enter the air force and retire in twenty years for a second career or seek a sports scholarship to earn a civilian bachelor's degree and enter seminary.

But both of these marvelous opportunities seemed out of reach as I lay in my hospital bed in the middle of the night. I felt so alone, I wondered if even God had forgotten me.

There I was, ready at the launchpad of my future, my mission on hold indefinitely. Both a prestigious military academy and a well-regarded private university were eager for my skills with a basketball. But now I couldn't even hold one.

I finally got back to sleep, but awoke in the morning still troubled by my situation. My thoughts went to the paper routes I was unable to throw and the morning basketball practice I'd miss for a team whose scoring I'd once led. I felt hopeless and desperate to make these thoughts in my head go away.

I knew what I had to do.

Almost falling, I slid out of bed and dropped to my knees. I vividly remember what I said next. "God, I've had this life for seventeen years, and basically I've done what I've wanted to do," I prayed fervently, my voice breaking with emotion. "I give my life to You, and I'll do anything You want me to do. Anything."

Peace flooded my heart before I could say "Amen." My disappointing injury became God's instrument for delivering my personal serenity. Instantly I knew that God had *not* abandoned me.

THE AIR FORCE AGREED to postpone my physical exam until my hand had healed. The exam was to be little more than a formality. I was to play basketball and baseball and run track for the academy while studying to become an officer. After that I might become a pilot.

But the air force never happened.

Abe Lemons, at Oklahoma City University, was then one of the nation's leading basketball coaches. He'd never seen me play but nonetheless came to Bowling Green to meet me, knowing I was on the injury list. Though I sat on the bench with my arm in a cast, my reputation was alive and well in college gymnasiums throughout the nation.

Lemons offered me a full scholarship to Oklahoma City University—then a premier basketball powerhouse—without seeing me play a second of regulation basketball. His offer included full tuition at the private college and a stipend for expenses. Best of all, I'd graduate with all of the academic requirements necessary to attend seminary. My parents had leaned toward the military scholarship, but I made my own decision, and made it abruptly. I went for Lemons's deal.

I resolved to leave Bowling Green for Oklahoma City and eventually preach the Gospel to anyone who'd listen. I felt I was walking toward God's plan for my life. My arm would heal with time, and be as good as new. Little did I know that other trials awaiting me would be far more dramatic than the formative challenges of my youth, and I would once again wonder whether I had chosen the right path or if God had abandoned me.

Chapter Three

I RODE THE TRAIN from Bowling Green for twenty-seven hours before it eased into the Oklahoma City station at 10:00 p.m. on a Sunday in September 1958. Although I was in an unfamiliar city, I knew exactly where I wanted to go.

Back to Bowling Green.

I wondered if I'd done the right thing in leaving home. I was just seventeen. Leaving home was the biggest life-altering decision I'd ever made up to that time.

My exit from Bowling Green had been attended by a warm mix of family, friends, and well-wishers. My arrival in Oklahoma City was the opposite: a welcoming party of one. At least he was a tall one—standing one inch shy of seven feet. "This is great," I thought. "I left my loved ones for the Jolly Green Giant."

Bill Johnston, recruited to play center on the Oklahoma City basketball team, was a full foot taller than I. He turned out to be friendly enough, but his big smiling face was no solace for the homesickness and doubt I had in my heavy heart.

On my first night at Oklahoma City University, I put my sheets on the bed, told Johnston good night, and buried my face in my pillow to silence my sobs if I accidentally cried.

The next day Abe Lemons watched as we did a half-court unsupervised practice. I stepped onto the court and felt right at home. I didn't need a home-cooked meal to cure my heavy heart. All I needed was a basketball. My longing for home vanished the instant the ball touched my hands, and I knew then and there that this is where I wanted to be.

Lemons oversaw grueling practice sessions during which I felt the pressure of playing basketball at the collegiate level for the first time. He was tough as nails and demanded more discipline than a drill sergeant.

"One day of practice is like one day of clean living," Lemons liked to say. "It doesn't do you any good." Our practice was constant, ongoing, and more rigorous than I could ever have imagined.

Lemons demonstrated the utmost dedication in every area of his life, even if it cost him. For instance, when he was offered a position at another school, he would not forsake his commitment to OCU.

"They wanted to buy out my contract," he told the press. "But I couldn't make change for a twenty-dollar bill."

Howard Cosell, one of the most prominent broadcasters of the day, once criticized Lemons on ABC.

"You may be big in New York," Lemons responded. "But you're nobody in Walters, Oklahoma."

Lemons didn't *let* players learn the game; he *made* them.

My high school coach, Denzal Barriger, had strongly sold my talent to Lemons, who *still* hadn't seen me play a game. I'd been drafted on the strength of a secondary school's recommendation as well as my scoring statistics. Those achievements, however, seemed as long ago and far away as Bowling Green.

Barriger had also told Lemons that I was a devoted Christian who'd initiated team prayer in high school. He'd said that I'd been the official captain of the Bowling Green team—and its unofficial coach. Barriger had emphasized, exaggeratedly or not, that I'd taught him more than he'd taught me about basketball. He said I was a master of the set shot. Years later, when three points were awarded to successful shots made from outside the circle, Barriger told a reporter that I'd have scored fifty points a game had that rule existed during my high school days.

That kind of praise is gratifying. But it also intensified the pressure on me to perform extraordinarily on the court and off.

I became OCU's first starting guard to play inside the sprawling, new Fredrickson Fieldhouse. Although I measured five feet eleven inches during my freshman year, my job was to contain players standing well over six feet. And I succeeded, playing most games with a one-on-one defense and a fast-break offense.

The pressure applied to Lemons's scholarship players was relentless. Year-to-year grant players could see their grant revoked if they didn't perform to expectations. Those on a four-year ride had no assurance of playing if they didn't perform well, as Lemons would put them on the sidelines. Then sportswriters would have a field day, publishing stories about benchwarmers not rising to athletic expectations and wasting scholarship money.

College athletes often experience the same academic pressure as other students. They don't, however, have as much time to devote to their studies. Perhaps that's why college sports figures often resort to mischievous pranks to vent the pressure. It happens to the best of us—I should know, because it happened to me.

I had bought a Volkswagen Karmann Ghia during a trip back to Bowling Green and drove it to Oklahoma City. My sleek new car became the buzz of the athletic dormitory. Boys being boys, the other players wanted to keep my ego in line and decided to give me a reality check by stealing my new car.

Forlorn, I searched all over the campus with some of my teammates, who, of course, were in on the joke but pretended to be helping me. No luck, no car.

Distraught and out of ideas about where to look, I went to the sports arena to shoot baskets. But I couldn't play. No one could. My car was parked inside the arena. It blocked the entrance to the basketball court.

Lemons decided that the ringleader of this escapade had been Harry Vines. It wasn't the first time Vines had been in trouble. He'd been cited repeatedly for removing the plastic cover from his mattress. (The administration mandated plastic covers to protect mattresses against bed-wetting. No kidding.) Vines resented the implication that he might be a bed wetter (though he wasn't). So each night he tossed the plastic into a wad on the floor. Though repeatedly punished for this and other minor offenses, Vines figured his value to the team was greater than the sum of his demerits.

Lemons decided Vines needed a role model. Can you guess whom he selected? Knowing that I was taking preparatory courses for seminary, Lemons thought I was a shoo-in for model behavior that might influence Vines to abandon his nonconformity. I was assigned to be Vines's roommate.

I'm not sure I effected as much change in Vines as he did in me. Together, we were questioned about a certain streetlight escapade.

It had to be Vines's fault that I shot out some streetlights, so the dean of men reasoned. If he hadn't been so rowdy, I wouldn't have tried to one-up him. But Vines offered a curious defense.

"Sure, I dared him to throw rocks at the lights, but it isn't my fault that he did," he said. "I didn't know he threw so well."

So the dean questioned me about my alleged misbehavior. At the end of the interrogation, he left—only to discover that his car wouldn't start. He raised the hood to check the battery.

Someone had stolen it.

I was falsely accused of organizing this caper as a ploy to divert attention from the other.

Vines eventually admitted to orchestrating the battery heist. His confession, however, was of no help to me. It came thirty-five years later—and the dean had long since died.

The wrongful belief that I had stolen the dean's battery could have resulted in limiting my basketball play. This would have damaged my athletic career tremendously and tainted my prospects as a student for the ministry.

I knew I had nothing to do with it, and I was pretty sure who did. I bided my time for the right moment, and it came one night when Vines went out for a cocktail. I didn't drink alcohol, but his stumbling return to our room told me he was tipsy. So did the slur in his speech.

"Larry, are you awake?" he whispered. "Say something if you're asleep."

Before long, he was in his bed snoring, and I knew what I was going to do. I got out of bed and placed a rubber replica of vomit on the floor beside his bed, ringing the disgusting pile with water for added realism. Vines awakened the next morning feeling sick. But he became genuinely ill when he caught sight of my bedside arrangement. I enjoyed a private snicker as I heard him heaving in the bathroom.

Unfortunately, things didn't end there. This episode only intensified the war of pranks between Vines and me. I had become an example for Vines all right, but not quite as Coach Lemons had planned. Instead of having a good influence on Vines, I was an exemplary practitioner of practical jokes, a partner in crime instead of a model of good behavior.

Even when I was acting responsibly, Vines would find a way to turn my behavior into a joke. He had occasionally voiced mild complaints about my nightly Bible reading by flashlight. I did my best to control the beam of the light, trying not to disturb him. When I prayed, I made every effort to keep my voice low—again, trying not to disturb him. I guess I disturbed him anyway. He said my constant drone sounded like a chant—and asked if I'd converted from Christianity to Buddhism.

One night I was so absorbed in study and prayer that I didn't notice Vines's slipping out of his bed and attaching a mysterious paper object to the wall.

I remained totally oblivious as he eased back onto his pillow, making sounds to get my attention.

I called to him. He didn't answer. I put down my Bible and let my flashlight slowly scan the room.

The beam fell first on Vines, who appeared to be sleeping. Then it continued to sweep along . . . only to reveal a naked girl.

Puzzled—and a bit panicked—I leaped from the bed to flip on the overhead light. Sure enough, there on the wall I beheld a sprawling poster of a woman—looking down on my bed and my Bible—wearing nothing but a smile. I found the situation definitely detrimental to my worship.

"You did this!" I yelled at Vines.

"Dean, I told Larry not to put that up there," Vines kept chanting, as if that's how he would explain the situation.

"I told Larry not to put that up there! With all his crazy antics I can't get any sleep!"

"You did this!" again I accused.

"Aw, Larry, you know God answers prayers," Vines responded impishly. "I was just trying to answer your prayer for a girlfriend."

With that, Vines took down the very, very dangerous picture.

I had had enough, and I told him so. After that evening, he and I declared a truce: we'd never again pull pranks on each other. We'd pull them on others—together!

The Greek community on campus became one of our targets.

A fraternity house was hosting a dance to celebrate the pinning of new members. Vines remarked that the frat boys looked like penguins in their tuxedos. He figured they'd look even more the part if they were all wet.

So Vines and I carried a load of large water balloons to the roof of a women's dormitory. Each time a frat boy came to fetch his date, a mysterious watery bomb would fall from the sky, crashing to the sidewalk and splattering him amply.

It was really funny for a while—until the Oklahoma weather pulled one of its instantaneous changes, with a cold front blowing in. The temperature was dropping probably twenty degrees an hour. Vines and I had undertaken our escapade in Bermuda shorts. We soon had chill bumps bigger than our water balloons.

We decided to call it a night—but not before someone had decided to search the roof! Vines realized that we couldn't return to the ground via the stairs we'd used to get up. Searchers were banging on the roof door—which, thank goodness, he'd locked. We waited there, freezing on the roof, for the would-be lynch mob to give up and leave for the dance.

Bare-legged and nearly frozen, we eventually sneaked from the roof by way of an alternate stairwell. From there, we walked stiffly on Popsicle legs to our room—while the fraternity crowd went dancing in wet trousers.

From that point on we began backing off on our pranks.

Our fun-loving antics at OCU had been child's play in light of the lawless, headline-grabbing aggression that eventually infected campuses from coast to coast. Student walkouts became cliché at major institutions, as well as the lead story on television network news. Our foolish behavior was just boys being boys—clones of Dennis the Menace—whose only threat was to ourselves and to our academic careers. The worst punishment we could imagine was being benched for a game or two. Students around the country were going to jail for their beliefs, and that put things into perspective for Vines and me, but it wasn't until many years later that I would understand the effect that our friendship had on both of us.

In 1995, Harry Vines watched the television coverage of Feed The Children's relief efforts after the Oklahoma City bombing of the Alfred P. Murrah Federal Building. The ministry received thousands of grateful letters—including a personal one from Harry Vines to me.

He started with a mock homage to my parents, reminding me of one important point of advice they had given me—and that I had shared with him: "Jerry's Hair Tonic has an alternate use as aftershave lotion." He went on to remind me that I had refused to share my bottle of the stuff while we were roommates. Then he informed me of his own discovery: that the tonic also made for a fine mouthwash. He urged me to try it.

Good old Harry—nothing, it seemed, had changed with him.

Then his letter suddenly turned serious.

He said I'd helped him grow into a responsible man and went on to relate what I already knew, that he'd become an Oklahoma high school basketball coach after graduating from college. He'd coached a winning team for four years, and then eventually took his skills to the public school system in his native Arkansas. Still enjoying his winning streak, he was approached by a man in a wheelchair. The guy wanted Vines to coach him and other disabled men, to win at wheelchair basketball. This was in 1978.

Vines had never been in a wheelchair. He thought he couldn't coach these men—coaching requires close empathy with the players. Nevertheless, he felt compelled to try. If not with their wheelchair-bound circumstance, he could certainly empathize with their determination.

His letter detailed his efforts, and he asked if we could discuss the potential involvement of Feed The Children. I stopped by to visit him the following July on my annual summer drive from Bowling Green through Arkansas to Oklahoma City.

From our conversation I quickly saw how Vines's quest could be of tremendous service to the physically limited. I sent one of our television crews to videotape his athletes. The resulting footage stressed that these chair-bound players had to absorb their own equipment costs. In those days a wheelchair with the mobility needed for basketball was a specialized device costing thousands of dollars.

Soon, viewers of our national telecast began to send donations earmarked for the players—and for Vines, a volunteer coach who worked tirelessly to adapt the play patterns shown to him and me by Coach Lemons all those years ago.

The play patterns worked. Vines's players, in time, were scoring as many as seventy-one points a game while dribbling and shooting from wheelchairs. His team, the Rolling Razorbacks, regularly rolled to victory and into the hearts of our donors. Eventually they won three national championships in competition consisting of more than two hundred teams.

Vines's sharing of his fond recollections, as well as the joy of his success as a coach, reminded me of the importance of maintaining relationships.

"A man should keep his friendships in constant repair," wrote Samuel Johnson, the author of an early English dictionary.

Vines and I had maintained our brotherhood through thick and thin, through laughter and anger, through practical jokes and their consequences. Two guys saw one friendship sustain them through the hapless days of youth and their transition to adulthood.

Both of us, not to mention countless wheelchair athletes, became better men for it.

Chapter Four

I RETURNED TO BOWLING GREEN IN 1961 to recruit Bobby Joe Parrish, the first black basketball player on Oklahoma City University's team. The Civil Rights Act that made racial segregation illegal was three years away when he and I traveled by car back to campus, stopping for hamburgers along the way and receiving heaping helpings of racial mistreatment instead.

Having grown up with blacks, I didn't think about racial differences. So I was embarrassed by a "Whites Only" sign affixed to the window of a roadside café where my friend and I pulled in to eat. I'd seen nothing like that in Bowling Green, one of Kentucky's largest cities. We both knew it was serious; we were also hungry. I went in for the food and carried it back to the car. Thereafter we ate and slept in the car or at rest stops to avoid unnecessary attention from less open-minded types. We talked about our hopes and dreams, about pressing on with our individual quests for a college degree that we believed would open the door to the entire world. We were naive about the struggles we would encounter passing through it; otherwise, we may never have set out in the directions we were headed.

～

AS A SOPHOMORE, I had become friends with Sue Hackler, a popular pianist and standout personality on campus. Our friendship brought my first experience with the heartbreak of personal loss.

Sue was killed in a car accident as she and her boyfriend were returning from an outing at Roman Nose State Park in Watonga, Oklahoma. A car failed to yield, and Sue was thrown from the vehicle.

Her head was pinned between the rear tire and the curb. She died instantly.

The tragedy shocked the entire campus and, for me, gave rise to a torturing question: How could God allow such a thing to happen to such an extraordinary person? I came up with no answer then. I still don't have one now.

Today, when tragedy strikes suddenly, I tell survivors to try to accept that some things are simply beyond our understanding.

"Trust in the Lord with all your heart and lean NOT on your own understanding; in all your ways acknowledge Him, and He will make your paths straight" (Proverbs 3:5–6).

We won't know the answer to everything in this life until we transcend to eternity. To know it all now would be the opposite of faith, which is the lifeblood of Christianity. I look forward to seeing Sue in heaven, and to asking God why He permitted her to leave this earth so early, as she provided such joy for so many.

I visited Frances Hackler, Sue's sister, the evening of Sue's death and did my prayerful best to console her. The next morning Sue's body was taken to Mountain Home, Arkansas, her hometown. I occasionally saw Frances after that, usually in the company of other students.

Frances was a sophomore when she was named OCU homecoming queen. Coach Lemons asked Harry Vines, my mischievous roommate, to crown the queen during pageant ceremonies. Vines didn't want to do it. He was afraid it might make his girlfriend jealous since he had dated Frances before her.

Then Coach Lemons turned to me. I had no way of knowing what monumental change my crowning Frances would bring. The school got its homecoming queen. I got the love of my life.

This was all in the unforeseeable future as I handed Frances a dozen roses and kissed her for the first time before the hundreds who attended the coronation.

The following night Frances was the guest of honor at a banquet and asked me to escort her. I accepted—guess you could say Frances asked *me* out on our first date!

Afterward, we had eyes, minds, and hearts only for each other.

Most of our time we spent together at church—or as I played and Frances watched my basketball games. Otherwise we went out to eat at inexpensive mom-and-pop cafés. Those were fun-filled times packed with all the romantic magic that goes with falling in love.

Except for this one evening when romance gave way to suspense.

Frances and I were returning to campus when we saw two boys, who appeared to be teenagers, entering a women's dormitory.

Something about the way they handled themselves told me they had a gun.

I leaped from my car, charging to the building's second floor. I sensed that an armed robbery was imminent. I didn't think about the consequences of their having a gun, only that these thugs might hurt an unsuspecting girl. I apprehended them. Frances called the police, who responded quickly. The cops took the boys into separate rooms, telling each that the other had tattled on him. At first each claimed innocence—and that the other was guilty. Ultimately, though, the delinquents fearfully confessed to carrying the gun that I had sensed they were carrying.

A close examination revealed that it was a starter pistol—one of the harmless guns used in track-and-field meets. The would-be robbers were eventually released. Frances, meanwhile, regarded me as her hero. The drama could not have played out better for me if I'd planned it.

About a year later, on December 4, 1961, I took Frances to a prayer chapel that was always open at Crown Heights Christian Church. On my knees, I asked her to marry me. She said yes before I could stand up. I'm sure my proposal did not come as a complete surprise. A week earlier, during Thanksgiving recess, I had accompanied Frances on a trip home to Arkansas, where I formally asked her dad for her hand.

I graduated from OCU and its basketball program in 1962. Frances had one year of study remaining. I had a spouse, a degree, and no job. Lemons and other coaches said they'd help me find work and in time procured an offer from Oklahoma Natural Gas Company. I was told I'd earn sixty dollars a week to read gas meters and avoid dog bites. I declined, instead accepting a sales position at

Rothschild's clothing store at the Penn Square shopping center. I made forty-five dollars a week in salary, drew a sales commission, and was never asked to face a dog, except for a few demanding customers who snarled a bit.

Frances and I underwent the noble marital apprenticeship of very frugal living. We were no strangers to that. In college we'd lived in a one-room apartment. Our landlady lived upstairs. It was an inconvenient arrangement. In order to get to her quarters, she had to walk through ours. Sometimes she knocked; sometimes she didn't. In either case, she always felt free to barge right through. People today talk about their privacy rights. Back then, we had no such discussions.

My life plan still included pursuing the ministry. So I enrolled in Phillips Seminary in Enid, Oklahoma, a ninety-mile drive north from Oklahoma City, and started preaching revival meetings. I'd say they were successful, as determined by the many who accepted Jesus Christ as their personal savior. One venue in McCloud, Oklahoma, was supposed to last for three days. It went an additional four to accommodate an ever-growing turnout.

I traveled during the summer of 1962 with Venture for Victory, a group of Christians who excelled in college basketball. We played seventy games throughout Hawaii, Japan, Taiwan, Hong Kong, and the Philippines, giving our Christian testimony during halftime.

I returned to Oklahoma City, where Frances entered her senior year of college. I worked at Rothschild's during the day and preached at area churches at night.

Around this time, I joined a group of former OCU and Oklahoma State University basketball players who played pickup games against the Harlem Globetrotters and the Harlem Magicians, talented squads that combined comedy with outstanding basketball. In these games my job was to restrain Marques Haynes, a show-off guard for the Magicians who dribbled behind his back—and mine, too. Many fans thought the Globetrotters and the Magicians carried an opposing team that only pretended to be competitive. Not so, at least not on the nights we played them.

We may have been younger and faster than the Globetrotters,

but they bested us with their skills. For instance, I was trying to guard George "Meadowlark" Lemon, with the Globetrotters, when he sank the ball from half-court with a hook shot. Luck? I don't think so. He did it twice in the same game.

And the best defense I could play against Marques Haynes held him to thirty-eight points. I had played NCAA Division I in college but was no match for the Globetrotters and the Magicians. They were wizards at basketball. While their comedic antics provided crowd-pleasing entertainment, they were masters of hard and fast full-court basketball.

Gradually we became familiar with the Magicians' style of play and lost one game by just one point. That's as close as we ever came to a win, no matter how hard we tried.

All the while, my preaching career continued to develop. While my desire was to become an evangelist, not a pastor, I was nonetheless given my own church, a Methodist congregation in Oklahoma City.

Frances and I took that first church in November 1962. The church had gone through nine pastors in ten years, so it was hardly a plum assignment. Most of the ministers who served there said, in hindsight, that this church had provided great training for the full range of problems a pastor is ever likely to face. I can vouch for that.

The first problem Frances and I encountered was during our relocation from our modest but tidy place into the shabby parsonage. While we were moving, Frances was driving ahead of me—speeding. I was afraid she'd get upset if I fell too far behind, so I accelerated to keep up.

Guess who got a speeding ticket!?

The church was only two blocks from the parsonage. As time passed, I found myself wishing it were on another continent—or perhaps another planet—given the ruckus some parishioners raised.

The parsonage had two bedrooms and no furniture, except for a living room chair and a dining table with four chairs. We moved in the day before Thanksgiving, when Frances's parents came for a visit. Good thing there was only two of them, else we might have been eating on the floor.

For a time the church had pretty much been run by an unofficial board of directors—three women who made administrative decisions that no one contradicted. That was our next problem.

I suggested that the church borrow money to buy furniture for the parsonage. The church would own it, the pastor would use it.

The three "directors" were against it. Instead, they suggested that Frances and I save Green Stamps and redeem them for furniture. The stamps were issued in those days at the rate of one stamp for every two cents spent at stores.

"Do you have any idea how long that would take?" I asked incredulously. My thoughts went to the marking of the new millennium, thirty-eight years away.

One member of the threesome mentioned an old couch that sat collapsing in the church office and suggested that Frances and I move it to the parsonage. It seated three people. One armrest was rickety, the other missing. But most people didn't notice that—the huge ink stain covering one of the cushions typically captured their attention instead.

One of the women said the couch had looked that way when it was purchased. I wondered what the buyer might have fed his Seeing Eye dog.

I suggested to the woman that she take the couch and let me take hers for the parsonage. After I said this, I realized I was out of line and apologized for my tone. They must have appreciated my change in demeanor. The church obtained a loan to purchase furniture for the parsonage.

The church building had no running water. The nearest faucet was inside the Sunday school building (which was actually an old army barracks). If a mother needed a drink for her child, she had to take the youngster from the church house to the barracks. To complicate matters further, the door was kept locked. To get the key, one had to approach the three domineering women—none of whom would respond to key requests during worship.

To provide reasonable access to the water, I suggested that they give me a copy of the key. But this was not to be. It seems I couldn't be trusted with the key. They didn't want me dirtying up the place.

I've got to tell you, though, given the poor condition of that building, a muddy footprint might have become its most appealing feature.

On my first Sunday as pastor, I discovered a church bill from the United Methodist Publishing House that was a year overdue. I believed the nonpayment of any debt was wrong. And this instance of a Methodist congregation failing to pay a Methodist bill was especially wrong.

I called for the offering that Sunday and collected ninety-nine dollars. Then, to everyone's surprise, I asked for a second offering earmarked to pay the publishing debt. This garnered another fifty dollars.

On following Sundays, I regularly petitioned two offerings—still failing to generate enough income to run the church and pay the overdue invoice. So I began taking a third collection—but this one indirectly.

I asked attendees to come forward during the middle of each service to place money on the altar, describing the gesture as an emergency relief fund for those in the neighborhood. If the revenue taken in by this method was any indication, their love for their neighbors was sorely lacking.

I WAS STILL IN SEMINARY and experiencing my first pastorate when Michael Allen Jones, our first of two children, was born. I drove 180 miles round-trip from Oklahoma City to school in Enid, leaving Frances to attend our newborn and to fulfill many of my pastoral duties. My salary was three thousand dollars a year, a paltry sum even for 1962, the nation's Camelot era under President John Kennedy's administration.

In 1964 Frances and I started a radio ministry. Trying to maintain that while serving as pastor and going to seminary became impossible.

I resigned my pastorate in May 1965 with two years of seminary study remaining. My hat will forever be off to pastors. People generally have no idea how difficult it is for one mortal to serve a pastor's dual role: preaching inspiring sermons and serving the never-ending pastoral needs of the congregation. As recently as the 1960s, it was fairly common for a pastor to prepare and deliver three sermons a week; supervise the church's cash flow and financial commitments; plan church outreach programs, including overseas missions; select the music; settle differences among parishioners; and be on call twenty-four hours a day. I've known preachers who have spoken twice on Sunday morning and once on Sunday evening, only to be awakened in the wee hours by a parishioner requesting prayer for a toothache.

I preached fourteen consecutive weeks of revival meetings in the fall of 1965 and another thirteen in the spring from community churches scattered across Oklahoma while commuting back and forth to school in Enid. Inevitably, I succumbed to exhaustion.

Frances, with my eighteen-month-old son, Allen, in tow, tried to accompany me on the evangelistic trail. The pace proved too grueling. We experienced marital difficulties. I tell people neither of us ever considered divorce, just murder.

Utterly depleted, I needed ministry for myself.

Frances and I sought marital counseling from Dr. Don E. Schooler. I was certain his wise words would bridge our riff. All he needed to do was help Frances understand that our conflicts were all her fault.

I was surprised to hear him say they were mine!

He told me, in Frances's presence, that I was failing her as a husband and personal pastor. I lacked sensitivity. I didn't know how to be a husband, good or bad, because the role was new to me. I had been learning through on-the-job training. And I was failing.

I resolved anew to heighten my sensitivity. I came home one day and Frances was crying.

"What's wrong, honey?" I asked tenderly.

"I don't know," she said. "But you're supposed to understand."

I didn't, and often don't to this day. I understood, though, then and now, that I've been blessed with an incredible woman. And I do my best to let her know that's what I believe and how I feel about her.

After I left my pastorate, my sense of personal pressure was intensified by two factors. First, I was a struggling Methodist evangelist, one of only two in Oklahoma. My counterpart was the Reverend Oral Roberts. He, of course, was a religious icon and way out of my league.

Related to this was the second source of anxiety—money. I had to buy airtime for the radio ministry and pay our living expenses. All together, the bills added up to about twelve hundred dollars a month. I resorted to knocking on doors, writing letters, calling people, and reaching out to relatives for financial aid.

I'd bought a house with a five-hundred-dollar down payment. After that, Frances, the baby, and I had ninety cents remaining. That was the extent of our entire net worth.

In June 1965, I went to our post office box, praying all the way for envelopes with contributions inside. The box was empty. The letdown I felt made for the lowest hour of my life at that point.

I was broke with a wife and baby. And we were out of food. I hadn't checked the mailbox at home yet. "Why bother," I thought. No one knew my home address. I had never mentioned it on the radio.

As the day wore on and my guilt mounted, I finally ambled out to the street to check the mailbox anyway. The box contained an envelope with no return address. The card inside read: "Larry and Frances, we're thinking about you." A five-dollar bill accompanied the note.

The money could not have been more appreciated if it were five hundred dollars. At that time, five dollars ensured that a family of three could eat nutritiously for three days.

Meanwhile, I was facing my first monthly house payment of one hundred dollars. Enough money came in to cover it, and Frances and I pressed forward, living on nibbles and prayers.

In retrospect, I realize that the start of my evangelistic ministry was slow because it was postponed. I had never wanted to be a pastor. But our Methodist bishop in Oklahoma insisted that I become one. He didn't see a need for new evangelists within his territory.

"Don't be foolish like Esau was when he sold his birthright, with your talk of evangelism," the bishop told me. "I don't need any evangelists. The day of evangelism is gone."

My former bishop is long since dead. I've often wondered what he'd think about the proliferation of evangelism today, as well as the growing trend among pastors to preach—and nothing more. Administrative and ministerial tasks are now more likely to be delegated to auxiliary personnel.

My mobile ministry continued through the 1960s despite the pitfalls—including the many collapses of my portable revival tent.

I had financed the purchase of a used tent that a crew of benevolent volunteers and I sweated in the baking sun to erect and take down. Too often the Oklahoma wind took it down for us at inopportune times. Years later, Frances told a reporter she had wondered about my sanity in trying to carry on a tent ministry in what was arguably the gustiest state in the nation.

Remember the Rodgers and Hammerstein song from the Broadway musical *Oklahoma*? A line of the lyrics declares, "Oklahoma . . . where the wind comes sweepin' down the plain." "Sweepin'" is an apt description. We put the tent up, the wind swept it down.

Between meetings, volunteers would help me find and mend the wind-inflicted rips. I mended them with hundred-pound-test fishing line. I was a full-time evangelist and a part-time seamster.

On several occasions, blasts of wind tore the tent to shreds. After one particular seventy-mile-per-hour squall I paid to have the tent hauled to and from Texas for professional refurbishment.

Often I continued preaching despite the threat of approaching storms—which in that part of the country can form in thirty minutes, sometimes less. I'd be trying to focus on my sermon while silently praying that the tent would not fall, capturing hundreds of uninsured believers beneath its heavy, wet sprawl.

Once I was preaching in Mannford, Oklahoma, a few miles west of Tulsa, when the tent was felled in the middle of the night. The steel support poles were bent into Ls. I was left standing on tattered canvas as driving rain put out my oratory fire.

Another time I was holding a revival in Stroud, Oklahoma, when a sudden bluster left the tent standing but severely tattered. I called the local electric company. They came to my aid with a hydraulic cherry picker that lifted me to the crest of the canvas. Using an industrial needle and heavy nylon thread, I rejoined the torn, ragged flaps that encircled the poles. That night's service went on as scheduled.

The tent and I parted company in 1974 after a seven-year relationship. The Bible talks about the danger of building a house upon sand. To that, I would respectfully add a caution against raising one made of canvas.

Chapter Five

*B*Y 1976 MY MINISTRY HAD BROKEN into national headlines due to my activism against pornography. I'd been leading marches, doing broadcast interviews, making citizen's arrests of smut peddlers, aiding the police in sting operations, and testifying against merchants charged with obscenity-related crimes.

I even received a handwritten death threat and turned it in to the FBI. They never found out who sent it. I'd received antagonistic letters before, but none as unsettling as this note. I reproduce it here exactly as written, excepting obscenities:

> *After viewing your genetically inferior program last Sunday*
> *about pornography; I only wish I could run across you in a dark*
> *alley or somewhere else . . . You pure clean Christian small Penis*
> *common Animal . . . you're Just Like the Rest of You're "Jewish"*
> *Kind . . . Your Son & Daughter need to be —— & Murdered*
> *before you're very eyes. Then I would Take Pleasure in bringing*
> *forth pain on you're Christian —— before I pumped a spent*
> *cartridge to you . . . After Gazing upon You're "Seeds" on Tele-*
> *vision it's easy to see They don't have a chance for a healthy sex*
> *life Around you're kind; They would be Better off in a Pool of*
> *their own blood . . . If I manage to Find out what Flight you're*
> *taking To D.C. in October . . . Then your only destiny lies in*
> *composition C4 . . . Don't sacrifice the Lives of others For you're*
> *ignorance! . . .*
>
> *A Psychopathic Killer*
> *666*

Despite the threat, my antismut campaign continued.

On one particularly active day, I bought pornographic magazines in front of plainclothes detectives. Seven retailers were arrested. My antipornography crusade infuriated many people, including the managers and stockholders of national chain stores that sold the lewd, filthy stuff.

Larry Flynt, publisher of *Hustler*, would eventually name me "A—hole of the Month" in his rag, which at that time was circulating twenty million copies annually. The magazine published a lengthy article (and degrading illustration) about my ministry and me, calling me an "outhouse preacher."

The *Daily Oklahoman*, the largest newspaper in Oklahoma, wrote a story about Flynt's pronouncement—bumping up *Hustler* sales in Oklahoma City by an additional sixty thousand.

His magazine repulsed me. I had incorrectly assumed it was another "skin" magazine that merely showed scantily clad women or frontal nudity. But *Hustler* went far beyond that. It was truly and shockingly degrading. Thankfully, I discovered that most Americans had never seen a copy of it.

Larry Flynt was, however, a complex and ironic person. At the same time he was publishing *Hustler*, *Chic*, and other smut, he was distributing a G-rated, slick women's magazine that offered recipes and ideas for better child rearing.

Some people were critical of my war against pornography. Still others were outright laughing at me.

I had taken a television crew and given an antipornography speech outside an Oklahoma City XXX-rated bookstore. The store owner sent two guys outside to intimidate me. One must have weighed close to 300 pounds, the other 350. They whispered threats into my ear as I kept preaching and the camera kept rolling. They talked into the sides of my head. I talked into the lens. I never noted their presence.

Their boss watched from inside his store, where he was spotted by two policemen assigned to ensure my safety. One cop recognized him as a parole violator. The officers went inside and brought the man out in handcuffs while I was still preaching. By then my viewers must have wondered what was happening among the cops, the thugs, and me. I was so focused on what I was saying that I never acknowledged or said a word about it.

The filth merchant made bond, then hired a knuckle breaker to frighten me. The first time he called me, the hair stood up on my neck. His voice on the telephone was faint but a bit edgy. Naturally, I wondered who it was, but not for long. My focus shifted to the menace in what he was saying.

"I got nothing against you personally," he whispered, "but I've got a contract on you. And I'm going to have to mess you up. I mean mess you up."

Luckily for me, the hoodlum turned out to be more greedy than loyal to his employer. After threatening me, he offered to let me buy him out. He would just take my money, he said, and disappear. But I had to pay him right away, he insisted. He needed funds to get out of town. And, of course, the transaction had to be hush-hush. No one else could know.

I asked him how much money we were talking about. He gave a figure. Even in the face of danger, my frugality spoke out. I said the amount was too high. Finally we settled on three hundred dollars.

I called the police the instant he hung up. I talked to an Oklahoma City detective, who told me to meet the culprit at the appointed time and place: Twenty-third Street and Classen Boulevard. I was to get some cash, mark only one bill, and then hand the loot over to the thug, as agreed.

On the Tuesday before Thanksgiving Day 1976, I left my office and went home to put on my bulletproof vest. I had bought it early in my anti-filth campaign, after receiving multiple death threats. I started out of the garage as Frances was coming inside.

"Where are you going?" she asked.

"Oh, I just have to go back to the office," I said, with manufactured nonchalance.

Apparently, my performance was less than convincing. She continued to quiz me even as a task force of cops was secretly assembling near the point of my dangerous rendezvous in hopes of capturing my thug in the midst of our transaction.

"Well, honey," I said, "I'll see you later."

"But where are you going?" she continued. "Why do you have to return to the office at this time of day? What's going on?"

She knew full well that I was up to something, but I refused to let on as to what it was.

I drove off. The closer I got, the less I wanted to go through with it. I'm like Woody Allen. I'm not afraid to die. I just don't want to be there when it happens. I thought about how dangerous it was to act as the bait in a sting operation.

The caller had told me that I'd know him by his black Yamaha motorcycle. He said he'd meet me in the back of a parking lot.

As I eased my car into our meeting space, I expected to spot some cops hidden in trees or perhaps lurking around the perimeter. But I saw no one—except a massive guy sitting atop a black Yamaha motorcycle.

I'll tell you this: I was scared.

My first thought was that the thug must be a bodybuilder. His arms seemed as big as my waist. I pulled my car to within what I thought might be a safe distance. Granted, he could shoot me, but I parked far enough away to jump back inside should he attack me on foot.

With my car still idling, I stepped out. The mysterious big guy just stared at me. He didn't move. Then slowly he swung one leg from over his motorcycle. He dropped both feet to the ground. He was braced. Would he charge?

I never broke eye contact as I approached. My footsteps were the only sound I heard. An envelope holding a marked bill and some blank paper protruded from my shirt pocket. I wanted him to think I had brought enough cash. I figured he wouldn't hurt me until after he'd received his bribe.

His stare pierced me as I gingerly pulled the envelope from my pocket. His hand was extended, and without a word I placed the money in his palm. He closed his fist. Then the clouds seemed to part.

It was raining policemen. I hadn't seen a one. But apparently ten or so had been watching me. To this day my hat is off to the Oklahoma City Police Department for their quick and fearless operation. A rescue like that belongs on TV. They slammed the thug onto the hood of my car, facedown. He cussed and cussed, calling me names—using words you might read in *Hustler*.

"Nothing would have happened to you, you son of a b——," he screamed.

A police car wheeled into the lot. The man, still kicking and screaming, was thrown into the backseat. The back door slammed. Though the windows were up, I could still hear the guy cussing me.

When things began to settle down, I asked the detective what would happen to him.

"Nothing," he said.

"What?" I gasped, incredulous.

"Larry," the cop explained, "he never laid a hand on you."

"But he threatened my life," I argued. "That's why we're all here! Now what are you going to do with him?"

The officer paused, and then gave me the surprising news.

"We're going to put him on that motorcycle, take him to the edge of town, and tell him not to come back to Oklahoma City."

"You're kidding!" I snapped. "And just what am *I* supposed to do?"

"Keep looking over your shoulder," he said. Then he walked away.

So the cop did what he said he was going to do. I did what I was told. The mystery thug and his motorcycle roared out of sight. Thankfully, I haven't seen him since.

But I do occasionally look over my shoulder.

ON TUESDAY, FEBRUARY 8, 1977, my car radio brought the staggering news.

"Larry Flynt, editor of *Hustler*, is sentenced by a Cincinnati jury to seven to twenty-five years in prison for obscenity."

It's no secret to anyone who's followed my ministry that the announcement translated into the first step of what became a love-hate relationship between Flynt and me. I hated then, as I do now, the filth he published. But through nothing short of a series of miracles, I came to know Flynt personally. Our relationship began when I called a friend in law enforcement to ask his help getting inside the Cincinnati jail where Flynt was incarcerated. I had decided to fly the 1,680-mile round-trip at my own expense to meet the man I considered an adversary. The only way I know how to address a problem is to attack it. I would attack *Hustler* by confronting its publisher. If I could get into his jail cell, maybe I could get inside his mind to exercise some Christian influence. He'd be my captive audience.

Less than twenty-four hours after Flynt was sentenced, I stood inside the Cincinnati jail along with twenty-seven news teams. My name was placed at the bottom of the list of those wanting to see him.

The clearance arranged by my law-enforcement contact held no sway with the Cincinnati sheriff. I tried every trick I could think of to gain access to Flynt first. I told the sheriff that Flynt wanted to see me—that it had been previously arranged. I asked him how he would feel if his son were in jail and his son had sent for a preacher.

"Wouldn't you want your boy to be allowed the visit?" I asked.

That did it. I was inside Flynt's cell in twenty minutes, while news crews from NBC, CBS, ABC, the Associated Press, and United Press International milled about impatiently.

Inside a cramped, soiled, and windowless room in the bowels of a Cincinnati jail I found myself face-to-face with one of the most notorious pornographers in the world. Flynt was to pornography in the 1970s what Al Capone had been to organized crime in the 1920s.

He was wearing a blue shirt with an American flag sewn to its back, which was intended to illustrate his advocacy for First Amendment rights.

"How much do I owe you for coming?" Flynt asked me.

"You don't owe me anything. I'm here because I wanted to come," I said.

"But you will bill me for the visit later, won't you?" he asked.

"No, I won't bill you, because I wanted to come."

"After what I did to you, *why* would you come?" He was obviously referring to the A—hole of the Month "honor" he had bestowed on me in *Hustler.*

I cited several reasons for having come. I mentioned that Flynt had obviously found wealth, but not peace of mind, and that he could through a personal relationship with Jesus Christ. I stressed the fact that God loved him enough to sacrifice His son on a cross, as evidenced by John 3:16. I added that I thought Jesus, if He lived in the flesh, might have come as well.

Flynt told me he wished he could say he was sorry about naming me the A—hole of the Month, but he wasn't. He said it was strictly business—a ploy to sell more magazines. His only regret, he said, was doing it to a nice guy like me.

This was not my first encounter with Larry Flynt. A few years before, Flynt had agreed to do an interview with me and publish it in his magazine. I had traveled to Columbus, Ohio, the magazine's headquarters, to meet him for the interview. Members of his staff and his wife, Althea, received me instead.

Althea herself had posed nude in her husband's magazine. But she balked when I suggested that Flynt might someday ask their daughter to do the same—perhaps even depicting a scene of child rape. He had done so with other children. I was convinced he would publish anything that might help sell more magazines.

"Larry, I don't know how much you know about me," Althea confided. "My mother and father were planning to separate when my father killed my mother. Then my father committed suicide. I grew up in an orphanage. Eventually I ran away. That's when I met Larry Flynt. Although you may not like him, he was the first stable thing to come into my life."

Stable? I had to wonder about the stability of a married woman who would pose with her genitals exposed for the entire world to see.

Though he never showed up to interview me that day, this was not my last encounter with Flynt or his family. He agreed to a debate with me on live radio, which the host Lou Staples broadcast on KTOK in Oklahoma City. Flynt and I went at each other for a full two hours.

I talked about the destructive effect of pornography on certain segments of society. I cited surveys that linked pornography to sex crimes. I protested the devastating effect on the young women who posed for his prurient photographs.

He talked about his First Amendment rights.

"He and I are in the same business," Flynt told the radio audience, speaking about me, "except he goes about it one way and I go about it another. He's repressive; I'm permissive. You see, I happen to feel that most of the social ills are caused by repression, not permissiveness, and his views are the opposite."

Flynt contended that the most heinous crimes in world history were committed by sexually repressive societies, citing the Germans before World War II, the Japanese, and hardened criminals, presumably those who live inside penitentiary walls.

His argument was sensible. It was also wrong.

I told Flynt and the radio audience that I was not against the sex business solely to be a suppressor. I told him I thought sex was good, although I'm not sure he believed me. Too many people think preachers are opposed to anything natural. Not so. I'm in favor of natural, healthy sex. The kind Flynt was espousing was just plain sick.

I refuted Flynt with an analogy.

"I can go to Dallas by taking I-35, a four-lane highway, or I can take off across the fields," I said. "I think God has not only given us something right and good (sex), He has given us the proper route (marriage). When sex steps out of those bounds, it can become bad."

As mentioned earlier, Flynt was eventually sentenced to seven to twenty-five years in prison. Lou Staples, the host of our radio debate, eventually committed suicide. And I eventually garnered more than fifty thousand signatures in an effort to stiffen the obscenity laws in Oklahoma.

Here's one eventuality no one could have predicted: Flynt became a born-again Christian under the ministry of Ruth Carter Stapleton (former president Jimmy Carter's sister). With that, his wife informed him that although Jesus may have come into his life, twenty million dollars a year would be going out if he gave up his pornography empire.

Flynt recanted his conversion and declared himself an atheist.

On March 6, 1978, a sniper shot Larry Flynt twice, leaving him crippled for life. A white supremacist was accused of the shooting. Authorities believed he shot Flynt because *Hustler* had published photographs of biracial sex.

From there, things got worse for Larry Flynt.

He moved from Ohio to Los Angeles's swanky Bel Air, where he lived in total seclusion. No one saw him except for Althea, his daughter, a few other relatives, and the domestic and security staffs. No more than a dozen people knew the activities of a man whose smut magazine was viewed by millions.

Flynt became hopelessly addicted to painkillers, and Althea became addicted to prescription drugs and cocaine.

Rumors circulated that Flynt had become a drug-addicted zombie who was being held captive in his lavish prison by his own security force.

On October 14, 1980, a twelve-member SWAT team carrying M16 rifles scaled the eight-foot wall surrounding Flynt's twenty-room, palatial estate to "free" the publishing magnate.

It was reported that the cops initially encountered only one security guard, who was not as well armed as they were.

A second police platoon scaled a rear wall and charged the compound door with a battering ram, reducing it to kindling.

Once inside, the SWAT team was fired upon by another security guard. After realizing he was outnumbered, the guard fled his post to hide under a grand piano.

Bill Rider, Flynt's security chief, responded to the commotion but dropped his gun when confronted with an array of rifles. He and the first security guard were placed in handcuffs. By then, more than fifty police officers were roaming the mansion, searching for Flynt, whom no one outside the residence had seen in months. Some speculated that he was dead, just as people had speculated on Howard Hughes's death when he became a recluse.

An uncle and a cook were also taken into custody. Even they did not know—or otherwise would not divulge—the whereabouts of Larry Flynt.

Still more cops came. Squad cars lined St. Cloud Road outside the estate. Unknown to them, deep in the heart of the house, confined to the gold-plated wheelchair he had used since he was shot, Larry Flynt was on the phone. Ironically, he was begging for the Los Angeles police to rescue him from the ruckus that was raging on his property. He had no idea that the police had instigated the raid in an attempt to rescue him.

A five-hundred-pound steel door stood as his last line of defense.

The police dispatcher with whom Flynt was speaking finally convinced him that the men banging on his bedroom door were indeed cops. Reluctantly Flynt pressed the button that let in the first people from the outside world to see his private chamber.

A police physician examined him on the scene. Despite the excitement, his blood pressure and heartbeat seemed satisfactory. Flynt assured officers that he was hiding of his own volition. No one, he said, was forcing seclusion upon him. And so the rescue effort that had taken weeks to plan was adjourned in minutes. The police left Flynt as they had found him—alone.

During his brief flirtation with Christianity, Flynt cleaned up *Hustler* magazine a bit. While it was an improvement over what it had been, it still fell short of most community standards. He apologized to American women for objectifying them like merchandise. He put up pictures of Jesus on the walls of his home.

When Flynt became disabled, though, Althea took over as editor in chief. She restored the previous levels of smut to the magazine's cover and pages. Slumping sales soon recovered.

But Flynt's personal recovery did not rival that of the magazine. Paralyzed below the waist, he was not only immobile but impotent. Perhaps to him, this added maddening insult to his injury.

I would have paid Flynt a visit in those dark days, had I been invited—or had I thought I could otherwise get inside. Unlike the LAPD, I couldn't force my way in.

Flynt had paid $2.5 million for a house once owned by Sonny Bono and then spent another $5 million on renovations, including building a lake in which he would never swim or fish.

In Columbus he had lived in a $375,000 house—no insignificant piece of real estate, given that market and the prices of the day.

Oddly, though, he longed for something he couldn't seem to buy, that he couldn't seem to touch: some remnant of the comfort and security of his boyhood innocence. He even went so far as to build a replica of the Kentucky cabin in which he'd been reared. It stood on the floor of his Ohio basement. But it failed to provide the peace he sought.

In California he continued attempting to reignite the spark of magic from his youth. He built raging fires in summer, turning down the air-conditioning as low as it would go. This in a vain effort to re-create the experience of a Kentucky winter.

He could never recapture that peace of mind, even on a nonstop diet of cocaine and Dilaudid, a morphinelike painkiller. Days and nights melted together in a drug-induced haze for this broken man, whose limbs throbbed with the pain brought on by the sniper's bullets. Althea said he sometimes screamed all night. Through it all, she refused to leave his side to seek sleep and respite in another room. Neither of them slept. Exhaustion overtook them. He anesthetized his body, she her mind, with more and stronger drugs. One report claims Althea was consuming twenty-five hundred dollars' worth of cocaine per day.

Flynt finally underwent a laser surgery that reduced his misery significantly. But he has never really recovered. Althea was found dead in a bathtub at the Flynt mansion in 1987, her fear of eternal damnation drowning with her.

My war against pornography has taken me down roads I never thought I'd travel. I've encountered people I never thought I'd meet. The further along the road I've traveled, the more I've become convinced that pornography is psychological and spiritual suicide to its users. There are precious few heroin users who didn't start with marijuana. There are precious few sex abusers who aren't regular users of pornography.

In 1994, two blocks from Feed The Children's international headquarters, police responded to an emergency in which two people were being held hostage by an armed man. He was an ex-convict who told police he would kill them both. For hours, authorities cajoled the pathetic figure, begging him to set his captives free and surrender.

They got half of what they asked.

He ultimately released the two hysterical people, but then turned a gun on himself.

When I heard the news, I recognized his name. He was the former owner of seven pornography stores—the very person who had put out the contract on me eighteen years before.

$\mathcal{M}$IRACLES OFTEN BEGIN with an experience that seems very ordinary.

Just such a miracle began unfolding for me on a sweltering night in Haiti in 1979. I had earlier spoken at a church where the temperature and the humidity were competing fiercely to see which could climb higher. A sauna would have seemed refreshing. I exaggerate—but not by much.

In my mind I was replaying a mental tape of my sermon. My words continued reverberating there, as they do for every preacher. Had I said too much about this? Not enough about that?

My thoughts wandered to the biblical story of the apostle Paul's conversion experience. He was a persecutor of Christians who was struck blind by God on the road to Damascus, and thus came to "see" God's purpose for his life so clearly that he ultimately wrote two-thirds of the New Testament. Then I recalled God's deliverance of Jonah from inside a big fish. I rather envied Jonah down there in the fish's belly, where it must have been cool. Even this might provide relief from the withering heat of Port-au-Prince on this evening.

As I returned to my hotel, these thoughts provided no escape from my sultry surroundings. I felt a powerful thirst.

Breaking my heat-induced reverie, I heard it: the voice of God. But not the booming, overpowering voice that the biblical Abraham reported hearing. I heard instead the weak, wispy plea of a starving young boy.

"Do you have a nickel for a roll?" he asked.

In that Haiti is the poorest nation in the Western Hemisphere, I was accustomed to children asking for money or food. But never before had a child asked so specifically—"a nickel for a roll." He was asking for what he needed at this moment only, no more. I engaged him in conversation.

His name was Jerry. He explained that the roll cost five cents and that with an additional three cents he could get some butter on it. I suggested that he'd need a drink to wash it down. He recalculated the total cost with lightning speed: he could get a roll, butter, and a soft drink for twenty cents.

This would in fact be Jerry's first and only "meal" of the day. It was past 9:00 p.m.

After giving him the twenty cents, I watched Jerry disappear into the store to purchase his bounty. Then the enormity of his situation dawned on me: My twenty cents had bought him a fraction of a meal. But what would feed Jerry tomorrow? And the next day? What about his brothers? Sisters? Parents? What about their next-door neighbors?

Pondering this, I walked inside to my room, where I removed my shirt. It dripped with perspiration. I wrung it out before hanging it up to dry.

All the while, thoughts of Jerry's plight haunted me.

I thought of the surplus wheat that was, at that moment, simply rotting in silos back in Oklahoma. I imagined how many rolls it might provide if it were made available here in Haiti. Nourishing food, a potential source of physical salvation, was going to waste just ninety minutes' flight time to the north.

This didn't make sense to me, so I decided to do something about it.

At the time, *Larry Jones Ministries* was broadcast on about fifteen stations, mostly in Oklahoma, Kansas, and Texas. Many of my viewers were wheat farmers. When I returned from Haiti, I made an on-air statement, pointing to the senselessness of our allowing wheat to rot while people were starving, virtually in the shadow of our silos. I presented this in terms of economic opportunity for the farmers: alleviating the surplus would bolster the price of wheat. Also, sharing our surplus in this way would ease the stress on taxpayers, many of whom felt outraged to be subsidizing the production of more grain than the market could bear and then ultimately paying for its destruction. All of this was a matter of simple common sense.

Many of my TV viewers also knew me more directly as a minister who had preached in their local churches. For years I had conducted weeklong crusades in their tiny sanctuaries—modest structures that continue to stand the test of time (and tornadoes) as they dot the two-lane blacktops across America's heartland. I knew many of the farmers by name. They trusted me.

Soon my telephone began to ring. These good-hearted people wanted to donate surplus to the starving children of Haiti—a country many of them knew little about.

I knew nothing about the logistics of transporting grain. But within eight weeks, more than two million pounds of wheat were scheduled to depart the farmers' bins into my eager-but-inexperienced hands. I was like a dog chasing a car. What does the dog do when he catches it? It all seemed to be happening so fast—but, in truth, not as fast as children were dying.

My thoughts returned to Jerry, the boy who had set all of this in motion. "What would he think if he knew?" I wondered. I suspected he'd ask for a roll. Maybe some butter. Maybe enough to feed his family.

We printed a brochure, itemizing how much it would cost to transport, clean, and bag wheat in Oklahoma, then deliver it to Haiti. The plan was to have locals beat it into flour upon arrival. But without proper equipment and trained personnel, this process would require precious time—time during which people would continue to die. Was there a way to process the wheat faster?

I began to pray nonstop. Imagining the faces of the hungry, I prayed harder. So did my staff, of seven full-time and three part-time workers. Starvation is a tragic and final deadline—one that comes daily in Haiti. I prayed for no more such deadlines to pass, not on my watch. I wondered who might be feeding Jerry now. I wondered if, indeed, he was still alive.

At this point, the number of responses to my televised plea was beyond tally. The ultimate miracle would be my keeping up with them.

In came a call from yet another farmer. And, as the grace of God would have it, he proposed a lifesaving solution. He owned commercial wheat-processing equipment. So he donated not only wheat but also processing services. And recognizing the need for an experienced supervisor to oversee the operation, he offered to do the job himself. He would accompany me to Haiti, unload the processing equipment, and teach Haitians how to use it.

Meanwhile, donated wheat continued to stockpile at our storage facility in Wellington, Texas. We had not yet raised enough money to transport the grain to its port of departure in Florida.

As luck (and the Lord) would have it, my plea for help reached Florida via a national cable channel. One fellow called from near Miami to say he could help with the transport. He owned trucks making hauls to California each week, returning empty. Picking up our wheat in Wellington would involve a detour of only seventeen miles. His fleet would drive the wheat to Florida, bound for passage to Haiti. Not only that—he'd foot the bill. All we had to pay was overseas passage. Thus, our distribution network was largely completed.

My staff included a cluster of devoted individuals, all of whom were now working full-time—actually *overtime*. One was Pastor Joseph—a Haitian by birth—whom I asked to be responsible for distributing the processed wheat to the starving. Joseph had attended seminary in the United States and had gone back to Haiti to minister. It was, in fact, his invitation to speak in Haiti that had occasioned my meeting Jerry in the first place. I knew without a doubt that Joseph was the one to be entrusted with Haiti's new source of food.

He was a winning choice, never once complaining, no matter how big his challenge. And he always got the job done, putting food on the tables of Haiti's needy children.

A few months later I spoke at a church in Wellington, thanking the community for its participation in getting the wheat to Haiti. Afterward a farmer approached me to say he'd grown too many black-eyed peas. There was no market for his surplus, and so he was preparing to turn the nitrogen-rich vegetables under. That way they would at least prove useful as soil enhancement. I asked him to give me the surplus instead. He responded by giving me sixteen tons.

Then this generous farmer traveled with me to Haiti, where his donation was delivered to Pastor Joseph. Embraced by Joseph, the farmer felt so moved that he wept tears of joy.

I, too, knew that joy. Of all the things I'd done in my Christian ministry so far, something seemed very right in what we were doing just then. It brought to mind the biblical teaching about loaves and fishes. On my subsequent rereading of the entire Bible, I counted more than 1,350 passages that essentially urge us to feed the hungry and clothe the naked. I noted thirteen major biblical famines and how transporting food from a place of abundance to an area of need eased the horror of each.

Feeling myself to be involved in some sort of miracle, I immersed myself in prayer and meditation. Without benefit of a mentor, I had found myself doing things I did not know how to do, acting on thoughts that had never before occurred to me. Unwittingly, it seems, I had enrolled in the College of Self-Education. My first course of study had been Hunger 101. Both my learning and the results that came of it had been profound.

While the Bible repeatedly commands us to love God, just as often it exhorts us to take love one step further—to love our neighbors as ourselves. The way I read it, allowing others to go without while I enjoy a life of plenty goes against what the Bible teaches. I found that I simply could not stand by and let that happen anymore.

Before this realization, Larry Jones Ministries had been an evangelistic organization dedicated to introducing people to Jesus Christ, urging them to accept Him as their personal savior. I had been ordained as a preacher who'd gone to seminary to fulfill this mission. Suddenly, though, I found myself no longer talking so much about eternal rewards in heaven. Less and less did I fill the television airwaves with sermons about Jesus' death on the cross for remission of human sin. Instead, I preached Christian love expressed as action to relieve human suffering and fulfill human need. My theme became the Doctrine of Sustenance.

This shift in emphasis raised more than a few eyebrows in the pastoral community. Some of my colleagues thought I'd lost my mind. Some began to pray for me. For this, of course, I would thank them. Then ever so subtly I would try to steer the conversation toward the hungry and how we might ease their pain.

I realized that my approach was not going to win me any accolades from proponents of mainstream theology. While my colleagues used their television airtime thanking God for the blessings He had brought into their lives and ministries, I continued thanking Oklahoma farmers for their wheat yields and their generosity. I like to think of it this way: what popularity I may have lost among young seminarians I gained among the Future Farmers of America.

Time passed. Our food ministry continued, ever growing. It was then that a colleague stuck his head in my office and casually asked, "So, what are you going to call the division of this ministry that feeds children?"

" 'Feed The Children' seems right to me," I responded. "Isn't that what we do?" And so that was that. There was no heavy pondering, no board meeting, and no focus group. Feed The Children was named in this brief exchange between a colleague and me—just two guys who felt we couldn't spare the time to think over the matter while there remained so many mouths to feed.

IN THE FALL OF 1979, I embarked on my second international wheat mission, this time to Nairobi, Kenya, in eastern Africa. I had never so much as imagined the kind of deprivation and misery I would encounter in that searing equatorial province. My efforts there came to focus on Dagoretti, a village that counted 150 handicapped children among its desperately poor inhabitants.

Upon arriving, I heard a story that communicated their desperation in no uncertain terms. A thief had stolen a goat, knowing full well he would be tried in the court of public outrage and killed if caught.

He didn't have time to enjoy the goat's meat. Hundreds of Dagoretti's starving mustered enough energy to chase him down. One found a discarded tire, which the mob placed around the body of the hysterical man, tucking his arms inside so he couldn't move. Others doused the tire with kerosene and set it on fire.

There's a horrible irony here: this man died for trying to stay alive. If only I could have gotten to Kenya sooner.

ABOUT A YEAR AFTER RETURNING FROM KENYA, I made another trek to Haiti. By this time, Feed The Children had provided the hungry there with untold tons of wheat. Even so, we had effected only minimal change in the plight of the Haitian people. Poverty remained pervasive. Someone directed me to a tiny room in which a child, Jonas, lay dying of malnutrition. His condition was so extreme that if I pulled the skin on his arm, it remained stretched, as if he were made of putty rather than flesh and blood.

I hurried Jonas to a doctor, who prescribed medicine and provided directions to a hospital. (In Haiti, emergency patients must buy their medicine before they enter a hospital.)

I continued a prayer vigil with Jonas intermittently for twenty-four hours. But my efforts proved to be too little, too late. He died. His body was taken to a mortuary. From there, it cost fifty dollars to have it removed for a funeral. Without the payment, the mortuary would simply have the boy's body destroyed. So I paid the fee, facilitating the body's release—but not before his mother asked me to conduct his funeral service. I'd never preached the funeral of a child before, much less one who'd died of starvation. I accepted, vowing to try to make it my last.

FEED THE CHILDREN WAS FOUNDED RAPIDLY AND HAPHAZARDLY, with an overwhelming sense of duty, as I've indicated. Recognizing a dire human need, I asked for wheat. Suddenly I found myself in possession of over two million pounds. That's fifty truckloads. Once I had it, I had to move it—or else lose any credibility I'd ever succeeded in building with my television viewers, not to mention my God. I was sincere when I asked for the grain; I was sincere when I asked God to help me distribute it. To this day I continue to be sincere as I begin each day with a prayer to bless Feed The Children's life-giving process, now supervised by perhaps fifteen hundred mission-driven workers.

Today, Feed The Children is essentially the same as it ever was. Where we discover a need, we try to bring it to public attention through our television broadcasts, exposing every tragedy we can—including those we find in major U.S. cities, where many viewers (and politicians) seem to be stuck in a state of denial that domestic hunger is shockingly pervasive. Thirty-three thousand children go to bed hungry each night in Chicago alone. That's a fact. In an attempt to reduce that number as much as we can, Feed The Children continues its food drops there.

This is not rocket science. One need not be a dietitian, logistics engineer, or any kind of specialist to do what we do. We're simply transporting food, supplies, and services from point A to point B, just like in the Bible.

I believe in Jesus Christ as the Son of God who died so that we might have eternal life. I also believe in sharing that Gospel with the world. I just go about it differently.

While I am an ordained minister, I don't use the title "Reverend" very often. Some people don't even know that I am ordained, and that's okay.

Religious ideologies tend to be divisive. People of one ideology often balk at entrusting relief aid—material or monetary—to people who champion another. To me this seems self-righteous and ultimately tragic, in stark contrast to the crying needs we might otherwise serve. Why can't we set aside our personal opinions, working together to cast the widest net?

Just as hunger is no respecter of politics, it's also no respecter of religious doctrine. I invite Christians, Jews, Muslims, Hindus, agnostics, atheists, humanists, and whomever else to work in harmony through Feed The Children. And that goes for corporations, LLPs, philanthropic organizations, and foreign governments as well. My mission is not about preaching doctrine. It's about feeding the hungry, just like when Jesus took five loaves and two little fishes to feed the multitudes. Jesus' own disciples criticized Him because they suspected He didn't have enough food to provide for the crowd. If people were then as they are today, no doubt some were still squawking after the whole thing was over and Jesus departed.

No matter what you do, somebody's bound to gripe about it.

Until I was thirty-eight, I preached to people, telling them how to live. After thirty-eight, I found it infinitely more satisfying and effective simply to live what I had once preached.

Chapter Seven

*C*HILD SPONSORSHIP was Feed The Children's first major one-on-one matching of American donors with needy children. Just ten years after the program's inception in 1981, more than thirty thousand overseas children were being fed by viewers of *Larry Jones Ministries'* broadcasts in eighteen small television markets. I was elated at the overwhelming response that enabled us to give food and medicine to youngsters who otherwise wouldn't have had them. As this outreach expanded, my staff increased to include six lovely, dedicated people who worked long hours for modest wages.

Previously I'd preached in Hollis, Oklahoma, where I met Don Richardson, a wheat farmer. While I was a guest in his home, we often talked about how the U.S. government made valiant efforts to address implacable hunger abroad but such efforts were often thwarted by corruption. We discussed rumors about nameless foreign officials who were said to commandeer donated food for personal profit.

Throughout the history of FTC, I've tried to prevent theft of goods intended for the starving. Those who do the stealing are often corrupt individuals in positions of power.

My first encounter with this sad reality unfolded in Central America in 1981. Don happened to be on a mission in Belize, where, coincidentally, I had recently sent tons of wheat. Half of it had mysteriously disappeared. Vanished.

"How could a small mountain of grain evaporate into thin air?" I wondered. I dispatched a staffer from our office in Oklahoma to investigate. In Belize he talked with countless policy makers, none of whom provided even a clue. The emissary returned to our offices weary and despondent.

Then I called Don.

Don had become a Christian in midlife. In many cases, people who accept Christ as their personal savior later in life feel especially grateful for His salvation when they do. They often feel as if they wasted many years and are determined to make the most of their remaining time on earth. Don was one of these.

"I sent wheat to Belize, and much of it has disappeared," I explained. "I wonder if you know anyone down there who might help us find it?"

"I think I might," Don replied.

He began querying his contacts, who worked inside and outside of government. One, currently a Christian, had previously lived outside the law.

After discussing the matter with this operative, Don called me to say, "I think I may know what happened to your wheat."

I had questions but didn't pose them. Don asked me to trust him, implying that he had his own scheme to recover the stolen grain. So I left the matter to him.

"Is Don going to steal back the stolen wheat?" I wondered, somewhat facetiously. After all, Don had alluded to some underground network, including someone he referred to as "streetwise."

I decided that what I didn't know wouldn't hurt me. More important, I knew something that would: a loss of food to feed the hungry.

Eventually Don volunteered some of the details. It seems that some commissioner had wanted a bridge constructed on his private property. A deal was struck between the commissioner and a builder, involving payment with multiple loads of wheat.

At this point Don let me in on his plan for how to get it back. He needed nothing from me except paper, a letter on the stationery of Larry Jones Ministries stating that grain, processed at the Wellington, Texas, center, had been sent by Feed The Children to churches in Belize.

Armed only with that unofficial contract, Don drove to a barn that was bursting with wheat but not located on a commodities farm, where Belize's grain supply is normally warehoused. How curious: a sizable surplus of wheat concealed inside a remote structure with no sensible reason for being there. Still more curious: the commissioner owned the barn! Even a rookie detective would recognize that circumstantial evidence strongly suggested hijacking for resale.

Stopped by a worker upon his approach to the suspicious edifice, Don produced my letter attesting to original ownership of the wheat. The laborer worked for the commissioner. He said his boss was away, visiting the United States. Someone speculated that the commissioner might be there trying to establish a network to intercept more food.

Keeping his composure, Don turned on his considerable charm. He said he had come to take the wheat to its ultimate destination, expressing gratitude for all the worker had done to keep the grain safe and dry.

Don's approach must have seemed appropriate to the laborer. This same fellow who had been assigned to guard stolen grain wound up helping Don load it into trucks.

Don had hired some Mennonite drivers to haul the wheat. Once the trucks were filled, Don and his hired help made a hasty getaway. In a few hours they distributed the bounty to a tribe of Kekchi Maya Indians who lived hidden within the thick vegetation of nearby mountains. There the grain was safely stored until ground into meal.

I learned about this sly rescue while viewing photographs Don sent to FTC headquarters. Some photos pictured grinning Indians holding what appeared to be sand but was actually processed wheat.

When I asked Don to elaborate on how he had recovered the wheat, he again alluded to his acquaintance with a streetwise man who had formerly been an outlaw. I asked nothing else, fearing I'd hear more than I wanted to know.

Thus, the competition between FTC and those set on exploiting its mission for their own gain had begun. This dirty contest would continue for years and years, but we had won round one.

ABOUT A WEEK BEFORE the Belize rescue I had mentioned my Child Sponsorship idea to Don. I offered to send him to El Salvador to oversee the campaign's launch with children uprooted by war. Don's assignment would be to take Polaroids of malnourished youngsters and to match the photographs with condensed biographies of each. Potential donors within my small television audience would then be promised a picture and the personal story of each child they pledged to support. After crunching the numbers, I'd determined that FTC could feed a starving boy or girl for twenty dollars a month.

The effort triggered a surprising lesson on the hazards of helping the downtrodden in countries torn by war.

Don was in Santa Tecla, just west of San Salvador, the capital of El Salvador. He had photographed only two children when others excitedly formed a line to let this strange American flash a light in their faces, then produce a paper bearing their likeness. They were giggling with fascination.

Working inside a small pavilion, Don had snapped his fifth photo when he felt a shock that will reverberate in his bones for the rest of his life. An explosion shattered the peace of the scene. In time, there would be others. And before long, he and I would be riding together in trucks topped by guards with machine guns to protect the delivery of FTC food.

That's just the way it is in a warring region. Others at the scene with Don were comparatively nonchalant. They were accustomed to living with bombs. Many spoke in Spanish, which Don could not understand. He had no clue about the politics behind the situation.

Suddenly someone burst into the pavilion carrying a hysterical woman with a blood-drenched towel wrapped around her head. As the blood flowed down her body, dripping off her elbows, Don was desperately trying to console her. He frantically looked for an interpreter to tell him what was going on.

Finally he found a local who explained in English that guerrillas had hurled a grenade into the woman's home, which she shared with her son, a member of the National Guard. The son had been the target but was not home at the time.

The innocent mother had been breast-feeding. The baby, torn from her arms and thrown against a wall by the explosion, died instantly. Her civilian son and husband were also killed.

Don eventually worked for FTC for almost thirty years, keeping a pictorial diary that included war casualties. There are hundreds. On this, his first brush with death, he realized he should photograph the outrageous scene for use in a television appeal on behalf of refugees. But he couldn't bring himself to raise a camera in the presence of such personal agony. To do so seemed disrespectful, an invasion of privacy. But if he didn't do it, how could decent people all over the world know what horrors were being suffered here? Eventually, he learned to force himself to rise to the grisly task at hand.

After this first dramatic exercise for Child Sponsorship, Don returned to FTC's headquarters with 212 snapshots of starving children, the charter beneficiaries of our flagship one-on-one outreach. In just one thirty-minute television broadcast, each child gained a sponsor.

In the glow of this success, I naively convinced myself that the grenade assault on the woman and baby in El Salvador had been an isolated incident. But my naïveté didn't last long. Upon returning to El Salvador, Don found it difficult to hire a driver willing to go into regions gripped by escalating violence. He wasted two days waiting for prospects who said they would meet him at his hotel but never came to call. On the third day he was greeted by two men who were prepared to transport him to a destination forty-five minutes from his lodging.

En route, the trio rounded a curve and came upon a swollen body lying in the middle of the road. The driver threw the truck into third gear and made a hurried swerve around the corpse without saying a word.

"Hey, man," Don protested, "somebody is in the road back there!"

"Yeah," the driver replied matter-of-factly, without looking back.

"Aren't you going to stop!?" Don pleaded.

"No," the driver murmured quietly. "The guerrillas have killed somebody during the night. They put his body in the road and ran to the bush to wait for somebody to stop. They'll remove it themselves after midnight. But if somebody goes to that dead man during daylight, the guerrillas will shoot."

The body was bait.

Thereafter, neither Don nor I ever tried to persuade a Central American driver to stop for anyone who was obviously dead. There were times when I was able to trick a driver into halting for people I thought to be wounded. I'd go to their side to see if I could help. Usually I'd come too late. Sometimes I had to sprint back to the vehicle as the driver yelled, threatening to leave me.

It was never my purpose to make myself a target, of course— although I would eventually become one.

DESPITE THE DANGERS WE FACED EACH DAY, our Child Sponsorship program continued to grow. We enrolled an average of three thousand children annually throughout the 1980s. The program was one of FTC's most successful antihunger offensives of the decade. Even so, my friends wondered about my sanity. They consistently asked viewers for money and in exchange told them how to live. I, too, asked for money, but just as passionately I solicited wheat so that others might not die. This was the difference in our ministries.

In the process I learned how to coordinate our mission with foreign churches and charities. My co-laborers and I would commit to deliver food or food products to a particular region if a local group would oversee the distribution. Our initial delivery to El Salvador expanded into thirty. Shortly afterward, we entered Honduras on similar missions.

Thankfully, our experience in Honduras proved not nearly so treacherous. Once we got through customs and past government employees, we could trust the local Sunday school teachers or educators to distribute the food where it was most needed without diverting it for personal gain. Our success continued at such a pace and with such beneficial results that it wasn't long before our efforts caught the attention of those who'd taught humanitarian relief and development for the United Nations and UNICEF. Feed The Children began to work with the sanction of each.

By the time we had labored for half of the 1980s, we were also feeding children in grades one through three in forty-one schools in Guatemala, including some remotely located in jungles.

We were accustomed to working on dirt floors inside thatched or adobe field kitchens. Owing to the scope of our operation, we needed something much more stable and waterproof for the Guatemalan staff.

Construction was out of the question. I had not yet mastered the skills of negotiating the costs of laborers and materials to erect a freestanding building. Don was equally inexperienced, given his background in agriculture. However, our intentions for Guatemala were far too ambitious to let that stop us. Child Sponsorship and other programs simply couldn't enroll a small army of hungry children and administer their feeding without an office.

I prayed vigorously about the need for accommodations, and God presented an option to rent. Renting carried the obvious advantage of no initial capital outlay to be sought from donors. It also meant that I would not have to wrangle financing through foreign banks, some of which were notorious for trying to exploit American customers.

I asked Don to head a team to evaluate existing structures, all the while appearing to be casual about our intentions. I'd learned from my mother many years earlier that the best approach to a real estate deal is to appear not to want it too much. The seller (or landlord) would otherwise "tear the pockets off" an enthusiastic prospect.

Her teaching proved advantageous. We leased generous square footage and ample amenities at the last place I would ever have expected to locate—the former French embassy.

Signs that once proclaimed the glories of France were removed and replaced with placards that heralded Feed The Children. Rooms that once hosted foreign dignitaries as they sipped the best vintage wine came to warehouse powdered milk and ingredients for porridge.

Once French and Guatemalan policy makers might have discussed how to feed Guatemala's needy within these walls. We didn't just talk about it—we did it.

As measured by FTC standards of the 1980s, our Guatemalan operation became one of our most effective ever. Child Sponsorship became a resounding success wherever we took it. Some charities were doing wonderful work by soliciting government funds. We were blessed to receive contributions from private donors as well as commodities from food producers.

The expansion of our overseas operations was shrinking the space at FTC headquarters in Oklahoma City. Our headquarters had begun in a residence. In 1981 we moved into a two-story office offering what I thought would be plenty of room. By 1983, however, staff members were walking on top of one another. Our space was so crowded that many claimed they could talk on the telephone and hold hands at the same time. To make their point, they demonstrated—which was actually pretty funny.

FTC employees began arriving at work earlier and earlier each day. I thought they were just eager to get started. No, they wanted to make sure they found a parking space. Those not there by 8:00 a.m. were out of luck—forced to park off the grounds and walk back to the office.

The staff was not amused. And I understood. For me, though, this seemed like a wonderful problem to have in the scheme of things. Being increasingly cramped for space meant that the ministry was growing.

AROUND THIS TIME, I learned of the Reverend Jim Bakker's problems: what eventually became a drawn-out, painful money and sex scandal involving the founder of the PTL network and former host of *The PTL Club*.

Before I continue, I want to be clear that it is not my intent to sling mud at Jim Bakker.

I believe that, as the saying goes, Jim Bakker has "paid the fiddler" for his wrongdoing. His personal pain and penance are made abundantly clear in his autobiography, *I Was Wrong*.

I bring up the whole sad matter here only to relate the Bakker scandal's indirect but devastating effect on our work at FTC. I cite only such things as were published in the 1980s and that remain on the Internet for all to see to this day.

The Jessica Hahn–Jim Bakker escapade rocked the world of born-again Christians, especially television ministries, which automatically became suspect in the public mind. The accusations against Bakker included drastic financial wrongdoing. Bakker's ministry received contributions of $1 million weekly, and he awarded himself $4 million in bonuses between 1984 and 1987, according to published reports. Other assets included a $600,000 home in Palm Springs, four condominiums in California, and a Rolls-Royce. News stories also claimed that Bakker once spent $100,000 for a private jet to fly his clothing from the East Coast to the West. The press had a field day disclosing Bakker's "Holy Roller" lifestyle. The negative reportage seemingly had no end, and it brought scrutiny on all television ministries, including FTC.

We were tarred and feathered along with Jim Bakker, guilty by association. After all, I was a minister pleading my case on television. Jim Bakker was a minister pleading his case on television. In some people's minds, televangelists were rotten as a lot. Never mind that FTC's accounting was an open book to supporters and the public at large. It was easier to skewer us first and ask questions later.

Here's how silly it all seemed to me: Roy Rogers had been on television. I had watched his programs, and perhaps he'd seen mine. But that doesn't necessarily mean he's ever been guilty of feeding the hungry or that I've ever been guilty of being a cowboy.

The fallout from the Bakker crisis nonetheless translated into the biggest monetary slam ever dealt to FTC. The ink on the tawdry headlines chronicling Bakker's fall from grace was barely dry before the fountain of FTC's contributions began to sputter and dry up.

Pledges to Child Sponsorship were among the first to go. People who had committed to care for the feeding of helpless, needy children were dropping out of the program. It strongly appeared that thousands of youngesters in poor countries were going to starve because of the sexual misbehavior and financial shenanigans of an American televangelist.

As the scandal widened, our financial situation deteriorated. Newspapers reported that Ms. Hahn had been paid $265,000 to keep her tryst with Bakker a secret. Bakker's staff members had tendered the payment, allegedly. Bakker resigned from PTL. Our contributions nose-dived.

News outlets continued to report unfolding developments alleging Ms. Hahn's dalliance with another self-proclaimed man of God, supposedly with the sanction of Bakker. The public was still buzzing when it was disclosed that Ms. Hahn would pose nude for *Playboy* magazine—which she did. Soon afterward, she and another former evangelist, the late Sam Kinison, publicly declared enthusiasm for their free-sex lifestyle.

As a television ministry, Feed The Children was getting burned by the mounting public outrage. The general sense seemed to be that if you're a preacher and you're on TV, you must be sleazy and crooked, no matter how worthy the ministry.

Feed The Children struggled to remain financially viable. Each time we'd see a light at the end of the tunnel, another incident would darken it, not the least of which was the continuing mass-media allegations that Bakker had used his contributors' money to subsidize a lavish lifestyle that included an air-conditioned doghouse.

Reporters from around the world seemed in hot competition to disclose the undoing of the largest television ministry of the day. Accounts leaped from newscasts to entertainment programming. *Saturday Night Live* spoofed the greed reportedly exemplified by Jim Bakker—which they seemed to generalize to all of television evangelism.

FTC's ability to underwrite the welfare of children continued to plummet. We were stretching to pay food suppliers, distributors, exporters, and others involved in Child Sponsorship, as well as the salaries of staff members in the United States and in nine countries overseas.

Our FTC computers, archaic by today's standards, took about sixty days to tally a bottom line that plunged us into the red. Revenue for Child Sponsorship, our largest and most life-sustaining outreach, had tumbled by 40 percent.

As a result, yet another storm cloud swept the corridors at FTC.

The typically buoyant, positive mood of our Child Sponsorship division hung low in a deep fog of worry. A small part of our contributions, as FTC's donors knew, went for salaries.

Once vibrant with purpose and joy, our office became like a mortuary. The silence was deafening. The staffers seemed to be wondering if they'd be let go due to insufficient funds.

They didn't go on wondering for long.

Payday for FTC employees came every other Friday. On one very sad Friday, our budget situation forced me to give notice to twenty-one valued, dedicated workers. Along with their final paycheck, I gave them two weeks' severance pay. Two weeks later, I had to let go eleven more.

Journalists and others who recognized us began to give Frances and me the third degree in airports and restaurants and on the street. They wanted to know if we had a Swiss bank account and owned private jets; they even asked Frances for a picture of her yacht. We were confronted with all manner of unimaginably silly questions, snide comments, and insults.

Once I was surprised by a woman jerking at my coat sleeve. She said she wanted to see my Rolex watch. I'm sure I disappointed her. I wear an inexpensive Feed The Children watch. Its face is a sketch of a child.

"Oh," she said, embarrassed. "Uh, I really only wanted to see what time it is."

"It's always time to feed the children," I replied.

Incidents like this hurt my feelings, of course. What's worse, though, they frightened me to my soul. I realized I was losing credibility with contributors, despite the innocence of the FTC mission and the integrity of our work.

In light of the televangelism crisis and its financial fallout that began with the undoing of Jim Bakker, I nonetheless struggled to reestablish credibility among church and charity workers across Central America. The FTC workforce had grown in proportion to the need. If FTC were suddenly to renege on its commitments, it might well be banished from countries whose governments had only reluctantly authorized its activities. Most likely, neither FTC nor I would ever be allowed to enroll their needy children again, nor would we succeed at recruiting personnel.

I pleaded with foreign host governments and organizations to stay with us, promising that not one child who'd been enrolled in Child Sponsorship would ever go hungry. Some officials nonetheless sought involvement with other charities—which was fine with me, as long as children's needs were tended.

Then FTC underwent new suspicion, once again the result of sex scandal headlines involving a televangelist who'd never been a part of our organization.

The Reverend Jimmy Swaggart was a high-profile Assembly of God preacher who conducted a ministry similar to Bakker's. Although I had remained publicly silent about Bakker's undoing, Swaggart had not.

He had denounced Bakker's behavior as "a cancer on the body of Christ." In many ways, Swaggart was balm to a wounded evangelical community. He struggled to sustain his own outreach, and his public comments on the issue had helped people feel a bit better about giving to television ministries (including FTC) after the Bakker debacle.

Then came the news accounts about Swaggart's own alleged improprieties with a prostitute in Metairie, Louisiana. In 1987 he was photographed at a motel with the woman after another evangelist had flattened the tires on his car in order to detain him. The whistle-blower evangelist then presented his photos to the Assemblies of God headquarters in Springfield, Missouri.

The Assembly of God hierarchy imposed on Swaggart two years of rehabilitation—a mandatory remedy required of ministers who commit sexual sin. Swaggart defied the church authorities, and reporters pursued him in a way usually reserved for public enemies.

Again I had no comment. My position was what it always is during crisis, to steadfastly continue walking the high road of my own ministry to feed the hungry.

As the Swaggart story heated up, contributions to FTC cooled substantially, just as they had after the Bakker incident. I felt as if I were fighting a losing battle in a senseless war that I had no part in making. FTC was an innocent bystander, suffering what military people call collateral damage.

By the end of the 1980s I thought the worst was behind us, as controversy involving evangelists had seemingly taken a holiday.

Then Swaggart put controversy back to work. On October 11, 1991, he was stopped by police in Indio, California, for driving on the wrong side of the road. His only passenger was a prostitute.

I, and millions like me, waited in suspense for Swaggart's public explanation. "God says it's none of your business," he claimed in internationally published reports.

Once again, my television viewership and financial support took a nosedive.

A SHORT TIME LATER I was called to Washington, D.C., to testify before a congressional committee investigating the stewardship of television ministries and benevolent charities. Giving sworn testimony wasn't stressful, though. I simply answered each question truthfully and as clearly as I knew how.

As you probably know, the oath specifies "the whole truth and nothing but the truth." Questions the congressmen intended to prompt a yes or no answer sometimes required more contextual information than a simple yes or no. I offered all the information that might prove helpful in a full assessment of the situation. I wanted to relate every aspect of how FTC takes care of donors' money and see it entered into the *Congressional Record*.

Someone on the panel raised the hypothetical question of what I'd do with a contribution sent by a senior citizen who, after the fact, was medically diagnosed with dementia.

I told him, the panel, the press, and the audience that I'd give back the money.

He wanted to know why committee members should believe me.

"Because I've done it," I replied.

As best I recall, I also offered to substantiate with a presentation of financial records. The chairperson pressed on with more questions and the remainder of the day's agenda.

A man rose at the opposite end of the cavernous room. He

walked around the sprawling committee table and approached me with a look of serious intent.

"I'm Congressman Charles Rangel from New York," he said to me. "I appreciate your directness."

He was familiar with Feed The Children and our efforts to ease hunger in the United States and abroad. He asked if we would commission a food drop in Harlem. If so, he would coordinate with local churches to distribute food, and cut red tape regarding the parking of our mammoth trucks.

Very soon thereafter, Feed The Children conducted the first of what ultimately became twenty-three food drops in Harlem. I'd be hard-pressed to estimate how many tons of food we've distributed in the heat of Harlem's blistering summers and bone-chilling winters.

We could not have accomplished it without Congressman Rangel's involvement. And it might not have occurred to him to seek us out had I not been summoned to testify before Congress.

It's ironic. I never know where or when opportunities to help may arise; they can even come up in the middle of a sworn testimony in the hallowed halls of government.

I HAD SET THE PATH of the FTC mission by tending the needs of one child in 1979. I'd rejoiced with the explosive growth of our outreach, which had fed more hungry children abroad than the total number of children who live in the state of Oklahoma. I had taken salary cuts, as had FTC staff, whose ranks rose and fell in proportion to the rise and fall of contributions to our ministry in the wake of scandals in which none of us had been even remotely involved.

Our faith and finances had been severely bent. Thanks be to God, they were never broken as we kept our eyes trained on the face of world hunger that constantly and mercilessly continues to ravage innocent children everywhere.

In the thick of it all, our sacrifices and persistence were rewarded. I remained clear and straightforward in my appeals to FTC viewers regarding our financial stress. While many did drop from the rolls of Child Sponsorship, others increased their contributions dedicated to our general fund. All who remained with us united to give money and prayers.

We sowed the seed, asking donors to fill the need. And God gave the increase, so that in the end the results of this long, painful chapter in Feed The Children's history can be succinctly told: not one of the thirty thousand children enrolled in our Child Sponsorship program was ever forsaken—or ever missed a meal.

Chapter Eight

𝓕EED THE CHILDREN was still under the umbrella of Larry Jones Ministries in 1981 when its workers began a quiet attempt to take it over.

Staff members were weary of what they felt was double duty, working for a parent organization and its offshoot with no increase in pay. Many called the situation unfair, and there was reason within their logic.

But FTC was rooted in love, not logic. Frances and I had always entered new outreaches by faith. We had historically provided the work and relied on God to supply the funds. He always had in His way, in His time.

Some of our workers weren't patient. Many saw their labor simply as a job, not as participation in a Christian outreach. They derived little or no emotional rewards from feeding the hungry. They instead wanted increased financial remuneration, and wanted it now.

I understood, but was powerless to capitulate. I couldn't raise salaries with new moneys. There were none, not yet.

The situation was seriously aggravated by an employee who wanted to assume the leadership of FTC. He had gone to Haiti and to Africa, and knew a lot about FTC's fledgling operation. He wanted to be in charge of the charity, and reportedly said that if he did not gain a leadership position, he'd lead a walkout.

Frances and I came to work one morning and found that our employees, and the person who'd organized them, had honored their threat. All personnel were gone.

My wife, our two children, one remaining employee, and I instantly assumed the tasks of the absentee staff. That meant that three adults and two teenagers inherited tasks formerly executed by eighteen people.

Our workforce of five tried to make television programs without a television crew, tally contributions and expenditures without accountants, oversee donations and dissemination of food with no one to monitor its receipt or distribution, and do all the day-to-day operations characteristic of evangelistic and feeding ministries, including the opening and sending of mail. We even performed janitorial duties.

Our busyness was a mental shelter. Frances and I didn't fixate on our disaster. We were too consumed with repairing it. No one can think about two things at once, and we thought only about clinging to the ministries.

Just before the walkout, the administration of Larry Jones Ministries had been converted to a computer system. In 1981 neither Frances nor I knew how to operate the terminals. Vital information for LJM and FTC was relegated to computer files we couldn't access.

Before buying the system, I'd entertained bids from IBM and other electronics giants. Mindful of donors' dollars, I opted to buy a less expensive system sold from an Oklahoma City company. I called the firm for instructions on how Frances and I could utilize our new technology. I requested that their technicians substitute for FTC's departed employees.

The business had gone bankrupt. All of their personnel had been dismissed. Freelance computer teachers were hard to find in those days. Larry Jones Ministries had a new ten-thousand-square-foot building that held computers where no one sat, as the staff had walked out before they could be moved.

For weeks a four-member family (two who worked after school) and loyal employee, Peggy Neel, exported all the grain needed for hungry people in Haiti and elsewhere.

How?

We did it with one other person who was then, and is now, the invisible partner in the mix: God. He had been with Frances and me when we started the missions. He was with us when we started over.

After many stressful weeks, new workers, most of whom had

computer skills, had replenished our staff. The assembly was soon bigger, and better, than the one that had quit. It was made up of people who shared our vision, and didn't expect us to share money we didn't have. They were people who took seriously the scripture that says, "Yet the Lord longs to be gracious to you; he rises to show you compassion. For the Lord is a God of justice. Blessed are all who wait for him!" (Isaiah 30:18 NIV). They realized that the key word was "wait."

The employees were told that they would work within the overlapping perimeters of two ministries and that their eventual pay increases would be based on merit. They were made aware that the competent fulfillment of their job description led to vocational security, not financial wealth. They were told that the ladder of success was measured by the number of people we fed, not the amount of salaries we paid.

They understood.

Larry Jones Ministries and FTC began to attract employees whose mind-set was that of co-laborers in the cause of Christ, not individuals whose incentive was a burgeoning portfolio.

Our combined outreaches had been interrupted, not stopped. They resumed their forward thrust.

No matter how many times I read the Bible, I always discover something new. In the wake of LJM's and FTC's repair, I revisited the Old Testament story of Shadrach, Meshach, and Abednego. I read again how they are bound and thrown into a fiery furnace. When King Nebuchadnezzar looks into the blazing structure, he doesn't see the ashes of three men.

"He said, 'Look! I see four men walking around in the fire, unbound and unharmed, and the fourth looks like a son of the gods' " (Daniel 3:25 NIV).

God is unseen when the furnace is ignited, is visible when it is extinguished, and has been present all along. So, too, the spirit of God had been with Frances and me during the most heated trial of our ministries. I continued to read the legendary biblical account and noticed something I'd intermittently overlooked since first reading it as a boy.

The only thing that burns on the three men is the rope that

binds them. Similarly, the ties of bondage that had gripped our ministries had been incinerated.

The realization translated into one of the most profound lessons in faith I would ever derive. I knew I'd rely on it for the rest of my life.

I'd call on it sooner than I ever expected.

IN THE MID-1980s contributions escalated in proportion to our television appeals, as the number of stations broadcasting our efforts increased. Our reputation was spreading as a hometown charity with overseas beneficiaries. More churches in Haiti and Third World nations were asking FTC for food. We consistently accepted donations, bought what wasn't donated, and underwrote distribution. I regularly promised food to a church or village and committed to subsidize its export. Contributions arrived by mail in time for me to keep my commitments.

Feed The Children remained a daily exercise in faith that was working.

I addressed my staff each week and relayed my testimonies of how God's blessings often seemed as if they'd be tardy, but miraculously never were.

I was increasingly asked to deliver similar devotions to employees at businesses throughout Oklahoma City. While speaking at a major automotive dealership, I was abruptly interrupted. An FTC worker had left word for me to call the office as soon as possible. The staff had an emergency.

Feed The Children had been robbed.

In those days FTC received the vast majority of its contributions by first-class mail. The post office held the envelopes to ensure the safety of their contents. FTC picked up the majority of its mail on Mondays.

The designated employee had departed the post office and was on his way to our headquarters when he stopped at the bottom of an exit ramp off the interstate. He was only a short distance from the FTC building when another car hit his from behind.

The driver in the offending car ran to the door of the FTC driver as if intending to ask if he had been hurt. When the FTC driver rolled down his window, the intrusive motorist brandished a pistol.

The FTC driver was frozen with fear, particularly when his passenger door was opened by an accomplice to the man with the gun. The two assailants wrestled the FTC driver out of the car and placed him facedown in an adjacent ditch. He no doubt feared he'd be shot point-blank.

He was left there, prone and helpless, as the two took off in his car, stealing the vehicle and the contributions it carried. Another thief followed in the second car.

I called an impromptu meeting of workers for another devotional service.

"We serve the same God this week that we served last week," I said. "He blessed us before the theft, and He'll bless us afterward."

I'm giving an abbreviated account of a story whose triumphant ending was that donations were replenished, at least in part. Food shipments were delayed, but not long enough to leave the recipients wanting. Some workers were asked to absorb other workers' duties while performing their own, and did.

We made it through.

Once again, I vividly realized that faith was not only positive believing but also an affirmative walk. I kept walking, trusting God to override the interruption in cash flow, and He did.

The results were not as good for the men who'd stolen from a ministry that wasn't mine and wasn't my employees'.

It was God's. I'm not going to say that God exhibited His wrath. I'm not going to say that He didn't. I'm simply going to relay the end of another anecdote in the compelling history of Feed The Children.

I'd haggled with FTC's insurance company for about a year, bickering about its liability for replacing the funds. The carrier had reimbursed cash losses for which donors had produced proof of contribution, as well as copies of checks. When the accounting ended, Feed The Children nonetheless failed to recover about $125,000.

Shortly afterward, I was called by an unidentified woman in Tulsa. She said she knew the names of all the robbers and wanted to reveal her information in person. She wanted to meet me at my office.

I told her I'd see her and warned that I'd be accompanied by police.

"That's fine," she said. "I'm on the way."

She kept her promise and so did I. As the woman entered my office, she came face-to-face with uniformed policemen, some of whom had probably participated in the robbery investigation.

Soon the authorities were certain the woman knew what she was talking about. She disclosed things about the culprits and their vehicle that were known to the officers but had never been made public. She recited unpublished facts that surrounded the crime. She established her credibility beyond reproach.

She told us the thieves had taken all of the hijacked mail to a remote field in Seminole, Oklahoma, about sixty miles southeast of Oklahoma City. By dark of night, they opened each envelope. They kept the cash and burned the checks.

Two of the three men who left the site were later killed on a motorcycle. The third was arrested on an unrelated charge and was serving time in the state penitentiary when the woman came to see me. Investigators visited his cell and procured information that verified his involvement in the robbery.

I was satisfied beyond a doubt that the prisoner and his dead cronies had robbed FTC. After huddling with a district attorney, I decided not to waste my time and taxpayers' money by prosecuting the remaining thief. He was already serving a sentence that would outlive him, with no chance of parole.

The local press reported the heist, and coverage had been offered to some wire services. The fortitude of FTC and its workers was apparent in published reports. The reportage increased our contributions.

The ordeal had been unexpected and unwanted. The results bolstered the survivors who ushered the ministry forward.

I WAS AS UNSUSPECTING regarding isolated employee theft as I'd once been in thinking FTC employees saw themselves as surrogate missionaries. Someone suggested that we take preventative police action against workers, the overwhelming majority of whom were trustworthy. I initially didn't believe the action was necessary, because I didn't want to.

There were no missing funds, as indicated by regular audits. Neither were there appreciable deficits in stored food or other commodities.

Except for a few items of donated apparel.

My storeroom manager one day mentioned that he occasionally noticed that his count of clothes was slightly inconsistent with the previous day's.

I took no chances.

Rather, I told no one about my contacting the Oklahoma City Police Department, asking that a plainclothes officer pose as an employee inside our warehouse.

The following Monday, FTC hired an undercover policeman, who reported for his first day of work unshaven and wearing dirty clothes. The clandestine cop looked as if he should be receiving goods, not helping store them.

Unbeknownst to anyone else, he accounted to me at the end of his shift.

He said he'd been approached by another employee who'd asked him if he'd like to earn extra money. The cop said he would.

The experienced worker told the lawman that he was regularly skimming from an inventory of culottes, women's slacks designed to look like a skirt. The "seasoned" employee told the cop that he sold the garments on Saturdays at a yard sale on his lawn. He also said he'd share his profits with him if he'd help him at the weekly sale.

The undercover officer arrived at the bazaar and watched his "employer" bring stolen merchandise from his garage. The host sold one pair of culottes, and uniformed policemen stepped from the surroundings.

The undercover cop arrested the FTC employee, who was put in handcuffs in front of his wife and children. He was tried and convicted on theft and related charges. The rulings were publicized, as well as reports of the sting preceding the apprehension.

Feed The Children gained a reputation within the local job market as being an employer who policed itself. It had zero tolerance for

I was five years old when
this was taken.
(Photo courtesy of author)

My parents, Lera and
Floyd Jones.
(Photo courtesy of author)

I caught these fish during a
family vacation in Florida
when I was seventeen.
(Photo courtesy of author)

My freshman year of
college basketball in 1958.
(Photo courtesy of author)

My back is to the camera as I sport my basketball uniform while crowing over Frances as Oklahoma City University's 1960–61 homecoming queen.
(Photo courtesy of author)

The first photograph of Mr. and Mrs. Larry Jones, taken in 1962.
(Photo courtesy of author)

I record my radio ministry
during the 1980s.
*(Photo courtesy of
Feed The Children)*

In the middle 1960s, I toured the Southwest with a tent, preaching revivals in
America's heartland. *(Photo courtesy of author)*

Crowds soon overflowed my touring tent, which was constantly falling down and tearing. After years of sewing it back together again myself, I finally got rid of it. *(Photo courtesy of author)*

Mother Teresa and I attended victims of the Armenian earthquake in 1988. *(Photo courtesy of Feed The Children)*

Recurring drought in Ethiopia during the 1990s produced merciless famine. Here, two dehydrated and malnourished women carry heavy loads of sticks across the desert. They'll sell them for the equivalent of a few American pennies. *(Photo by David G. Fitzgerald)*

Frances and I join Garth Brooks during his 1990s tour in conjunction with Feed The Children. *(Photo courtesy of Feed The Children)*

On April 19, 1995, Feed The Children was the first relief organization to reach bombing victims at Oklahoma City's Murrah building, in middle distance, left. Our ministry grew significantly as America's television viewers saw this shot and others like it for the six months we remained at the scene. *(Photo courtesy of Feed The Children)*

A 2001 earthquake in El Salvador reduced a church to rubble. Frances and I stand in front of the cross that sat atop its steeple, the only part of the structure that wasn't demolished. Feed The Children has established more than thirty feeding centers across the country. *(Photo by David G. Fitzgerald)*

In San Pedro Sula, Honduras, street children lie side by side each night in an effort to remain secure against nocturnal human assailants and predators. *(Photo by David G. Fitzgerald)*

From 1991 to 2002, Sierra Leone was besieged by a civil war in which the rebel militia cut off the hands of men, women, and children to prevent them from fighting. This man and his son were victims, and among thousands given food and supplies by Feed The Children inside a country with the world's lowest average per capita income. *(Photo by David G. Fitzgerald)*

After the September 11, 2001, attacks in the United States, Afghanistan was thrust into the global spotlight as a breeding ground for terrorism. The United States attacked its Taliban strongholds, leaving children as victims. Here I escort two barefoot youngsters in freezing weather. Feed The Children later sent 14,000 pairs of shoes and 18,000 pairs of socks to internally displaced persons in a camp outside Herat. *(Photo by David G. Fitzgerald)*

We at Feed The Children have been serving the Dagoretti Children's Center in Africa longer than any other facility housing disadvantaged children. Here I visit with a child with no arms who has learned to paint with her feet. *(Photo by David G. Fitzgerald)*

I often find time to play with disadvantaged residents of the Dagoretti Children's Center outside Nairobi, Kenya. *(Photo by David G. Fitzgerald)*

Contemporary Christian singer Carman, center, joins me inside a shanty in Kibera, also outside Nairobi, where we arrange to feed and medicate a family whose mother is HIV-positive and whose children were born with the disease. *(Photo by David G. Fitzgerald)*

Frances locates an abandoned baby in Africa (Kenya) and takes it to the Abandoned Baby Center. *(Photo courtesy of Feed The Children)*

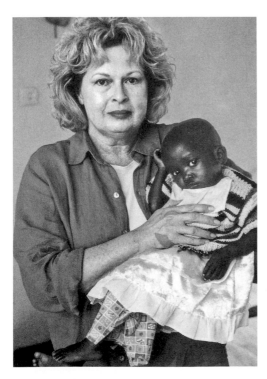

My wife, Frances, embraces a malnourished and HIV-infected child during his admittance to the Frances Jones Abandoned Baby Center, which was opened on August 1, 2001, near Nairobi, Kenya. *(Photo by David G. Fitzgerald)*

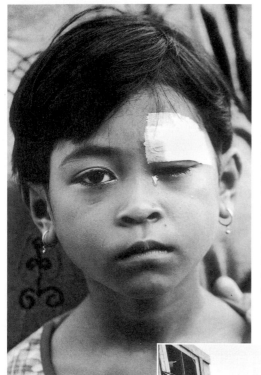

Feed The Children's relief efforts after the Indian Ocean tsunami of December 26, 2004, brought me into contact with many inspiring individuals, including Suzy, pictured here, who, along with her mother, was the only member of her family to survive the devastation. Her people were among 186,000 killed or 42,000 still missing.

Feed The Children workers and I found streets like this in Indonesia following the 2004 tsunami. Within two days after the watery strike, FTC sent its first planeload of food, carrying 38,000 pounds of nutrition and medicine. We eventually moved 700 tons of food and supplies to the worst disaster I've ever seen during FTC's twenty-eight-year history. *(Photo by David G. Fitzgerald)*

Here I am with Suzy, a survivor of the tsunami of December 2004. *(Photo by David G. Fitzgerald)*

Former United States Secretary of Agriculture Mike Espy joins me with children at a refugee camp inside Angola in 2004. Stomachs were bloated from hunger and the presence of worms. *(Photo by David G. Fitzgerald)*

For more than twenty-five years, the southern African country of Angola was wracked by civil war that ended in 2002. Refugees, including children, still live inside internally displaced persons (IDP) camps. Here I visit such a camp where Feed The Children supplies hot food, medicine, clothes, books, and other school supplies to children such as this deformed boy, who struggles to walk with the aid of a stick. *(Photo by David G. Fitzgerald)*

A caravan of Feed The Children trucks hauls the first installment of more than 600 million tons of food and medical supplies delivered to victims of Hurricane Katrina. The mission began in August 2005 and continues, in part, to this day. *(Photo by David G. Fitzgerald)*

Mississippi Governor Haley Barbour, front right, joins me in Jacksonville in August 2005, when I explained how the National Basketball Players Association and the Women's National Basketball Association had formed an alliance with Feed The Children to initiate relief efforts for survivors of Hurricane Katrina.
(Photo by David G. Fitzgerald)

A photograph of the Larry Jones family. From bottom right are Larri Sue, my daughter, and Frances, my wife. From top left are Allen, my son, and me.
(Photo courtesy of author)

Mike, my late brother, was an avid fisherman.
(Photo courtesy of author)

A contemporary shot of yours truly.
(Photo courtesy of author)

Frances and me today. *(Photo courtesy of author)*

embezzlers. That lent to the reputation I wanted, a benevolent organization that accepted in-kind gifts and financial contributions from everyone and tolerated sabotage from no one, not even our employees.

WITH THE EXCEPTION OF TELEVISION, nothing has done more to raise FTC's national awareness than its namesake trucks. They are identified with our charity as much as blimps are associated with Goodyear.

Fifty-five diesel cabs pull eighty trailers from coast to coast, criss-crossing the nation twenty-four hours a day seven days a week.

"Feed The Children" is emblazoned in twelve-foot letters on both sides of the eighteen-wheelers, familiar sights at Hurricane Katrina, the World Trade Center collapse, the Murrah building bombing, and innumerable other major disasters for more than two decades. The long-haul trucks are seen almost weekly at various major food drops, such as the Christmas 2006 New York City distribution, where ten thousand Harlem families were given enough food to feed forty thousand people for a week. The dissemination was covered by ESPN and commercial network affiliates and prompted the participation of numerous professional athletes from the National Football League Players Association, the National Basketball Players Association, and Major League Baseball teams.

At the forefront of the feeding marathon sat thirty over-the-road semitrailer trucks, which served families around 138th Street. It was called the "Miracle on 138th Street."

The rigs are big enough to monopolize the setting of news coverage afforded to our charitable missions and have been seen on NBC, CBS, Fox, and ABC, as well as countless cable channels. They've served as collection repositories at major entertainment and sports events, from regular-season games to the Super Bowl.

We receive countless requests annually for the trucks to be a part of parades in America's major cities. I can't justify using them simply as visual attractions with no benevolent benefit to FTC. I instead lend their striking presence to philanthropic organizations that have pledged donations. The trucks are ultimately about food and clothing.

I eventually authorized the scale-model building of a replica truck, a motorized and glorified toy. Civic groups pay FTC to use the novelty vehicle in community parades.

Many major entertainers who've participated in our collections have agreed to park the trucks outside their concert venues. More than one million fans saw the rigs parked outside many of the nation's largest arenas and NFL stadiums during a Garth Brooks tour in the early 1990s. People were asked to bring canned food to Garth's shows, and those who brought the most were photographed with the singer. A list of public figures too long to mention here has headlined similar collection campaigns.

There is virtually no major market in the United States where those trucks haven't been a recurring and visual pillar of collections. Additionally, they are an imposing and reassuring fixture of disaster relief, and even moved up and down the Mississippi River during the Great Flood of 1993.

Despite the trucks' advertising value, FTC's trucking company wasn't rooted in public relations. It, like all of our endeavors, was anchored in human need.

By 1982, FTC was receiving tons of in-kind gifts from manufacturers of food, clothing, and medicine. For delivery, I solicited gratis participation of trucking companies. I'd coordinate the time for a trucking outfit to have a unit in Chicago, for example, to pick up and transport a load to Atlanta. All systems were go unless the trucking company suddenly got a paying customer who wanted to hire the rig intended for FTC. The company would usually accommodate the payer, and no truck would arrive to haul FTC's donated food or nonperishables. The frustrated donor would then clear its warehouse. The charity would miss perhaps $100,000 worth of products. As a result, desperate people were forced to forgo necessities.

The scenario repeated itself time and time again.

I frequently prevented the problem by leasing trucks. Because I always negotiated for the lowest price, the trucks at the last minute were sometimes leased to another entity that was willing to pay more than FTC. Once again, I'd lose the gift from a contributor whose main incentive was to void his warehouse. The goods were given to another organization or were discarded.

It became increasingly evident that FTC was going to have to buy a truck, the first of what became the major fleet adorning U.S. thoroughfares today.

In 1982, I knew as little about the trucking business as I'd once known about exporting wheat to Haiti.

Many friends and advisers urged me not to buy that charter truck, insisting its financial overhead would be the death of the ministry. Trucks instead became its life.

Feed The Children was soon able to commit to appointed times for hauling food from suppliers who wanted to move it for floor space or for tax reasons. Whenever we received commodities on schedule, the contributor called us again. From Oklahoma City we could pick up goods anywhere in the United States within seventy-two hours. That immediacy made FTC a major source of relief to blue-chip companies needing tax-deductible reductions of swollen inventories.

As donations of goods increased, I had to buy more and more transportation licenses from the states where our first truck traveled. I had to hire an alternate driver, as the former Interstate Commerce Commission forbids a single driver to work more than a twelve-hour shift. That first old truck was worn out when FTC bought it. It soon became a relic.

Members of the staff began to joke that our truck was running on diesel fuel and prayers.

The truck broke down constantly about two years after its purchase. We'd already begun to expand the armada.

I had quickly seen the folly of paying expenses to send a truck from point A to point B, where it picked up cargo for point C. FTC then had to pay the cost for the truck's return from point C while hauling nothing.

A truck without cargo travels "deadhead miles," in the lingo of truck drivers. Deadhead miles generate no revenue and are financed at a loss.

After prolonged feasibility studies, I decided that FTC would start its own trucking company. The trucks would meet their original intention, the hauling of charitable goods, but would otherwise be available for lease.

The Internal Revenue Service cited regulations pertaining to a nonprofit organization's ownership of profitable enterprises. The IRS performed an unnecessary exercise in scrutinizing me to be sure I wasn't using the charity's trucks to gain personal profit. I didn't own the trucking company, FTC did, and all profits have always gone to the charity. Given the expensive costs of tractor-trailer rigs, and the escalating cost of diesel fuel, the trucking company hasn't shown significant profits.

But the decision to alternately use the trucks for private hauling has made it possible for FTC to absorb the cost of their overhead during well-disposed outreaches. That said, I concede that managing a trucking company has been one of the most stressful endeavors of administrating a charity.

On two occasions our trailers were blown over by high winds in Wyoming. Imagine my dismay when someone in the nation's most sparsely populated state called to ask if I knew that a truck saying "Feed The Children" was lying at the side of the road while blocking an interstate. Consider my perplexity when it happened again.

The repairs cost several thousand dollars.

We had a truck involved in a wreck in New Jersey in which it lost hundreds of gallons of flammable diesel fuel. Men from the Environmental Protection Agency wearing white fire-retardant suits were dispatched for cleanup. FTC was billed ten thousand dollars for the work. An aerial news photograph of the miles-long traffic jam was seen in several newspapers.

I earlier mentioned the Goodyear blimp. Imagine how Goodyear would be besieged with telephone calls if the aircraft were to become entangled in power lines, or its pilots were seen engaging in questionable activity before liftoff.

The same kind of reaction occurs when people think they see similar things in relation to trucks that belong to a charity. People, especially donors, are outraged.

A friend of our ministry one day reported that an FTC truck

driver was selling watermelons out of the back of one of our trailers in rural Oklahoma. The observer assumed the driver was using the truck for personal gain. That would have been true had he been selling the melons. He wasn't. He had instead asked permission to buy melons for his family. There was no wrongdoing, and a lot of people were exercised for no valid reason.

Not all reports, however, have been without substance.

Someone sent a photograph of a truck whose trailer said "Feed The Children" before a backdrop that said "Adult Bookstore." The driver was fired. Another was dismissed after he was seen relieving himself beside a gasoline pump because he couldn't wait to get to the men's room.

Still another driver claimed he injured himself when he tumbled from the cab of his truck. He filed a personal-injury lawsuit against FTC. Medical X-rays confirmed that the plaintiff had been injured. His legal action failed, however, after records proved that the injury had been sustained not on a truck but years earlier in South Vietnam.

Lawsuits are public record and available without risk of libel to the mass media. Press coverage of bogus lawsuits has resulted in a smattering of bad publicity for FTC. That has been damaging. Even a little publicity gets a lot of word of mouth.

One of our truck drivers was once transporting a woman who may or may not have been his wife inside an FTC tractor trailer. The woman was hurled from the vehicle at sixty-five miles per hour. It was never determined if she'd been pushed. She died.

The driver was exonerated in a publicized legal proceeding.

The driver had nonetheless broken an FTC rule and federal laws by having a passenger inside his long-haul truck. He'd been fired as soon as the incident was reported. Following the failure of charges against him, he called FTC headquarters. He seriously wanted to know if we would like to hire him back.

Years ago, many truck drivers brandished a bumper sticker that said, "Trucks Bring You Better Living." God knows they've brought mountains of food and relief to FTC's beneficiaries. They've carried life-sustaining nutrition and materials to our export centers for desperate people around the globe. FTC's trucking entity is one of the nation's most stable of privately owned companies, and its public relations value has been as pronounced as its functional worth. In 2006, FTC Transportation was honored with the Truckload Carriers Association National Fleet Safety Award: first place in the Small Carrier Division. I made the announcement during FTC's weekly chapel service, where our employees rose to applaud our drivers, many of whom were present.

But my learning to acquire the trucks and administrate the company's operation, before eventually hiring seasoned trucking executives, was an exercise in heartburn versus hilarity. Our drivers, by and large, were dedicated men who saw themselves as ambassadors of our ministry. The few who saw otherwise sometimes managed to be seen by the public at large.

An FTC supporter called our Oklahoma City office to report that a driver was running around a truck stop parking lot in his underwear. To that caper, I simply didn't know how to respond. I passed the ball to Frances.

"The only thing I can say is thank God," she replied. "Thank God he was wearing underwear!"

Chapter Nine

*F*EED THE CHILDREN was only five years old when I was asked to undertake what stands as one of the largest international relief efforts in our history.

In 1984 more than one million Ethiopians starved or dehydrated to death after unspeakable and prolonged suffering as one of the most ruthless famines of the twentieth century ravaged their homeland. Competing for attention in the news that same year, Hulk Hogan defeated the Iron Sheik for the World Wrestling Federation Championship, and Michael Jackson's scalp was burned by pyrotechnics during filming of a Pepsi television commercial.

The celebrity stories commanded more interest, it seems. In the train of events following his newfound fame, Hogan was asked to name a cooking grill after himself—which ultimately became the George Foreman grill. Hogan laments that he missed out on his part of $400 million in sales. And Jackson was retained as a spokesman for the soft drink company that boasted sales exceeding the sum total of Americans' donations to casualties of the famine.

Nonetheless, there were concerted efforts for relief from the United States and throughout the international community.

The Ethiopian mission offered my first depressing opportunity to look on helplessly as thousands of people perished for no good reason. Lifesaving grain, rotting in harbors a few hundred miles away at Djibouti or Assab, was withheld from processing by corrupt officials who wouldn't send trucks to haul it off the ships. To them the food was currency. They could sell it, or they could trade it— but not if it was used to feed the perishing population. They decided to let the people die. Meanwhile, various militia groups hijacked food distribution efforts, feeding hostility among internal factions whose skirmishes had ravaged the nation for years.

So the most heartbreaking element of the 1984 Ethiopian famine was not the famine itself. It was the fact that surplus food was available from a multitude of sources, but it was kept from the needy by the greed and corruption of those who held positions of power and responsibility.

In 1984 surplus grain within the European Community alone was enough to feed fifty times the combined populations of Ethiopia and the Sudan. Yet African officials declined its receipt. Such an infusion would spoil the market for the food they intended to barter or sell.

I boiled with anger over such callousness. But my fury toward crooked governments shifted to empathy for the suffering people once I arrived in Bati in Wollo Province, site of a death camp 250 miles north of the Ethiopian capital, Addis Ababa. There, my mind was burned indelibly with the image of a sea of seemingly interchangeable, emaciated bodies. For days I reached out with my hands to listless Ethiopians who were too weakened to reach back.

Bati was intended to be a distribution site for food, water, and medicine serving three thousand. Within two weeks eighteen thousand Africans lay dying on its parched ground. Even more continued staggering or crawling onto the site. Previously I had seen pockets of the dispossessed, starving in clusters. I'd interacted with them one-on-one. But here the ground was thick with starving people. They were spread out, inert and dying, like some horrific carpet, as far as my eyes could see. And they just kept coming—stretching the outer perimeter of the carpet on and on and on.

I saw thousands of women in the surrounding countryside digging in the dust for roots and dormant seeds. After a day they might scrape up enough to cover their palms. Then they'd close their grip to compact the forage, and they'd bury it. The next morning they'd divide the handful of ration among their family members. They'd spend the remainder of the day repeating this grim process.

Nothing in my life had prepared me for the Ethiopian holocaust. I found myself wrestling with the temptation to hate the men responsible for this genocide. Resisting this temptation required the constant mustering of all my spiritual resources, and then some. I vigilantly reminded myself of my personal priority: *always* to be Christlike. I repeated and repeated to myself the primary Christian principle: hate the sin, but love the sinner. The evil actions of Africa's leaders were rooted in the love of money. The apostle Paul said that the love of money is the root of all evil. I would challenge anyone to come away doubting this after bearing witness to such a travesty.

Put starkly: my Bati effort was my first experience watching masses of people struggle for their lives without any realistic hope for survival.

As a medical layman, I often assessed a victim's condition by the flow of his or her blood. As a person's condition deteriorates, the blood flows very slowly, pushed along by a weakening heart, until the heart drains of the will and energy to beat on, then ceasing altogether. But this experience shattered my preconception that death by dehydration or starvation is a process wherein the victim is gently sedated by a lessening of sensation and energy. In the scheme of things, that might be preferable. But it's nothing like that.

Dr. David Stevens, head of the Christian Medical Association (not affiliated with FTC), has described precisely the death by starvation and dehydration that I witnessed in Ethiopia, and have continued to see in my mind's eye ever since. He worked in Africa for thirteen years before publishing a report in 2005 that described the agony of demise from the absence of body fluids.

"As dehydration begins, there is extreme thirst, dry mouth and thick saliva," he wrote on WorldNetDaily.com:

> The patient becomes dizzy, faint and unable to stand or sit; has severe cramping in the arms and legs as the sodium and potassium concentrations in the body go up as fluids go down. In misery, the patient tries to cry but there are no tears. The patient experiences severe abdominal cramps, nausea and dry heaving as the stomach and intestines dry out.

By now the skin and lips are cracking and the tongue is swollen. The nose may bleed as the mucous membranes dry out and break down. The skin loses elasticity, thins and wrinkles. The hands and feet become cold as the remaining fluids in the circulatory system are shunted to the vital organs in an attempt to stay alive. The person stops urinating and has severe headaches as their brain shrinks from lack of fluids. The patient becomes anxious but then gets progressively lethargic.

Some patients have hallucinations and seizures as their body chemistry becomes even more imbalanced. This proceeds to come before death occurs. The final event as the blood pressure becomes almost undetectable is a major heart arrhythmia that stops the heart from pumping.

During my first eighteen-hour shift at Bati, sixty-seven people died. This was on Thanksgiving Day. That number, along with death tolls from the ensuing days, burned themselves permanently into my memory. This is not something I choose to remember. Nevertheless, I do. Seventy-one died on Friday, eighty-seven on Saturday, ninety-one on Sunday, and so on.

People often succumbed without anyone noticing. Their deaths were eventually discovered as they lay, with sunken eyes wide open, unblinking and covered with flies. The presence of insects on the eyes often provided the first clue. The living could still blink— although they tried not to, as their eyes produced no moisture and closing them was painful. Other times, doctors investigated with stethoscopes to detect the faintest heartbeat. It was hard to separate the living from the dead by observing their breathing, or lack thereof. Breaths were so short that chests didn't always rise and fall.

Families constantly badgered medical personnel, pleading for them to listen to their loved ones' hearts, hoping for any assurance that their rigid bodies were not yet corpses.

Whenever someone was pronounced dead, his or her survivors would scream like panthers. These noises served as wordless, broken-spirited eulogies, spreading a dense blanket of sorrow across the human expanse. They punctuated the ever-present low-level sound of sobbing among those fearing that their parent, spouse, or child would be next. In fact, the yelps often segued one into another, producing a prolonged, dissonant concert of wails, the last sounds ever heard by legions.

Sanitary arrangements also bear comment: there were none.

Diarrhea accompanies starvation. People expelled their bowels, urinated, and dry heaved into a field only yards away, the maximum distance that many could stagger before their physical urges overcame their weak constitutions, or otherwise they simply collapsed. There was no barrier to the heavy, acrid stench carried by breezes across the field.

By this point, I had spent half a decade getting food to hungry people. Although FTC's food relief often arrived at the eleventh hour, in Ethiopia we were surprised to learn that 11:30 can be too late for some who yet remain alive. Some victims were simply too weak to ingest anything, liquid or solid. And in the final stage of dehydration, nothing will save the victim, not even swallowing liquids. This is also true of malnutrition. When it advances to the final stage, food simply cannot save the sufferer.

Earlier in these pages, I recounted occasions when noticing the plight of one person signaled to me the predicament of thousands. In Ethiopia the reverse was true. At first I saw nothing but the hordes. And attempting to deal with the multitude directed my focus to one boy. His name was Ali. He was seven.

It may seem insensitive to acknowledge that charity workers sometimes have a favorite among the victims. But in the practice of relief, the bottom line is people treating people, usually one at a time. Sometimes, especially when offering relief on a mass scale, a worker can find it therapeutic to focus on a single victim for a while. It reminds you why you're there in the first place. Taking a bit of recess from the majority can help to revive you emotionally. Then you're better equipped to address the needs of the masses again. It was just such an occasion that gave rise to the bonding betwen Ali and me.

Ali's weight was perhaps half of what it should have been when he arrived at the camp with his father. He had left his mother behind, knowing she was too weak to make the perilous journey. When he told her good-bye, he was unknowingly bidding her farewell. He never saw her again. Through word of mouth, Ali learned his mother had died before he arrived at the destination intended to save his life. He was then told his sister had also died from the drought.

Additionally, Ali's grandmother had stayed behind. Ali feared he'd find the old woman dead when he returned. But he never went back. I later learned that Ali had plodded thirty miles without food and water to the rescue station. He was determined to stay alive, and I was drawn to his spirit of determination. His face appeared as loose flesh sagging over a skull, featuring prominent eyes that bulged from sunken sockets. Someone had given him a new home—a cardboard box that had previously provided refuge for a train of other children, now departed.

The daily range of temperatures in the desert was extreme. It was hot in the daytime, chilly to downright cold at night. Dehydrated, starving people have little immunity and tend to be quite susceptible to cold, owing to their sluggish circulation. Lives were frequently lost to hypothermia about two hours before sunrise. Four o'clock became the grimmest hour. Piercing screams among the bereaved came almost nonstop. Some mourners put their hands over their ears, hoping to muffle their own hysteria. All around me, people were bawling. Ironically, not one had enough fluid in his or her body to produce a single tear. Survivors felt their dying loved ones had beaten the odds if they lived through the grim reaper's daily 4:00 a.m. sweep.

A new dawn had broken when my rounds took me to Ali's side. His father looked at me in a way that rather suggested a smile. Weakness had reduced his ability to animate his ever-diminishing features. His son was still alive. I had a sense that the father felt more joy than his emaciated face could convey.

I felt safe in asking the question.

"How is Ali doing?" I said.

Answering with the faintest of whispers, barely audible, he replied that Ali had made it through the night.

Rejoicing silently, I removed my hand from Ali's fragile chest. Before moving on to another young patient, I looked squarely into Ali's determined eyes—those that had led him on his ten-day walk without food or water. Then, for a split second, I looked away.

As I did, Ali's father let out a yell. For an instant I wondered where he found the stamina to exert the volume.

My eyes darted back to Ali. He was dead.

Staring helplessly into the blank, lifeless eyes, whose last sight had been my face, I felt a sense of panic rising. Perhaps hoping for a moment of retreat from this overly poignant moment, I turned my attention back to the other child.

In the space of seconds, he had died, too.

I felt suffocated by the sad events that were closing in quite personally. On the outside, I may have seemed to be the model of composure. But inside, a storm of unspeakable terror raged. Two boys whose combined ages didn't add up to fourteen had died within seconds of each other, right there in my presence. Their stilled bodies lay huddled together in a space no broader than my shadow. If I moved, my silhouette would touch someone else. For seconds that seemed like hours, I simply sat still, staring into space and seeing nothing.

A SLIGHT RISE IN THE LANDSCAPE (what passed for a hill) was where the dead were buried, eight to a grave. I escorted Ali and other victims there to the makeshift cemetery, where we had created mounds of unmarked graves. Many of the dead were carried here from an area designated for the quarantine of people with incurable and contagious diseases. They had been sent there to die. People called that zone "The Ward Nearest Heaven."

In the process of burial, I learned a haunting lesson about Ethiopians and their uncompromising respect for their dead. Each corpse was "washed" with filthy water that had to be used again and again since the number of the dying was so great. Desperate for water, some people were tempted to drink the rancid liquid.

After the washing, each body was wrapped in cotton that people had brought to the camp as preparation for death, which they expected to come either for themselves or for their children. Each time the eight-body quota of departed was reached, the casualties were stacked atop each other in a shallow earthen vault. The next day birds of prey would pick at the cracked ground that fumed with the odor of human decay. The stench seemed to intensify as it filtered through the parched earth. The cracks remained open as if waiting to welcome a rain that just wouldn't fall. Bati had baked in the relentless sun without so much as a drop of rainfall for three full years.

I RETURNED TO THE UNITED STATES after distributing an entire shipload of wheat flour, a donation made by the National Baptist Convention worth $1.2 million. Television news had been awash with the tragedy, airing scenes of the vermin, the filthy conditions, and all the horrors of death that I had witnessed firsthand. It was real reality television, not the scripted manipulation that draws millions of American viewers today.

Wheat farmers and processors from across the nation had called FTC, wanting to donate grain to Ethiopia. I accepted anything and everything they offered. I bargained with ship lines for transport and sent several FTC workers to oversee the distribution of tons of food.

Through contacts in the U.S. and African governments, as well as the private sector, I was able to arrange agreements with the foreign governments to ensure that the cargo would be successfully unloaded and transported to our distribution points.

Not all donors were so fortunate.

Some ship lines that volunteered to transport food found that there was no way to get their bounty unloaded and transported farther once they reached the African harbors. The captains of the ships could only wait and hope that arrangements for transfer of the goods could be made. Meanwhile, anxious paying customers awaited their return. Many threatened to cancel contracts and use another transportation service if the ships didn't immediately come to pick up their shipments. Responding to the economic pressure, several ships then left the port, reportedly dumping tons of lifesaving food into the sea.

Humans were not responsible for the drought that caused the Ethiopian famine. But the blood of hundreds of thousands will forever stain the hands of those who prevented the feeding of famine victims.

Famines are a part of biblical history. The Old Testament reports that they were almost always relieved by transporting food from places of plenty to places of need. The world had no shortage of food or donors during the famine of 1984. Government officials of the affected region had a shortage of concern, human compassion, and leadership. I wonder if the world has ever before seen such outrageous greed. A few selfish officials must now live with knowing the carnage they caused. Should they finally develop a conscience, perhaps this will haunt them for eternity.

In time, I was able to pray for their souls. In time.

Chapter Ten

*I*N 1984 IN KENYA'S RIFT VALLEY, an FTC employee noticed a solitary woman walking dejectedly along a dirt road. She was gaunt, emaciated, carried no food or water, and clutched a filthy and empty plastic glass.

Our worker followed her. He watched as she joined a line behind hundreds of others who tightly gripped dry receptacles. Each person took his or her turn lying beside a spot where water leaked from the earth in a stop-and-start stream the diameter of a pencil. Thirsty people policed each other, making sure no one consumed more water than one glass could hold. Each drank, and then carried the water left in the vessel to family members in villages miles away.

Most were depleted from dehydration. With cup in hand, many passed out while wrestling the land to harness its moisture. Others prodded the faint, telling them they'd fallen asleep, forfeiting their turn to procure lifesaving liquid. The weakened struggled to their feet, and left with whatever water hadn't spilled from their containers.

Through news accounts, I'd been thoroughly watchful of Kenya's recurring drought. When I heard this narrative from one of my coworkers, I wanted to see it for myself. I'd soon decide I'd never seen anything like it.

Physicians agree that most humans can live for about forty days without food if they have water. For the malnourished, time is even shorter. Such was the case in Rift Valley in 1984, a burgeoning death camp where baked earth had swallowed the sparse rainfall, making agriculture impossible.

Water was abundant, but was hidden deep underground. Desperate people using sticks and cups could never tap its flow.

Two years later I received an unsolicited telephone call from Jim Halsey, the legendary country music booking agent whose corporate offices were in Tulsa, 110 miles northeast of FTC's headquarters. Halsey had seen our telecast from Rift Valley.

The agent said he and some of the celebrities he represented wanted to get involved with FTC. His call translated into a God-sent array of luminaries and their millions of fans, some of whom became advocates of our missions. That lonely woman walking to Rift Valley's feeble water well indirectly activated legions of supporters.

Halsey's clients included the Oak Ridge Boys, a quartet whose fame the late Johnny Cash had nurtured. The group went on to garner multiple Grammy Awards and numerous number one songs. They were a headlining Las Vegas attraction that had released their second volume of greatest hits.

Halsey told me the group was getting top billing at a world-renowned music festival in Nice, France. The Oaks wanted to donate their fee to FTC to help the starving.

Overwhelmed, I suggested the money would be better spent for water, more specifically, for Rift Valley's buried reserves to be tapped and pumped aboveground to outlets. I'd made up my mind to somehow build water wells in that part of Kenya.

Research had shown that pure water eradicates twenty-seven diseases. These poor Africans were desperate enough to drink anything, including the foul puddles standing in shrinking cesspools. They had nothing to lose. If they forwent water for fear of disease, they'd die from dehydration.

I knew that Kenya's nomadic tribes constantly moved in search of any trickle of water. History had proven that once a tribe found water, it would settle at the source for as long as it lasted. Someone would erect a food stand or little store where outlying farmers would bring what few crops they could raise. That food would be sold or traded to tribal members. If the water held out, and if it didn't breed disease, charities such as FTC could then help fashion a tiny, makeshift school. A constant source of freshwater, I surmised, would enable us to eventually build an agricultural center where we could teach people how to grow food. FTC or other charities could also consider construction of a medical clinic and maybe a school. But our first concern wasn't saving souls; it was saving lives, and this depended on continuous, consumable water.

I determined that four wells would be needed to support the work within our outreach sixty miles west of Nairobi. Feed The Children could drill the wells for about $125,000, procured through television appeals. I asked Halsey if he and the Oak Ridge Boys would agree to our using their donation as start-up money for the drilling of wells. I promised to name each well after a member of the quartet: Joe Bonsall, Duane Allen, William Lee Golden, and Richard Sterban.

My idea was approved. Exploration commenced for drinkable water in a drought-ravaged valley halfway around the world. The undertaking was simultaneously steady and haphazard.

The first two drillings produced dry holes. Don Richardson, the project manager, had a deal with three men who worked as contractors. It called for them to move the rig, free of charge, if it sunk a hole that failed to yield. They honored their commitment, and a month into the pursuit two rigs were moved, and two more holes were drilled. They hit, and thousands of Kenyans had water.

Thousands more still needed it. Countless died of thirst and disease-related contamination during the four months needed to finish our exploration. As people waited on water, I observed first-hand the loss of lives without it.

There was the matter of mechanical disrepair, as evidenced by the continual breakdown of drilling equipment. Don had a long-time background in irrigation. He had overseen the transfer of water along the seared wheat farms that line the sweltering south-western United States. He had personally grown high yields of grain during dry summers where temperatures exceeded a hundred degrees.

He knew how to find underground water and how to disperse it for miles across thirsty and cracked terrain. He'd seen nothing like the antiquated drilling equipment he encountered in Africa.

In 1986 he saw machinery powered by a 1927 motor. It ran on diesel fuel that ignited only two cylinders. Don was trying to pull water from underground with compression that would barely pull the hat from his head. The task was especially challenged by one well whose depth was 450 feet, more than some Oklahoma oil wells.

Don was accustomed to American laborers and their work ethic. In Africa he encountered workers who moved at a snail's pace, partly as creatures of habit in a culture where no one rushes, partly due to listlessness from lack of fluids.

The men toiled a couple of hours and rested a couple of hours. The machinery was broken a couple of hours, and repairs took a couple of hours. That pretty much filled an eight-hour shift, and drilling was passed to the next crew, who worked in a similar manner.

There was another problem, one we've seen repeatedly during FTC's missions. Corruption.

The contractors had assured Don that they'd studied hydrology maps at Rift Valley's county office. They were sure, they said, that they could pinpoint subterranean pools and streams. They knew nothing about Don's background.

He'd been busy overseeing the move of the first well from its initial dry hole. Meanwhile, the man in charge of the second had taken it to a place Don hadn't seen. When Don was sure the first was in production, he wanted to visit the second.

The contractor didn't want Don to go, assuring him that he could handle things without him. Don's gut told him something was wrong. The more Don was told he needn't come to the site, the more he determined to go.

Don pulled onto the drilling locale about two hundred miles away, off the map of Rift Valley. He estimated its elevation at three thousand feet.

The spot was a wheat farm owned by the contractor's brother. The man had been secretly intent on irrigating his sibling's land.

Don is a gentle man who's slow to anger, and intolerant of lies. He didn't ask the contractor what he was going to do; he told him. The drilling rig, Don said, would be moved back to Rift Valley at the contractor's expense. Exploration, Don told him, would resume at no cost to FTC. It would continue until water was found for needy people, not for anybody's family farm.

Don said those things plainly, and said them only once. The Kenyan spoke limited English, but understood the tone of determination. The man moved the well and subsidized the costs, labor and all.

Within days, all four wells were producing. Within months, FTC began to work with other charities to develop communities near the wells. For years, people have drunk, bathed, and washed clothes in the lake of water that has been extracted by four wells that still grace the horizon of a formerly dirt-dry valley.

The wells were subsidized by the Oak Ridge Boys and FTC donors. It was a onetime expense whose maintenance has been absorbed by Kenyan workers, motivated by flowing water on which they depend to live.

In 2001, Frances was in Kenya on an unrelated mission that happened to be near one of the wells. The demeanor of her interpreter indicated he wanted to tell her something personal. In so many words, he thanked Frances for helping save his life.

She didn't understand.

"When I was a little boy, I watched them drill that well," he said. "Each well casts a shadow that's a shrine to life," he implied, in limited vocabulary. She knew what he meant, and he knew she did. The man might not be alive today were it not for the water well that revived his ebbing childhood. He might instead be buried beneath the very soil from which the well extracts water.

The man listened to my wife and relayed her English to the masses that spoke Swahili. He told them again what God and FTC had done to save their lives.

The wells' development had begun due to the need of one woman. More than two decades later, throngs still drink from them. A cliché says there's power in numbers. There is. The most powerful is often found with One.

"The Lord will guide you always; he will satisfy your needs in a sun-scorched land and will strengthen your frame. You will be like a well-watered garden, like a spring whose waters never fail" (Isaiah 58:11 NIV).

MY TEAM AND I WERE three hours outside Addis Ababa, the capital of drought-plagued Ethiopia, when we again encountered an individual who indirectly abetted the treatment of countless others. We were doing follow-up work at an agricultural center, another place where we had developed a water source to enable people to grow food. We irrigated and bought oxen to break the hardened land. We were making additional plans for additional needs.

The task became routine, meaning it was routinely difficult. People who've lived short lives with little food were not always adept in learning how to grow it. I therefore was fixated on assessing the functions of a potential food center. Once again, FTC was importing food to a center where people could eat while learning to cultivate their own.

Movement was restricted for outsiders. Each country had its own shaky government with its own rules. Civil wars erupted in many. Visitors from the United States, even relief workers, were heavily policed. Governments wanted to be sure we weren't supporting insurgents during internal conflicts.

Permits were required to move from one location to another. We needed approval in order to use government vehicles and were assigned "minders," men who accompanied us to ensure we passed through checkpoints at our assigned times. The idea was to guarantee we didn't work on missions after nightfall.

We were filming our agricultural center for an appeal I'd later make to stateside donors. The plan was to show them where their money had gone, and where it was needed. On one particular day, the process was surrounded by setbacks. Time got away from me.

I expected Don to regularly monitor my schedule to keep each day's time from running out before sundown. Don knew that should I fail to negotiate three checkpoints between Addis Ababa and us by nightfall, the FTC workers and I would be thrown in jail. There would be no arrest, no trial, and no guarantee as to when we'd be released. We'd simply be hurled into a cell overcrowded with desperate men in remote Africa.

"Larry," Don said, for the third time on this difficult day, "we've got to go."

The sun was high in the sky—the western sky. It was dipping into the horizon when we at last departed. If our caravan ran without breakdown, if roads were just right for passage, we'd still be late. We'd be lucky to reach the first checkpoint by nightfall. Making all three was impossible.

We were embarking on our journey, racing from our camp, when something caught my peripheral vision. On closer look, I saw that it was a baby. Although dusk inhibited vision, I could see from perhaps twenty yards that the infant was seriously ill, evidenced by its limp body draping around the frail arms of the woman holding it. To demonstrate her desperation, the woman lifted the baby above her head. She clearly needed help and had obviously heard that Americans near her village could provide it. The sight was heartbreaking.

I wanted to stop but decided against it. Nightfall was tightening its grip. I rationalized the obvious: that I'd be of no use to one baby or anyone else if I landed in jail. Besides the wasted time from incarceration, I'd risk losing the permit that would enable me to return the next day to the agricultural center. I'd also jeopardize the film permit that was the eyes through which our supporters saw our efforts. I reminded myself that I was currently involved in developing a long-term feeding mission, not an immediate medical undertaking. After all, I told myself, no one on the team had pharmaceuticals. We'd brought along no medical personnel. No matter how dire the baby's needs, I had no resources to address them.

I could not construct a logical reason to stop.

God isn't always logical. More frequently, He's miraculous. Always, His voice is relentless.

"Do not withhold good from those who deserve it, when it is in your power to act" (Proverbs 3:27 NIV).

Don was riding in the lead car when he called mine, the second in the convoy.

"Larry," he said, his voice cracking through a two-way radio. "Did you see that baby on the shoulder of the road?"

"Yes," I answered. "I did."

"Oh" was his only reply.

The sight had obviously shaken him as much as me.

"Why would he, the timekeeper of our schedule, call my attention to something that would detain us?" I asked out loud.

I called Don back and said I wanted to stop. He didn't get to respond. His voice was overridden by the shouting of the government minder inside his car. The man's angry tone leaked into Don's microphone. The minder repeatedly said that in no way was the caravan going to halt. We had to make the checkpoints without being any later.

We must have ridden another mile before impulse overtook me. I had always trusted God to direct my ministry, and to do it with His whispered inclinations, and with visible signs.

His whisper had been in my heart. The live sign of a dead or dying baby had been thrust in my face.

"Stop the cars," I said into my radio. "We're going back."

One of the minders took Don's handset. He told me what I already knew, that if we were late, our losses would include the forfeiture of government cars.

I didn't argue with him. How could I? I had no reasonable argument.

"We're going back," I said again.

I heard disgusted moans from the minder.

The baby was still asleep when I got to it. Actually, it was unconscious. The mother was of no help. I couldn't understand her. I, of course, didn't know her. But I knew her look. I'd seen it on others thousands of times. It was the gaze of relief, cast toward a person who she'd been told could save the life of her child. She didn't know it wasn't that simple.

Her stare simultaneously uplifted and frightened me. I was blessed with the opportunity to serve and terrified that I probably couldn't do a thing.

The weakened woman handed me her baby and virtually fell at

my feet. I don't know how long she'd been standing on the side of the road holding the infant, but she could hold it no longer. Its life was now in my hands—literally.

I helped the mother and child into my car. I held the baby in one arm and used the other to call the lead car.

Don relayed all of the awful things, as described by the minder, that were awaiting us in jail.

"We're going to the nearest hospital," I said.

There are times when my mind becomes so overloaded it simply cannot provide a rational explanation for my actions. During those times, I ignore my mind and listen to my heart. That's the only route to peace, the catalyst to right thinking and all that goes with it.

Our schedule wasn't dented; it was totally destroyed by the lay-over we had inside a primitive hospital before we ever reached our first checkpoint. I didn't leave the baby until a doctor could treat it.

I waited for two hours. The drivers were threatening to leave us and had to be persuaded to take us as far as the first checkpoint. There, they planned to go on to the Ethiopian capital. They said nothing about returning to retrieve the rest of us from jail.

Someone asked why they couldn't return the next day. A minder said he had no assurance we'd be released by then.

A doctor finally confirmed he could treat the baby and initiate its recovery with fluids and medication. I made arrangements to pay the costs. Because FTC had earned a credible reputation in that part of the world, the doctor took me at my word. FTC later paid his fees, and the hospital's, in full.

Our convoy resumed, en route to the first checkpoint, where everyone agreed we'd be put in handcuffs. Somehow, I wasn't sure.

The lights of the first stop were visible from perhaps a quarter mile away as we approached. Still in the second car, I waited for the first to slow down. It didn't. In fact, its driver accelerated, and so did mine. I bent down to look through the windshield and saw two uni-formed men in the middle of the road sporting rifles. Their hands stretched skyward and waved us forward, directing our motorcade straight through the checkpoint. Obviously, they did not want us to stop.

The guards were a blur as our cars whisked by them.

The same scene was repeated at the second and third check-points. In the middle of the night, we arrived at our Addis Ababa hotel, where Don and I visited with the minders and drivers. Most had ushered American visitors, including missionaries, for years. None had ever seen them get through a checkpoint after dark. None had ever imagined that visitors would ever pass at any time of day without detainment.

There's no logical explanation as to why it happened for us. No one had called ahead to ask for permission to pass. We had no mobile telephones in those days. Our two-way radios wouldn't connect with the checkpoints.

I'd been consumed earlier in the day with the overwhelming agricultural needs of the tiny farming community created by FTC. It was peopled by Ethiopians who were besieged by hunger, not glaring disease.

Yet the distance of a hospital from our agricultural center underscored the immediate need for medicine at the farming site.

This insight came via one suffering baby.

Feed The Children was not that old, and our focus had primarily been on feeding, with ancillary emphasis on medicine and clothing. Back then, we treated the sick wherever we happened to find them.

The way I became aware of the conspicuous medical deficiencies in rural Africa almost a quarter of a century ago, through the dire straits of a baby, may seem naive. But FTC has always been focused on relief, the immediate meeting of needs as they arise. We had responded to the life-killing demands of famine and had been shown the life-sustaining need for medicine.

And all by the predicament of one baby.

⁓

ONE PERSON'S HARDSHIP has repeatedly instigated ministries that have addressed the multitudes. The situation has also been true in reverse.

In the mid-1980s I encountered the desperation of hundreds of children, and it was alleviated by one individual whom I'd never met at the time and whom I haven't seen since. The scenario set a precedent and has unfolded countless times since then.

I've often told my staff that we'll always respond to needs that are put in front of our faces. The faces of little children were thrust into my own in Nairobi, not far from the mansion where filming took place for *Out of Africa,* starring Robert Redford and Meryl Streep.

The site where I found these distressed youngsters was hardly mansionlike.

Feed The Children had set up another feeding center and Child Sponsorship program outside Nairobi. I had returned to shoot a video to show my television audience how its contributions were being utilized.

I was speaking to a class that held 60 kids in various grades, all taught by one teacher. There were three other identical classrooms inside the building. That meant 240 students, none with textbooks, were instructed by four women using a blackboard as their only learning aid. The need for expansion was irrefutable.

I addressed youngsters who were distracted, as was I, by the scratching of other children on the exterior sides of the walls and broken windows.

I stepped outside to face perhaps two hundred children who wanted to come inside a school where there was no room, not even to sit on the dirt floor.

Don had preceded me on this mission. Before he departed Oklahoma City, I'd told him that FTC had reached a new low in its general fund and admonished him not to commit money for any new projects. We were still reeling from fallout over the Jim Bakker scandals. The ink was barely dry on the pink slips I'd handed out to former employees due to financial cutbacks.

That day in Nairobi, I asked Don why kids milling outdoors weren't in school somewhere. He said all schools in and around their community were full. They weren't in school because, for them, there was no school.

Don also said the school I was addressing owned land where a schoolhouse could be constructed. The school had no funds for expansion.

I stood among the children that education was forgetting. They literally spent their days on the outside looking in at other kids who were being taught.

I could feel my spirit of contradiction rising, as I was going to go against my own directive to Don.

I had no idea how I'd get the money. Rather, I had no idea how God would provide it.

My television crew finished shooting the children under instruction and steadied cameras on those who were not. Meanwhile, I stepped off the footage of the land owned by the existing school and confirmed there was enough to situate a new, four-room addition. Within a day, Don and I talked to a contractor who could build it, complete with a floor, windows, rock walls, and a roof, all for sixty-five hundred dollars.

In retrospect, it's hard for me to believe the operating fund of what had firmly become an international ministry would not allow a few thousand dollars to educate so many students. But that was the cold reality.

I had a potential contractor in sight and needy children all around me. I told the man to start building. The credibility of FTC again showed itself in Africa. The fellow began construction without a contract, accepting my word that he'd be paid.

I returned to America and aired footage of the education-starved children. I asked viewers to send contributions earmarked for the project. The following week no designated money had arrived. The scenario repeated itself during weeks to come. Meanwhile, building continued in front of children who sat for hours, watching workmen erect a structure where they'd been promised they'd learn to read and write.

I'd never made a commitment on behalf of FTC that wasn't kept. I knew God would provide the revenue in His time, and hoped it coincided with the time that construction was finished. God had a lot to remember. Had He forgotten the children and my promise to attend them?

The prayerful and anxious vigil continued for weeks, and finally I was told the builder was only days away from placing a sheet-metal roof atop the new school. Excited children continued to walk for miles to the site each day. Their mounting enthusiasm couldn't be contained. Someone said they clapped when workmen arrived at the project each morning. Youngsters often got there before laborers.

We at FTC were opening mail Monday through Friday while hoping for a check. Our people approached the bottom of the pile. There were donations, many specified for Child Sponsorship and other designated programs. There was one more, sent by a former schoolteacher who'd liquidated a part of her retirement portfolio. The check contained a letter that assigned the amount for school construction in Nairobi, enough to cover the entire cost of the structure.

One woman had sent one check that paid for a school that, to this day, has steered the educational process for thousands of students. The envelope was opened in seconds. Its results will last indefinitely.

A FINAL RECOLLECTION COMES TO MIND about one person's unexpected but dramatic impact on many.

In the mid-1980s I read an article about "Jane," an impoverished woman who was worshipping God one day under a tree, the only landmark for miles within an African desert. Someone was drawn to her audible praise. Soon, so was another person, another, and more.

Shortly afterward, Jane could be heard praying each Sunday beneath the barren foliage, and her few onlookers increased to scores. Many participated with her in worship, and the open-air site was quickly named "Jane's Church."

While en route to one of Rift Valley's water wells, I was unknowingly traveling near "Jane's Church" while accompanied by Dr. Stan Mooneyham, former president of World Vision, an international relief organization. He had brought along the man who'd written about "Jane's Church."

I told the scribe that I'd been fascinated by his article.

"Would you like to go to Jane's Church?" he asked.

"What?" I replied, bewildered.

"We're going to pass it on our way to Rift Valley," he said.

"Yes," I almost shouted. "I'd love to see the tree and meet Jane."

"Fine," he said. "Would you like to preach there?"

Taken aback, I instantly said that I would.

The wind was hot and foul, as if nature had bad breath, on the morning I stood beneath that withering tree. Seventy-three women and children sat on logs that had been pulled for miles to surround the tree, still the only permanent fixture of Jane's Church. Twenty-five men stood in the encircling bush. Each was partially invisible and within earshot of the branches.

I was told that the men wouldn't approach, as they were ashamed to be the failed providers of their women and children who had nothing. Literally nothing.

I don't remember what I spoke about that morning.

During earlier weeks, some of the people had individually accepted Jesus Christ as their personal savior. They were more joyful than any "congregation" I'd ever addressed.

They raised their hands, closed their eyes, and opened their souls as they sang "Amazing Grace" in Swahili. Their voices drifted like the breeze over the parched terrain.

Some wore only enough clothes to cover their gender, and those tatters were their only possessions. They had nonetheless walked as far as ten miles, and planned to walk back, just to stand under a dried tree and worship God.

I felt simultaneously guilty for all I had back in America and envious of all they had within.

Relentless sunshine glistened on their bodies and would later set on their hunger. Sweat streaked their faces and mixed with joyful tears. Their spirits soared toward heaven, defying their earthen hell.

I'd come to preach to them, but their charged demeanors ministered to me. Overcome with what I saw and felt, I wept while utterly penitent.

Life had never taken anything away from them, as they'd never had anything. I took their time, of which they had plenty, and I took memories of them. Those recollections have taken me through many struggles that I realize now were the product not of my circumstances but of my lack of faith.

Those forgotten people never knew they changed the man who'd come to change them. But they will, when we meet in heaven.

If heaven has a tree, it surely will be Jane's.

And so the ministry continued. To this day I continue to drive past the site whenever I'm en route to Rift Valley. On weekdays it's just a withering growth enveloped by empty space. No one would suspect that it's been the scene of hundreds who eventually assembled, and that countless have made decisions to accept Jesus Christ as their personal savior.

Once again, one person was used to change the multitudes. This time the multitudes made for lifetime changes in one American preacher.

"I raised you up for this very purpose, that I might display my power in you and that my name might be proclaimed in all the earth" (Romans 9:17 NIV).

I'll always believe in the power of one.

Chapter Eleven

*B*Y THE MID-1980s I'd recognized the obvious: nothing is more effective than national television for promoting an international humanitarian outreach.

As a curator of donated funds, I'd often tried to avoid coming to this conclusion. Television time was (and still is) expensive compared with other mass media, such as newspaper or magazine advertising.

Still, no other medium proved so powerful in recruiting donors from viewers as well as the corporate community. And television's magnetic appeal was becoming even stronger as basic cable service was fast becoming a part of every community in the nation.

I would invest FTC contributors' dollars to buy television time, and the return was astronomical in terms of donated food, goods, and services.

Back then, critics said what some continue to say now—that I, a steward of private contributions, could not afford to spend donations on expensive television time. I'd concluded, however, that I couldn't afford not to.

Nonetheless, I continued to wrestle with uneasiness about television's high cost when compared with that of other media. Sometimes I engaged the services of various professional television time buyers who claimed they could buy blocks of airtime more cheaply than I could. Many talked a good game, but not all delivered. Some were more interested in their sales commissions than in the welfare of suffering people. Many agents saw their work as only a job. I viewed their services as FTC's most valuable channel for publicizing and financing its lifesaving missions.

In 1984 I attended a conference in Washington, D.C., where I met Van Dalton, a political science graduate who'd recently managed a campaign for a candidate from Virginia running for state senate. I'd been searching for someone to handle FTC's in-house public relations, and I immediately knew Van was my man. He was among those select individuals in my life with whom I instantly clicked. He saw affiliation with FTC as co-labor in improving the human condition. This was made clear when I asked him to move from the lush scenery of Washington's Potomac River to the comparatively bleak flatlands surrounding FTC's Oklahoma City headquarters and he agreed.

Larri Sue, my daughter, picked up Van at the airport, where she drove over a speed bump as they were departing the terminal. The bump, she told Van, might be the highest landscape he'd see in the entire state. Obviously she meant this as a joke, but Van's attitude toward the mission was no joking matter. He'd come to garner publicity for an organization that fed the famished. He didn't care where he lived, as he lived to work for FTC. This mission, he felt, might take him anywhere.

I relished his attitude.

As I observed Van's dedication, I considered using him to purchase television time. He had a limited television background. Mostly he'd learned about buying for a nonprofit charity the same way Frances and I had learned to gather and disseminate food—through on-the-job training.

Shortly afterward, a political insider from the Washington Beltway became an FTC worker who commuted to the bleakest parts of the globe. Van changed with the change in his environments.

I remember Chad in 1986, when FTC workers and I had to take armed guards with us into dangerous refugee camps that had formed after Libya had bombed the region. Van was still naive about the volatile desperation of those we attended. He'd wondered why we were accompanied by armed escorts. To him, this seemed to be a show of force that contradicted the loving spirit of a feeding mission.

Van had never seen people who were starving to such a degree that they would kill each other to be the first in the food line. The mission marked the first time he witnessed dire drought where dead leaves were the only pitiful reminder of what had been plant life. He saw emaciated people struggle to climb trees to eat the brittle foliage. Its sharp dryness cut their tongues, so they ground the leaves into anything that would hold water and swallowed the filthy mix.

We took Van to Ethiopia, where drought-stricken people were almost catatonic, dazed with thirst and hopelessness. Their bodies were too dehydrated for their eyes to tear, even as their parched throats leaked the sounds of subtle sobbing.

Van had to shut down his senses.

He had to postpone his natural human reaction to the desperation so he could fixate on a solution. He waited until he returned to America before finding a place to fall apart.

Van, I confirmed to myself, was someone who understood the premise of Feed The Children, a relatively new coalition addressing mankind's oldest quest, the search for survival, whose first priority is food.

During the rest of the 1980s and well into the 1990s, under Van's administration, Feed The Children's television exposure experienced its greatest growth. Van mastered the art of bargaining, convincing himself that anything for sale is negotiable. He witnessed television stations' discontinuance of selling time for religious programming in the wake of the evangelistic scandals of the 1980s. Van made it clear to station general managers that Feed The Children's thrust was not evangelical but humanitarian, intending to address the needs of the world's starving. He persuaded stations that had dropped our program to renew it.

Like any good man, Van considered the purpose of his job to be more important than the person who filled it. He was willing to share or surrender his work to anyone who could do it better. In time, he found this in a man and his wife who'd started a new company to buy television time for religious organizations.

Today, Ray and Betsy Davis's Affiliated Media Group represents more than one hundred ministries. It still represents the only humanitarian client it has ever had—Feed The Children. By 1991, FTC had become firmly established with AMG, now the nation's biggest buyer of television time for religious programming. Ray consistently promised clients that AMG could buy more time for less money than any other agency. His vision fit perfectly with mine—which is to spend donors' dollars wisely. Recognizing this, I was instantly tempted to go with him. But I wouldn't until he passed a test.

IN RECRUITING FTC AS A CLIENT, Ray proposed a no-obligation challenge. I accepted. The terms were that AMG would approach television stations in twenty-five of the nation's markets where time buying was most expensive. Ray said he'd renegotiate my deals and procure the same time slots for lesser rates. He said he'd charge me nothing for the service.

If he failed to pull it off, he and AMG would go away, he said. If he succeeded, he wanted me to retain his company for future buying.

It was a no-lose proposition. And it worked.

Ray first approached a Los Angeles station where he reduced FTC's rate by 40 percent. The annual savings amounted to more than one million dollars, which was plowed back into FTC's general fund and used to procure more food and necessities for casualties of hardship and disaster.

I didn't pry into the mechanics of Ray's time-buying techniques. To a degree, his business was none of mine. I was mostly concerned with the bottom line, and it was more indelible than it had ever been.

Nonetheless, Ray shared part of his business strategy with me. He kept FTC's purchase prices down by making them part of buying blocks shared by multiple clients. Instead of purchasing thirty minutes specifically for us, Ray would buy four hours to be divided among religious shows and our outreach. This block-buying technique cut the rates for all of the ministries, including our humanitarian efforts.

The public relations skills of Jim Shaffer complemented Ray's talents perfectly. Jim knew how to buy time by selling himself, if that makes sense. He's a bright guy who's as likable as he is savvy. His warm demeanor is accessible to anyone, from television's general managers to those who work for them. His charisma is subtle but compelling, in that he naturally calls attention to himself and his credibility without being obnoxious. What you see in Jim is exactly what he is, and seemingly everyone likes what they see.

RAY AND HIS STAFF, including Van and Jim Shaffer, also shared some of the more dramatic ordeals behind the overhaul of FTC's television buying. One television station, for example, had threatened to break its buying contract with FTC and to sell our time to someone willing to pay more for it. Some station managers plainly didn't care that their stations, by airing Feed The Children, were helping mankind. They were concerned only about raising their financial profits.

Ray persisted with some highly aggressive negotiation techniques. He'd threaten to sue stations for their implied mistreatment of hungry people, and remind them that the lawsuit would be public record. He'd say that he'd see to it that the action was publicized. He'd ask if that was the kind of publicity they wanted for their company.

He also used other aggressive ploys that, back then, were foreign to me. He never hesitated to call on the relationships he had cultivated within the television industry. A former television station general manager himself, Ray had amassed a list of business contacts that was worthy of a big business conglomerate. He approached those powerful men with the social graces of a diplomat and the determination of a pit bull—as did all the members of his team.

Reportedly, Van once threatened to expose a questionable aspect of a television mogul's personal background. His pressure tactic was voiced after the man's representative had warned he'd break a contract with FTC and sell its time to another buyer at a higher rate.

The magnate's representative countered with a threat to sue for slander and libel. Van asked the representative if he had a dictionary and suggested he look up the definition of those words. Van contended that charges of slander and libel won't hold up if the spoken or published words are true. The tactic worked. A station that had threatened to take a valuable time slot from FTC did not. Our message about hunger and our missions to address it went forward.

By 2006 Ray and his team had put together a number of channels to air Feed The Children programming, consisting of ABC, CBS, NBC, and FOX affiliates, as well as national cable channels—often as many as thirteen. Through bulk buying and AMG's trade secrets, the savings to FTC were phenomenal.

Ray Davis and crew had unquestionably proven themselves as FTC's key to economical buying of broadcast and cable time. Their tried-and-true approach translated to savings the charity used to aid people on five continents.

Ray's efforts toward furthering the cause of FTC remained unceasing. I spoke to him an average of twice daily, even through his diagnosis with cancer to the time I learned it had killed him on February 16, 2007. He'd been fighting the disease for many of the same years he fought to bolster the humanitarian efforts of Feed The Children.

Someone wondered if I'd been asked to preach Ray's funeral. The fact is I had—by Ray.

He and I were fishing one day when he surprised me with his final request. He asked me and others to participate in his eulogy. I was glad to accept and touched when able to deliver. I meant my words as nothing less than a celebration of a man who had breathed so much life into Feed The Children through broadcasting our cause on television.

Some mourners wondered if I'd decided to speak because FTC was Ray's favorite client. The answer was no.

The Joel Osteen ministry was his favorite client. Dr. Creflo Dollar, with his national Christian outreach, was his favorite client. The Reverend Benny Hinn, with his worldwide crusades, was his favorite client. The small church in Middle America whose sermons are broadcast on one station was his favorite client. Ray treated each client the same in that he made each equally special. The combined ministries reached millions of people each week. Our outreach was largely attributable to Ray Davis and his brilliant business savvy, which is clearly shared by his widow. A co-laborer with Ray, Betsy mastered the fundamentals of television buying. She has that most important characteristic of executive leadership: she knows her strengths and her weaknesses. She gives 110 percent to the tasks she selects, and delegates those she feels could be better executed by someone else.

A former pillar of support for AMG, Betsy is now its capable leader. Someone asked if I thought she could walk in Ray's tracks.

"She can walk in his tracks," I said, "and she can fill his shoes."

I have no agenda in saying that. Feed The Children doesn't need to obtain the services of AMG; it already has them.

I have no incentive to issue the above superlatives except that they're true. Feed The Children has become a staple of America's television programming because of a man, his wife, and his dream—coupled with the efforts of like-minded visionaries such as Van and Jim.

I sincerely thank all of them.

So would FTC's beneficiaries, if they knew about AMG and its crucial role in furthering both the extent and the effectiveness of FTC's outreach. Many of them have encountered some of the AMG crew as volunteers who regularly work food drops or rescue missions.

The company's executives and employees have walked the lines of FTC's food missions to lovingly mingle with the rank and file of the needy we serve. Many food recipients have told me there was something special about these kind strangers—a feeling of connection.

The fact is, they *were* connected—very directly, in ways they'd never know.

Chapter Twelve

I HAD NOT HEARD FROM the FBI since I received a death threat during my antipornography crusade of the 1970s.

In June 1985 the bureau initiated a series of secret investigations into my ministry—and me, personally. In many cases the agents were merely going through the motions, as it wasn't hard to see that the allegations were ludicrous. Nonetheless, they were bound by law to pursue any accusations of wrongdoing.

Today, I'm the subject of a 125-page FBI file kept by the Justice Department of these United States. I obtained the cache in 2006 by exercising provisions within the Freedom of Information Act.

Entries show that I was investigated numerous times by the nation's most powerful law-enforcement agency after allegations were made against me by persons whose identities weren't revealed as a matter of bureau policy.

I'd be remiss as a curator of financial donations if I didn't disclose charges of misconduct or misappropriation filed against me. The resulting probes vindicated me, ratified my innocence, and validated the integrity of Feed The Children. Not one investigation resulted in my arrest. Not one initiated an investigation of anyone with whom I did business. All revealed me to be what I am in the eyes of the law: squeaky-clean.

That doesn't mean, however, that no damage resulted from the FBI investigations. They caused a lot of raised eyebrows—even among my associates, employees, and personal friends, who were contacted by agents seeking information about me. People are susceptible to the perception of guilt by implication. The inquiries implied that I might be embroiled in nefarious activity, and some people seemed to think me guilty until proven innocent.

The mere fact that I was under scrutiny damaged my reputation in the eyes of some. That's why I have never made public the fact that I have an FBI file—until now.

Thankfully, many who learned of the investigations instantaneously vouched for my good character and the legitimacy of FTC. One fellow repeatedly told agents that he'd be glad to participate in all surveys, that he was positive none would incriminate me.

"You'll never find him guilty, because guilt isn't there," he said. Toward the end he asked an agent how many other people could consistently emerge blameless after so many recurring probes.

I appreciated my friend's confidence and loyalty.

Some agents seemed to become weary of assessing and reassessing me. I never had anything new and incriminating to say.

"Come to me at the start of these things," I urged. "I'll tell you exactly how things really are. It will save you a lot of time and the government a lot of money." Nevertheless, their inquisitions usually didn't work that way. More than once I got a call from a government agent telling me I'd been vindicated in an investigation that I didn't even know about.

A 1985 inquest claimed that FTC was receiving one million dollars a month in donations and alleged that I was skimming part of the funds for personal use. It also contended that I had established a business selling wheat intended for distribution by FTC. The bogus leads came to the FBI by way of "informants" they declined to name.

My bank accounts were examined. My telephone records were checked. My buying and spending records were scrutinized. The Internal Revenue Service was called into the investigations, owing to its easy access to personal financial and property information. Tax agents reportedly checked my income against my expenditures.

People from whom I accepted gifts of grain were interviewed, as were those who shipped it overseas. Nary a discrepancy was uncovered.

When I found out about being investigated, I was astonished to be under the watchful eye of the most powerful law-enforcement agency in the world and never to have suspected it. I asked to see my file. When eventually I did, one line of text leaped out at me.

"All of those interviewed have 'gut' feelings Jones is not dealing fairly with the public, but are unable to provide specifics of his manipulations . . . As far as the FBI and IRS are aware, Jones does not know he is under investigation."

Why would the FBI waste time and resources on the basis of unsubstantiated "gut" feelings expressed by random accusers? Like I said, I don't know who they were. The FBI would not disclose their identities. But it would make more sense, it seems to me, to investigate first whether the accusers might be disgruntled former employees or associates, or perhaps workers for other charities who viewed FTC as competition for fund-raising. This might have offered some needed perspective on their "gut" feelings.

Similarly, the IRS would never disclose the sources that prompted their investigations into my finances. During one such investigation, I was being interrogated by an agent who accidentally dropped his file folder. Paper bearing the name of my accuser floated across the floor. It was someone who'd been an adversary of my management at FTC. In the past he'd taken steps to undermine my leadership of the charity I founded. When those maneuvers failed, I suppose he resorted to making false allegations about me to the IRS.

In this case, as in all the others, the investigation resulted in my vindication—and the waste of a lot of a major government agency's time, money, and resources.

Never was this demonstrated more clearly than during a three-month FBI inquiry into the alleged theft of ten tons of baby food. The accuser reported that I had commandeered one shipping container of a two-container, twenty-ton donation offered to FTC by a major food supplier and intended for distribution in Poland.

After more than ninety days of investigations that spanned two continents, I received a surprise visit from federal agents inquiring into the whereabouts of the missing container. While the agents waited, I put the question to FTC's warehouse supervisor. His records showed that FTC had been given only one container of baby food rather than two. I then contacted the supplier. His documents confirmed that FTC had been sent only a solitary, ten-ton package.

Case closed.

Again, I have to wonder about the thoughts of people who were interviewed before agents approached me. It's likely they were asked what they knew about Larry Jones and FTC stealing baby food. It's a loaded question, like "are you still beating your wife?" It presupposes the crime. No matter how a loaded question is answered, it creates suspicion that proves immeasurably damaging. Like charities, corporations do their best to avoid controversy. Who's to say if the food supplier might shy away from making future donations to FTC? This robs the world of goodwill.

In May 1986 someone told the FBI that I was laundering money through a gold and silver store in Haiti, one of the poorest nations on the planet. It was almost as if accusers were competing to see which accusation could be the most absurd.

Expenses in Haiti are paid not in U.S. dollars but in Haitian currency—gourdes. When we conduct transactions in Europe, our currency must be translated into euros. We abide by the same, completely uncontroversial process in Haiti. "This transaction is common practice between companies in Haiti seeking U.S. dollars and missions funded outside Haiti attempting to maximize funding dollars whose expenses in Haiti are paid in gourdes," read the FBI conclusion that ended with my proven innocence.

Be that as it may, how many people were given a dim view of our organization simply because authorities raised the question about FTC's supposed laundering of donated funds?

This sad parade of accusers seemed to have no end. Five months after the Haiti investigation closed, yet another of the FBI's secret inquests began. Once again, the allegations are laughable. Yet the ramifications remain tragic.

In this amazing episode the FBI responded to a contention that I was the brother of the late reverend Jim Jones—the missionary infamous for taking his own life while leading the 1978 mass murder-suicides in Jonestown, Guyana. The allegation suggested that I was feeding children potatoes laced with cyanide.

I know the FBI has its policies. I know that agents don't create these policies; they simply obey them. That said, how could they justify a serious, prolonged investigation into my family ties? Wouldn't a simple check of my birth certificate, on file as public record in Kentucky, establish that my parents were not the parents of the late Jim

Jones? Couldn't they have interrogated anyone who graced my child-hood or social circles, who would have told them the names of my family members?

As for the matter of cyanide? Wow. Give me a break. Cyanide is a lethal poison that kills instantaneously. It's the poison Adolf Hitler chose to kill himself and Eva Braun with. The children I was feeding remained alive—and to all observation, better nourished for FTC's charitable efforts. Surely this might indicate the absence of cyanide in their food.

I know the FBI agents who investigated me were just doing their jobs. But I find it exasperating that bureau policy mandates that they take seriously allegations as outrageous as some of those leveled against FTC and me. It seems to me that shifting the policy toward a higher degree of sanity would be a step in the right direction. It seems clear that agents investigating preposterous allegations could better spend their time chasing criminals. I'm sure the agents would be the first to agree.

So who fabricated the claims that I was related to a mass murderer and also was bent on killing the very children whose needs I live to serve?

According to FBI records, he was an unidentified caller described in a report that read, in part: "The voice was that of a white or Indian male, possible age 50, possibly drunk." The document went on to say that the complainant was "a blustery, belligerent red-neck (Bohemian), possibly from South Texas, and possibly a disgruntled farmer."

Why was such a call ever taken seriously?

For whatever reason, it was. And the official FBI report on the probe reads, in part, as follows:

> Extensive investigation conducted concerning Jones and
> his activities has developed no information indicating food
> tampering. Based on investigation to date, and knowledge
> of Jones' operation, allegations of food tampering appear to
> be unfounded. Further, Jones is not known to be a relative
> of Jim Jones of Guyana.

On October 28, 1986, aforementioned TCP allegation

was related to Food and Drug Administration, Oklahoma City. Subsequently, FDA visited LJM (Larry Jones Ministries), Oklahoma City. FDA inquiry determined that LJM coordinates the shipment of potatoes domestically in conjunction with various food programs for the needy throughout the USA. LJM receives orders for the potatoes which are donated by one or two farmers, one in Texas, the other in South Dakota. LJM is charged only a small handling fee by the farmers. The potatoes are then delivered fresh in one-hundred-pound bags by the truck directly from the farmer to the customer. LJM owns the trucks, which are driven by independent truckers hired by LJM. No potatoes are handled by LJM at Oklahoma City. The last shipment coordinated by LJM was delivered October 8, 1986. LJM has reportedly received no complaints regarding contaminated potatoes.

That was it. And so I was cleared again of ridiculous allegations.

The FDA office in Oklahoma City is only a few miles from FTC. People who work there know people who work here. I wonder how many FDA employees are FTC supporters themselves. I wonder what they were thinking when they were asked to investigate our operation. I wonder how many withheld their support after the question was raised about our poisoning the food we distribute.

Of course, I'd prefer that the stupid investigation had never happened. But since agents had no choice, I wish they had simply come unannounced to FTC's warehouse and derived their conclusions immediately and firsthand. The gossip grapevine could have been cut before it climbed out of control.

And a lie doesn't care who tells it. Because the total effects can prove subtle and far-reaching, there's no measuring the damage done by such lies.

Who was the liar who sparked the investigation that wasted the time of federal agents and therefore the money of American taxpayers? Who was the mysterious "informant" whose tip from a phone in rural Oklahoma commanded the power to activate government agencies in the nation's capital?

A follow-up probe revealed his identity. A black mark replaced his name as well as an alias in my FBI file. While I don't know who he is, I now know some things about him.

The FBI found him on November 4, 1986. His first call alleging my relation to Jim Jones and involvement with food contamination was made to the Grady County Sheriff's Office, Chickasha, Oklahoma, and was relayed to the FBI, whose report says:

> The potatoes possibly being poisoned was merely conjecture and he has no facts supporting this. —— was obviously irrational in his thoughts and when cautioned not to make interstate calls regarding tampering of consumer products, which would be a federal violation of furnishing false information, he responded by stating that he would "take it to the world court."
>
> During the week of October 27, 1986–October 31, 1986, —— had previously been interviewed by bureau agents from the Boise (office) in connection with a similar call to a boy's ranch in Idaho, also regarding potatoes.
>
> Contact with the criminal identification bureau, Boise, Idaho, reveals that —— has an old criminal record dating back to the 1950s . . .
>
> In light of the above, no further investigation is being conducted by the Butte division.

The results of the investigation were forwarded to Assistant United States Attorney Ted R. Richardson, Oklahoma City, for a "prosecutive opinion." Unbeknownst to me, FTC and I were still not out of the woods. The FBI was still considering federal charges against me—but not for long.

My FBI file reveals, in part:

> Richardson states, due to the fact that —— has a history of mental instability due to his alcohol-related problems, this case does not have prosecutive merit, and he will decline prosecution of this case.
>
> Since the United States Attorney's office, Oklahoma City,

has declined to prosecute this matter, no further investigation will be conducted and this case will be closed.

It would be tiresome to itemize each entry on the list of hard legal looks that the FBI has cast my way. In retrospect, it's probably a good thing I was unaware of each study while it was happening. I'm thankful for that. Because knowing that I was the target of FBI attention would surely have distracted me from my work.

If ignorance is bliss, I have blissfully kept walking on the path that, to this day, I'm convinced is God's will for my life—a life I am able to use to make a difference in the lives of millions of deprived people the world over. FTC continues to provide. And I thank God for that.

Chapter Thirteen

Iₙ 1987 the very farmers who'd been so generous with their donations suddenly became tightfisted. I was mystified. Farmers, after all,
had been Feed The Children's charter donors.

Oklahoma farmers had, in some years, offered more of their
bumper crops of wheat than I could distribute. In these times they
came to me, not vice versa, wanting to know where to deliver grain
that Feed The Children could pass along to the feeding centers we
had established in the United States and abroad.

Their attitude seemed different all of a sudden. I wondered what
was breaking our food chain.

I asked around and quickly learned that America's farmers were
in crisis.

I discovered early what the press would eventually report internationally—that farmers were paying more for supplies and selling
crops for less, in a losing game of farming economics. Almost invariably, their bottom line presented itself starkly in red ink, resulting in
foreclosure on their farms and the loss of everything they'd spent
their lives building up.

"Despair Wrenches Farmers' Lives as Debts Mount and Land Is
Lost," pronounced a headline on the front page of the *New York
Times* on February 10, 1985.

"Economic problems of a size not seen by generations of Americans are wrenching farm life and rural communities across the
country's principal food-producing regions," the story's first para-
graph declared.

Conditions continued to spiral downward. By 1987 the crush of
the crisis threatened to squeeze out an entire realm of traditional

American culture. Testimony to this fact was reported with the icy calm of statistics.

The nation's 2.37 million farmers struggled to pay interest on liabilities that had bloated by 63 percent since 1979, the year Feed The Children was founded. The debt of American farmers had exploded from $132 billion to $215 billion in less than ten years. They were paying more than $21 billion a year in interest while their income had averaged only $23 billion in 1986 and 1987. Debt blew through the heartland like a nuclear blast, its fallout hanging over mom-and-pop farms like a mushroom cloud.

Bank foreclosures soon reached an epidemic level. Experts reported that the worst of the problem was confined to about 641,000 farms—family-owned operations with little or no outside income. In contrast, approximately 25,000 of the nation's largest farms—with gross annual sales exceeding $500,000—were taking more than half of all farm profits.

That's approximately 25,000 large corporate farms winning, 641,000 small family farms losing. From a lofty perch some economists and captains of industry may count this as progress. To me, and to the salt-of-the-earth people involved, it seems a travesty and a crying shame.

The seeds for the crisis were sown in the 1970s after the removal of American sanctions against grain trade with the Soviet Union. Anticipating an expanding market, farmers increased their holdings based on escalating land loans. Perhaps they did this too rapidly. Also, they did not anticipate the devaluation of the dollar or the ruthless price competition. A cynical person—or even a realist—might say, "They brought this crisis on themselves." That's harsh and unhelpful. These people are local farmers, not global economists. By and large they're not the kinds of people who are looking to get rich. They're the kinds of people who try to do a good job at farming and at looking out for one another—even looking out for strangers, as was made evident by their generosity to FTC over the years.

Here's a little perspective on the economics of farming. In 1950 a postage stamp sold for two cents, a bushel of wheat for two dollars.

In 1987 the cost of a postage stamp had escalated to twenty-eight cents—and wheat was still selling for two dollars a bushel.

So land that had been in families for generations was, during the 1980s, being sold at sheriffs' auctions, sometimes for no more than back taxes. The foreclosures were tearing apart farm families, a bastion of Christian values.

I went to some of those auctions. I saw neighbors split into two groups. One refused to bid on anything that had been seized by a bank from a destitute family. The other bid in a feeding frenzy, like piranhas that sensed blood in the water. Fistfights broke out among neighbors. The air was poisoned with acrid accusations. The sharp word "traitor" was flung at bankers, deputies, and in some cases farmers who had previously been friends. I heard flurries of cussing. I saw floods of tears.

During this period a sociologist at the University of Missouri reported that suicide rates among persons in agriculture had risen to a rate 40 percent higher than those in the nonfarm sector. Forty percent.

Just when things seemingly could get no worse, in 1988 they did when the nation was stricken with the fourth-worst drought in the history of meteorological record keeping. It struck during the early, sensitive stage of the growing season. By year's end, barges could not move grain down the Mississippi River to the Gulf of Mexico for export. They ran aground on sandbars exposed by receding water.

The boats backed up for miles as the nation's largest river fell to a record low. A fleet of stranded barges sat stuck in the mud along their southbound route until freed by the spring rains of 1989. By then, their cargo had rotted.

President Ronald Reagan and Congress responded with a $3.9 billion drought-relief fund to reimburse farmers for their losses. This compensation, coupled with the higher prices paid for grain as a result of the drought, marked the beginning of the end of the farm crisis—almost a decade after former president Jimmy Carter had placed an embargo on the sale of wheat to the Russians because they had invaded Afghanistan.

I know President Carter intended to punish the Russians, but

American farmers actually caught the brunt of it all. The ultimate effect of our government's policy made life miserable for the men and women responsible for putting most of the food on the world's table.

When I learned what was going on in 1987, I became an outspoken critic of the government's handling of the situation with my weekly telecasts. The American farmer is the backbone of our nation and Feed The Children's greatest ally. I felt duty-bound to speak out for the farmers. Depressed farm prices, after all, had been a factor in spawning the Great Depression of 1929. And in 1987 agriculture was as much a part of the gross national product as it had been sixty years earlier.

In the fall of 1986, America enjoyed a 3.2-million-bushel surplus of corn. Our government spent seventeen million dollars a day on storing corn, wheat, and other grain that could and, in many cases, did spoil. The waste itself is pretty sad. Sadder still, it fell far short of helping farmers lift themselves out of their financial hole. The entire scenario made for a national tragedy being played out on a grand scale, and the audience was asleep.

That's when we at Feed The Children woke up and determined to touch farmers not at the soil but inside their souls. We vowed to supply financial and psychological balm to the hurt behind the headlines.

We had no idea what awaited us.

Television cameras in tow, my wife, Frances, and I drove for hundreds of miles along America's dusty country roads. We had no trouble finding desperate cases to document with video footage. Our way was marked by "For Sale" signs on farmers' lands, by the defeat we beheld on their faces and deep in their spirits.

Frances and I were astonished at the ruthless measures taken by lawmen against their neighbors. Sheriffs' deputies and SWAT teams came like thieves in the night to evict farmers from their homes. Right here, in the United States of America—home of the brave, and land of the free. The supposedly compassionate nation of people to whom France gave the Statue of Liberty, which stands with the inscription "Give me your tired, your poor . . ." Many farm families were evicted from their homes with only the clothes on their backs.

It was a real-life enactment of the John Steinbeck tale *The Grapes of Wrath*—only no one was standing up for these poor uprooted human beings.

We reported the brutal activity in television stories, implying that someone should be policing our police. I'm sure our reports angered a lot of people in law enforcement, and no doubt added pages to my growing file with the FBI.

One of the reports centered on Irving Boldridge, a Kansas farmer who saw his holdings repossessed piece by piece over two years. The last to go was his herd of sixty-six cattle.

A banker, accompanied by a deputy sheriff, showed up one morning to begin collecting the livestock. Mrs. Sophia Boldridge, Irving's wife, used a pencil and paper to keep a record of the repossessions. She counted the cattle as they were loaded into a truck and told the authorities when the tally reached sixty-six. The few remaining cattle belonged to the Boldridges' daughter, an elementary school student.

"You've got all of our cattle now," Mrs. Boldridge said. "These others are our little girl's."

The men kept loading the bawling cattle despite her protestations.

"Lady," Mrs. Boldridge quoted one man as saying, "don't you know that we're going to take everything you've got?"

One year later, authorities visited the Boldridges again without notice. One of their three youngsters ran into the house alarmed, reporting that men in camouflage uniforms were approaching the home. Mrs. Boldridge looked out a window to see a team of uniformed men carrying high-powered rifles, accompanied by the sheriff—a man she knew personally.

The sheriff shouted from the yard, ordering Mrs. Boldridge to take her three children to town. Terrified, she loaded the kids in the car and drove off.

Alerted by the commotion while working out back, Irving Boldridge stepped from around the corner of the house to see what was going on. He was ordered off his land, prohibited from entering his own home.

Boldridge, a craftsman, had been whittling a wooden horse for his children, which he picked up and carried with him on his walk to town. His wife had taken their only vehicle.

He walked for miles to the west, facing the most forlorn sunset of his life. Life as he and his family had known it was behind him. He never returned. He never even looked back.

Apart from war or natural disaster, human experience can't be much harder than this. Nevertheless, if God created a creature more resilient than the American family farmer, I've yet to see it. Throughout our involvement in the crisis, I never ceased to be amazed at the strength of the farmers' faith.

"We'll stay together and pray together and change our life, because that life [farm life] is gone," Boldridge said. "Most people [farmers] think the farm belongs to them. That's where they're wrong. It belongs to the Almighty. They didn't take that farm away from the Boldridge family. They took that farm from the Almighty and called it their own."

I don't think the average American has any idea how close this country came to another depression due to the farm crisis of the 1980s. Before the stock market crash of 1929, 650,000 American farm families were evicted from their land. That's about the same number of people who lost their farms during this crisis.

Even as the American farmer was being foreclosed upon, thirty-two million other Americans were living below the poverty level. Twenty million of those went hungry at some time during each month. Meanwhile, fertile fields lay fallow and grain decayed in government silos. Does that make any sense to you? Does it not seem outrageous? Scandalous? People nationwide may have been praying and fasting about the farm crisis, but as the prayers wound toward heaven, folks were going hungry and broke here on earth.

"When we get off our knees, we'd better give more surplus to the hungry," I said. We delivered food to forty-two states in 1987.

Beyond feeding the hungry, we also knew that American farmers needed help getting back on their financial feet. I could think of no better way to aid them than by trying to buy the nation's surplus food—the grain they'd already produced, then rotting in the government's silos. I knew at the time that it was an ambitious undertaking. Many thought my goal was unrealistic. Those same folks were among the critics of Willie Nelson for his annual Farm Aid concerts that have raised more than fifty million dollars over several years. Given the scope of need, that was only a drop in the financial bucket. But if a few more people had acted with his enthusiasm and ingenuity, who knows what could have been accomplished.

For our part, we wanted to accomplish two things: (1) use the nation's surplus to help the hungry, and (2) by eliminating the surplus, force a rise in the price of crops, thereby making it profitable to farm again. With this aim, I turned to my television audience for help in 1988.

I solicited eleven-dollar pledges from viewers. Eleven dollars is all it took to buy one hundred pounds of surplus beans, rice, potatoes, wheat, flour, or cornmeal that would otherwise simply be allowed to rot in government storage facilities. Eventually, I cut a deal to include apples and oranges in the discounted price. Then, in addition to the eleven dollars, I began asking for one more dollar to start a farmers' fund. The fund was used to buy personal necessities for farmers such as gasoline, medical supplies, what food Feed The Children couldn't give them, and the like. Along with their dollars contributed, viewers added their signatures to a petition protesting the unfair treatment of farmers, which was delivered to President George H. W. Bush in 1989.

In response, the administration offered a thank-you letter, but no remedy to the situation.

THROUGHOUT THIS PERIOD Frances and I toured America's heartland continuously. One such trek introduced us to the plight of William and Linnie Parker. What remained of their tiny farm was little more than a backyard garden after land that had been in the family for four generations was taken by the bank.

William had applied for a loan to buy seed. It took the bank so long to process his application that the check wasn't issued until after planting season. His family then used the money to cover living expenses. Needless to say, there would be no crops to sell to repay the loan or support the family. Their only collateral was the farm itself. Therefore, the Parkers faced foreclosure.

"A farmer is like Job," Linnie mused, citing the Bible story in which Satan pounds Job with catastrophe after catastrophe in an attempt to shake his faith in the Lord. She equated her creditors, as well as their tactics, with Satan. The Parkers came from a world where personal honesty, integrity, handshake agreements, and helping one's neighbors had served as the primary currency of life for generations. They could not relate to the seemingly cold-blooded, impersonal ways of business. They were not alone in this orientation. They were just one family among perhaps hundreds of thousands whose grandparents, parents, and children knew no other way.

Thus the Parkers were left destitute by the ways of the "modern" world. By hand, often on all fours, they worked their small, parched plot. Much of the time it was watered with nothing more than their sweat and tears.

Despite their abject poverty, the Parkers had taken in William's mother and their two grandchildren. When we first talked, Linnie was on her hands and knees cleaning scarred linoleum. There were so many holes they seemed to be part of the design pattern. Her relating of the story was broken by sobs.

"I don't see why they have to come down so hard on the farmer," she said, crying. "I don't see why."

No amount of explaining could ever have helped that woman understand. Frances and I certainly couldn't explain it to her. How could we sell her ideas we weren't sold on ourselves?

"What will you do if you lose your farm?" Frances asked William. William was a man's man. Real men, in his mind, bled when they were cut, but they didn't complain. Frances's question brought him to tears, which was as much of an answer as he could muster.

I watched his craggy face, etched with wrinkles, melt into a pool of tears. The man had never read a book on agriculture. And yet he had brought in a yield every year for as long as he could remember. He had whipped drought, floods, hail, insects, and more, often with only primitive tools.

But he couldn't whip the legal papers ordering him off the land out of which he and his family had sprung. He didn't have the right tools for that.

THE STORIES ARE ENDLESS, sad, and, for the most part, senseless.

Nothing about the farm crisis made sense. In 1988 the American farmer was buried under thirteen billion bushels of surplus wheat. At the same time, mayors in sixteen major American cities complained of food shortages.

We at Feed The Children bought as much surplus wheat as our donations would allow—which, in the scheme of things, was a drop in the bucket. Thirteen billion bushels is a lot of surplus. There are small nations on earth that could be fed with that much wheat. But it rots if nobody buys it.

We scrambled to think of other ways to help farmers. We televised more programs addressing their plight. We earmarked more incoming funds for their cause. We even acquired seed corn and gave it to drought-ravaged farmers in North Carolina contingent on their giving the surplus back to us. God must have liked that plan. North Carolina yields averaged 120 bushels an acre that year. The farmers saw a profit, and we saw to it that the surplus grain moved to hungry people here and abroad.

Sixteen-hour workdays became the norm at our Oklahoma City headquarters. Someone remarked that the task of trying to financially and psychologically tend the needs of those who once fed the nation would put Feed the Children staffers in our graves.

During our weekly devotional service, I reminded the staff that there is no work beyond the grave, and of my lifelong motto: "Keep walking." And that's exactly what we did.

To this day, no matter what happens, I don't stop and stew. I don't waste time wondering why. I don't demand that things not be the way they obviously are. I maintain movement in what I believe to be the direction in which the Lord would have me go. I just keep walking. And when death finally stops me, I want those words engraved on my headstone.

IN ALL OUR TRAVELS, I don't think Frances and I encountered a consequence of the farm crisis more dramatic than that of Art Kirk, who, until then, had farmed in Nebraska.

Art was working on his broken-down farm equipment when three Hall County sheriff's deputies came to serve legal papers.

According to an article written for Nebraskastudies.org, Kirk pulled a pistol (one of over twenty-five stockpiled guns, a gas mask, and an army helmet) and threatened the lawmen, claiming that a sign with the words "Posted, Keep Out" barred anyone from coming uninvited onto his land. The officers drew their guns, shoved the papers into Art's fence, and left.

Arrest warrant in hand, deputies returned and blocked the gravel road to Art's house. Then they moved in with a court-ordered SWAT team. The aggression transpired under cover of nightfall. Art could not see the men in dark uniforms with high-powered rifles approaching his house.

Unable to reach her own home due to the blockade, Art's wife, Deloris, went to the local highway patrol station to use the phone. She called her husband to tell him their property was sealed off, and then reportedly urged him to hang up and remember "the plans" they had. Those were the last words he ever heard her speak.

Before the farm crisis, this had been a fairly close-knit community. Under friendlier circumstances, the men now stalking Art had visited in his home. They knew the location of the phone. Therefore, they could pinpoint the spot where Art stood while talking to his wife.

Just then, her attention was drawn to a desk where someone had inadvertently left a two-way radio activated. Over it she heard a lawman barking ominous directives.

"Move from the west . . . You on the north—close in."

A team of officers seemed to be encircling a major criminal.

Then Deloris realized they were stalking a farmer. Her farmer. Her husband.

She demanded to talk to the county sheriff. She insisted on being allowed to go onto her own property, confident she could neutralize what was quickly becoming an explosive situation. The sheriff refused, saying it was too dangerous for her to go to her own house. She countered, insisting that the danger would not exist if she was allowed to go there.

It seemed as if these agents of law enforcement were seeking to ignite rather than defuse the situation. Did they, in fact, want to make an example of Art Kirk?

The fuse continued burning. Though information remained sketchy at best, Deloris discovered that a psychologist was on the line negotiating with her husband. Again, she insisted that she be allowed to go to Art's side.

Summarily, she was told she'd be arrested if she left the sheriff's office.

This was madness. What would be the charge? Trespassing? Had some secret court already ruled that the land was no longer hers and Art's? What, actually, could be their legal grounds for holding her? She was in defiance of no warrant. She was not a suspect in any crime. She was a material witness to nothing.

Nevertheless, Deloris obeyed the senseless directive. These people were, after all, the local representatives of the law.

Eventually she was led to a conference room where she was met by an assistant district attorney. He told her that her husband had been shot. Shot dead.

"When," Deloris demanded, "did they shoot my husband?"

"I'm not at liberty to say," the prosecutor replied. "That information will be included in the autopsy."

The tight-lipped prosecutor also declined to say where Art was shot. And here's yet another bit of information he did not volunteer: Art Kirk did not die immediately. He was shot, and then allowed to bleed to death. He perished alone as his lifeblood drained out onto the fertile ground that he had walked as a child, and where his own children had played.

Before all this insanity set in, some of the same deputies who shot Art Kirk had no doubt hunted wild game on his land. And here they had hunted Art himself down like an animal.

Deloris was not arrested. She was allowed onto her own land the next morning, after Art's body had been removed and the gore had been washed away. There, she discovered bullet holes in the walls, and inconsistencies in the deputies' stories.

The SWAT team heard Art screaming and yelling as he ran from his house to a windmill fortified by sandbags and steel curtains—as if Art had anticipated a standoff. He was believed to be carrying an automatic army-type rifle, sporting a gas mask, and wearing a steel army helmet.

To shore up the rickety structure's stability, Art had once set logs around the windmill's base. It couldn't, after all, serve his farming purposes if the contraption collapsed. And the so-called steel curtains were, in fact, flimsy nylon irrigation socks. They wouldn't stop penetration by a snowball, much less a high-powered rifle.

The reportage went on to say that Art had first fired twice upon the SWAT team. They had merely returned fire—a total of about thirty rounds.

If this was true, routine crime scene tests could confirm it. But routine tests were never conducted—no test for gunpowder on Art's hands, no ballistics tests. We have only the officers' word that Art fired his weapon.

The late Art Kirk doesn't get a say in the matter.

All things considered, a reasonable person is compelled to wonder if the local authorities were interested in the facts, or if they were even interested in doing everything in their power to prevent a lethal escalation of the situation. They claimed to fear for Deloris's safety, so they would not allow her on the scene. Was this gender prejudice? If so, why didn't they call someone else whom Art knew and trusted? His pastor, for instance? Art did belong to a local church.

In considering this outrage, I used to think there were too many unanswered questions. More recently, I realized there is one answer that covers them all: the authorities failed to act with the good judgment their responsibilities demand. Nobody who was empowered to do anything did. Apparently, they thought it was easier to shoot Art Kirk than to deal with him.

A report released in December 1984 by a former Lincoln, Nebraska, judge, Samuel Van Pelt, said, "The death of Art Kirk could have been prevented, but police acted in a prudent manner under difficult circumstances. The slaying of Kirk by the Nebraska State Patrol SWAT team occurred because of too many unrelated and coincidental factors and wasn't an orchestrated killing by police. The farm crisis was the real cause of the killing."

And so the soil Art once tilled today holds his body. The earth that was once his livelihood is now his grave.

Chapter Fourteen

O<small>N A FRIGID NIGHT IN JANUARY 1988</small>, I received a call from Pat Jones, my sister-in-law, that temporarily interrupted my work regarding America's farm crisis and renewed my awareness of the uncertainty of life.

Her husband, Mike—my thirty-nine-year-old younger brother—had suffered a brain aneurysm. Pat insisted I needed to come to Bowling Green right then. I arrived before the next sundown.

I found my brother awake, but not entirely lucid, tethered to monitoring devices in an intensive care unit. After a few days he was moved to a hospital in Nashville.

Two weeks later I preached his funeral.

Mike was my only sibling, eight years my junior. From the time I received Pat's long-distance call until his passing, a constant stream of reminiscences played involuntarily through my mind. Just as I'd put one precious memory to rest, I'd be ambushed by another.

I remembered how our age difference had once seemed to inhibit our bonding. That notion seemed silly as Mike lay dying. My only thoughts about time had to do with my hope that God might miraculously give Mike some more. But this was not to be. I had my hopes, God had His plan.

I recalled the support Mike had shown to my ministry, especially after it evolved into Feed The Children.

Just a year earlier, Mike, his wife, Pat, and their son, Baron, had accompanied me to Honduras. Before we departed, Mike had wondered if he'd relate well with starving children. Before the experience was over, he found himself wanting to adopt two. This never happened, though. In those days governmental red tape regarding the adoption of foreign children was even more of a tangle than it is now. It continues to be a monumental undertaking.

"What am I supposed to do with these children when we get to Honduras?" Mike had repeatedly asked.

"You're supposed to love them and keep them from becoming afraid while being carried from one doctor to another," a volunteer physician advised.

Mike absorbed that lesson about loving in minutes. At that, he was a natural.

I reflected on the innocuous symptom that had brought me to my brother's deathbed—a headache. Headaches are common. Everybody gets them. And they're curable—you just take an aspirin, right? Mike had been having these headaches for months, and he didn't die then. Why now?

I revisited the matter with Pat just to hear once more the scenario behind the headaches that I'd mistakenly underestimated.

Mike had gotten sick and tired of feeling sick and tired, so he'd gone to Vanderbilt Medical Center in Nashville for a complete physical examination. Doctors discovered nothing irregular.

He then decided that the headaches might be blamed on eye strain, as he'd been reading more than ever in connection with his work. An ocular test revealed nothing. Still, the headaches persisted. He bought reading glasses. He could see better, but his headaches recurred.

On the night of the second Saturday in January 1988, Pat lay beside Mike in bed when he made an unusual sound. She spoke to him over and over, with increasing urgency. No response. She called an ambulance, and Mike was rushed to the hospital. There the diagnosis was returned: Mike had suffered a devastating brain aneurysm.

At that time, as I pondered the past, I petitioned God to intervene in the present. I asked Him to heal my brother. Actually, I pleaded.

On February 1, 1988, God answered my prayers. His answer was no. I was taken aback, and Mike was taken to heaven.

As Mike's condition deteriorated, my mind occasionally returned to thoughts of America's suffering farmers. I'd temporarily left my work tending hardships to attend my brother, who, ironically, had maintained close relationships with many farmers in Kentucky. He'd done business with them, fished the streams on their land, and socialized with their families.

I also thought about the farmers because their lives tend to be so stressful. At that trying time during the farm crisis, some feared that the stress over the pending loss of livelihood, through foreclosures, might actually take their lives—just as a ruptured blood vessel was slowly taking Mike's.

When I'd told my brother about Feed The Children's involvement in addressing America's farm crisis, he'd insisted that I not take time from my work to be with him. He said I was needed back on the farms.

Earlier, Mike's doctor had predicted, almost to the day, when he would pass, saving a dramatic miracle. The only miracle lay in the wonderful sedatives that kept Mike comfortable in his final days.

And so my thoughts continued to vacillate between my dying brother and the farmers, who were losing everything except their health, even as Mike's was slipping away.

Funny how the mind will seek affectionate humor during a loved one's darkest hour. It's a defense mechanism for the survivor and a tribute to the dying.

My thoughts ran to Mike's occupational genius: salesmanship.

He could sell anybody anything—*if* he believed it was something that was truly needed. He had the power of conviction and conveyed an air of trustworthiness that was deeply rooted in personal character.

I thought about the times he'd extended a hand of friendship and aid to farmers, unlike the people foreclosing on their property after pretending to be their friends.

Mike once visited a farmer at 5:30 a.m., the only time the man was available before disappearing into his sea of acreage for the rest of the day.

Mike told him he needed to buy a two-way Motorola radio that would enable him to stay in constant contact with coworkers, instead of seeing them only after wasting time to chase them down amid the plowed furrows.

The farmer understood but insisted he didn't need Motorola handsets. He was feeling the pinch of falling crop prices and rising production expenses. He said he could find a two-way system that was cheaper. Mike told him he was right.

"But your repair prices will overshadow what you would have paid for a Motorola," Mike said. "The Motorola won't break, and it comes with an unlimited guarantee if it does. Don't wait and call me when your off-brand radios break down. You need a Motorola! Then you won't have to call me later."

Perhaps the farmer thought Mike was brash. He definitely thought he was telling the truth. That kind of frankness is rooted only in honesty.

The farmer paused for a moment's thought, and then asked where he should sign the purchase order. Later, he wound up calling Mike after all. He wanted him to sell similar Motorolas to his friends.

If Mike hadn't been dying, I can imagine that he might have tried to persuade me to recommend Motorolas to help save the time and energy of the midwestern farmers whose land I was trying to save.

As his life was easing away, I reflected on Mike's participation in outreaches to the impoverished people of rural Kentucky. They lived in shacks with empty pantries and no public services. It was bad. But this deprivation was nothing compared with what Mike had seen in Honduras, where people had no shelter of any kind. Their water supply had been turned off not by the water company for nonpayment but by drought. And it flowed not through clean underground pipes but across ground littered with animal waste.

Mike was a Christian who lived his convictions more than he talked about them, and was often busier serving God than he was in studying His teachings. Once he quit going to church, which my mother equated with heresy. She was an old-school Christian who insisted that believers belonged in church on Sunday mornings just as they belonged at work Monday through Friday. Mom believed that for a Christian, skipping either was an unpardonable sin.

"Mike's not going to church and you have got to pray for him," she commanded me in an impassioned telephone call during that period.

"Mom," I replied calmly, "here's what we're going to do. The Bible says, 'If two people agree on one thing it shall be done by the father who is in Heaven.' Notice, Mother, it will be done by the father in Heaven, not by you or me. I don't want you to say another word to Mike about not going to church. If you actually quit bothering him about it, that will be the first miracle."

She called shortly thereafter to say that without her ever mentioning it again, Mike had resumed church attendance.

I told her that she and I would keep praying, and I reminded her that neither of us would say a word to Mike about his return to church.

Soon, she called again to say that Mike was teaching Sunday school. She called yet another time to report his paying of tithe, or 10 percent of his income, to the church.

My brother suffered his seizure the night before another anticipated Sunday morning in church. He never made it back, though, except for that day inside his coffin.

More than five hundred people attended his funeral. Reportedly, it was one of the largest in Bowling Green's history.

At Mike's graveside, I spoke a simple sermon to the grassroots, God-fearing people in attendance. To bring everyone to a sense of closure, I used a plain illustration.

I had handed out balloons to all of the children and teenagers. "To be absent from the body is to be present with the Lord," I said, quoting scripture. "The best way I can exemplify this is by asking you to turn your balloons loose on the count of three."

On my count, the helium-filled orbs floated across the heartland, no doubt catching the attention of farmers working their fields. There's a good chance that some of those farmers excitedly called each other to report the spectacle, talking on radios sold by Mike and made by Motorola.

Chapter Fifteen ～～

GIVEN THE TANGLED WEB of laws that govern exporting and importing, and that vary with each country, the international distribution of food and medicine is always difficult. It's particularly so when done spontaneously in response to emergencies occurring half a world away. Such was the case on June 21, 1990, in the aftermath of the earthquake in Iran that killed 40,000, injured 60,000, and left 100,000 families homeless.

Some analysts raised hope that the tragedy might lead to improved relations with the West. Iran expressed openness to accepting aid from any nation in the international community, except Israel and South Africa.

Actually, few nations responded to the dire needs in Iran—a hated country that, eleven years earlier, had taken sixty-three diplomats and three U.S. citizens hostage. Three weeks into the ordeal, the captors freed several women and African Americans, leaving fifty-three hostages, who were held for fourteen months. But this selective release of prisoners provided little consolation in the eyes of the outraged West.

Any sympathy that might have remained for Iran evaporated after Operation Eagle Claw, a foiled U.S. rescue effort that resulted in the deaths of eight servicemen. A majority of pundits later agreed that President Jimmy Carter's handling of the Iranian hostage crisis cost him his bid for reelection in 1980.

At the time of the massive earthquake, the United States maintained no diplomatic ties with Iran. The ideological walls between Iran and the free world seemed insurmountable.

I chose to ignore them.

Hungry, suffering people tend not to place a high priority on political ideas. Natural disasters tend to draw people's focus to concerns that are very concrete.

The media learned that I was marshaling Feed The Children's human resources to aid earthquake refugees inside a country that Americans loathed. They seemed to recognize that I was trying to operate beyond the politics of the situation, in the interest of addressing the suffering of innocent victims.

Had I been responding to the needs of people victimized by political unrest, I would surely have been criticized. But because the damage was done by nature's unrest, my response was, thankfully, celebrated.

I was surprised to be summoned by the producers of *Nightline*, the late-night news show broadcast by ABC.

"During a time of natural disaster, we need to set aside political, religious, and racial problems and reach out to people in need," I told Ted Koppel, the program's moderator at the time.

The late Peter Jennings, past host of ABC's *World News Tonight*, also contacted me. Each week, Jennings made a practice of airing a segment called "Person of the Week," often featuring someone involved in humanitarian undertakings. I was pleased to be chosen for this. They prepared a video profile featuring Feed The Children and its work in Iran. It was narrated by Diane Sawyer and aired during the segment's usual Friday night time slot.

I was very touched, humbled—and mystified—by this. The former South African president Nelson Mandela was visiting the United States the same week the honor was bestowed on me. I would have expected that he would be that week's featured personality. I, like most of the world, for years had applauded his valiant work in advancing the fight against apartheid.

An ABC reporter asked me about FTC's caring gestures toward a country that had once held Americans hostage.

"I didn't like what happened to the hostages," I replied. "But right now, my own personal humanity demands that I reach out to those people who are suffering."

Ms. Sawyer echoed my sentiments. I felt gratified when she referred to me as a man "reminding us that true human kindness doesn't stop at the boundaries of nationality or politics."

The broadcast did wonders to call attention to Feed The Children's multiple missions. Our war chest in the fight against suffering increased substantially. For example, I received a call from an executive at one of the nation's foremost pharmaceutical companies, offering four million dollars' worth of medicine. This was coupled with forty tons of donated food, earmarked for Iran.

I was pondering how we were going to transport it all over there when Harut Sassounian, president of the United Armenian Fund in Washington, D.C., offered the services of a cargo plane about the size of a DC-10.

Thus, within days of the earthquake, many of my coworkers and I were airborne with five million dollars' worth of medicine and food in tow, en route to desperate people in the volatile Middle East.

Iranians were so accustomed to the harsh conditions of war that they had developed a sense of humor about the ongoing conflict with Iraq. As Iranian volunteers rapidly unloaded a small mountain of wares from our aircraft in Tehran, I remarked to one of them, "I've never seen such efficiency. How did you guys get so good at something like this?"

"We're fast," he replied. "After all, we've been distributing supplies for our fight with Iraq for nine years."

In retrospect, I believe that FTC's response to that tragedy served to improve the United States' relationship with the people of Iran, if not their government—at least to some degree. We acted as representatives of a Christian nation, administering the principles of Christianity in a hands-on way. We turned the other cheek to political differences, attending the needs of children who were the offspring of our adversaries. Many responded with heartfelt appreciation, seeming to undergo a change of attitude toward Americans.

Hospitality extended to FTC personnel had never been more gracious. Officials of a former Hilton hotel provided our lodging. We were given free access to the ruined regions where we delivered supplies. Their allowing us to work without restraint spoke volumes. Historically, Iran had been leery of foreign relief workers, fearing some might be Iraqi spies. Our collaboration was an exercise in reciprocal trust, the likes of which I'd never seen.

Whatever hostility they may have felt toward Americans before simply dissolved. A substantial portion of the Iranian people placed themselves at the disposal of FTC, determined to help us help them.

Their response validated my earlier thinking about the value of reaching out to distressed populations. A helping hand can work wonders at shifting popular sentiments. Human experience has proven time and again that guns and bombs are not going to settle the differences among people of conflicting lifelong convictions. Even benevolence may not alter their basic ideologies. But it will give pause for thought.

Be that as it may, FTC was there to restore health and fill stomachs. As for effecting a shift of sentiments in minds and hearts, God works alone there, in mysterious privacy.

On leaving Iran, we took nothing but pictures; we left nothing but food, medicine, and blankets. The people we served seemed to recognize that while Americans could've stayed home, some of us chose to come and help. With tearful embraces, they expressed their thanks.

If nothing else, FTC made it a little bit harder for people who live in political bondage to hate those of us who live in the land of the free.

FEED THE CHILDREN'S NEXT MAJOR OUTREACH was in Bosnia and Herzegovina, assisting refugees of the armed conflict that raged between March 1992 and November 1995.

As in Iran, we encountered people of starkly different political persuasions who expressed high levels of hostility toward those they considered their enemies. I won't get into analyzing the grievances behind that clash or the events that preceded it. It's always been my belief that humanitarian gestures must operate outside of politics.

Suffice it to say that the need we encountered was massive. An estimated 110,000 military personnel and civilians died, and 1.8 million people were displaced by warring factions made up of Bosnians, Serbs, Croats, Muslims, and smaller groups in western Bosnia.

On most missions to Bosnia, I sent associates ahead to assess needs. On the first trip of this mission, however, I wanted to see firsthand if the agonies were as pronounced as news reports had indicated. I found Sarajevo, once as modern and vibrant as many Western cities, pounded to ruin by artillery. What remained reminded me of Berlin after World War II.

Upon arrival at the Sarajevo airport, I was told to stand behind barricades while waiting to be placed inside an armored transport vehicle that resembled a tank. When I climbed into its cramped quarters, my knees almost touched my face.

An FTC volunteer—a Londoner—escorted me. As our "tank" approached the sites of inner-city destruction, we were told to vacate the vehicle. The driver felt it was unsafe for him to continue farther. I asked how my companion and I were supposed to proceed. He suggested that we take a taxicab. Seriously.

Our ultimate destination was a Holiday Inn, located about three miles farther into the heart of the destruction. We found some Bosnian cabdrivers operating vehicles smaller than American compacts.

"How much will you charge to take me to the Holiday Inn?" I asked.

"Seventy dollars!" a driver replied.

"Just to go two or three miles?" I was incredulous.

"Yes," he insisted. "And you must pay before you go."

I soon understood why. The exorbitant fare was hazardous-duty pay. Our route to the hotel took us along "Sniper Alley," where shooters burrowed into the refuse along the way, intent on murdering anyone who stopped to rescue those they'd already tried to kill.

We were driven along an eight-lane highway. The driver steered crazily, hoping to make the car a difficult target for the shooters. Were we ever shot at? Who knows? I couldn't hear anything over the roar of the engine and the squall of tires. My companion and I were tossing around the backseat like rag dolls while trying to keep our heads beneath the windows.

I have been in a lot of dangerous situations. I've got to say this experience took the prize for inspiring high anxiety.

My long trip by air, followed by our three-mile zigzag in the cab, left me longing for rest. The sight of the hotel, however, was anything but restful.

Most of the windows at the Holiday Inn had been blown out and replaced by plywood. Outside, dead bodies were being discovered with intermittent sweeps of loud, motorized road graders. Mortar fire had severed electrical power. I had to carry baggage up eight flights of stairs to my room.

If I thought getting to the hotel in Sarajevo was tough, I had not yet seen the worst of the challenges to come in transporting relief supplies into outlying Bosnian war zones. One drop point required a fifteen-hour drive from Mostar to a temporary FTC outpost in Tuzla.

In making this trek, I was accompanied by Frances and the American broadcaster Geraldo Rivera, as well as film crews. We traveled in a convoy of cars interspersed with trucks hauling food. We never knew when sporadic gunfire might erupt as we traversed the turf of various Balkan militia groups.

On another trip, I traveled in a similar convoy with my film crew departing from Split, Croatia, a port city where FTC received goods from America. We were destined for the mountains, where we were to deliver supplies to refugees amid volleys of artillery and ground fire. We all wore helmets and flak jackets.

We were accompanied by British troops serving as United Nations peacekeepers. A British tank led the procession; another brought up the rear. Crossing the various militarized zones was literally like running a gauntlet. Approaching each, we were told via two-way radio to prepare. This meant to assume a crouching position inside our carriers.

The convoy would then accelerate. We'd speed through the middle of skirmishes to the sound of gunfire that was not supposed to be aimed at relief vehicles, but sometimes was, accidentally or not. The metal exteriors of cars and trucks offer no defense against the armor-piercing bullets from combat rifles and machine guns. At any moment, any of us could have been struck down by hostile snipers who hid camouflaged along the roadside.

We continued our ritual of crouching then sitting up repeatedly for hours as we made our perilous way to the mountains. The motorcade was halted a couple of times in "safe" zones, where drivers attempted to catch their breath and flush the fear from their minds.

Eventually we stopped at Vitez, a small Croatian village surrounded by mountains that concealed Bosnian Muslims whose intermittent gunfire was intended to keep residents from leaving the area and insurgents from entering. I prayed repeatedly that they would recognize us for what we were—relief workers with food and medicine for the suffering.

Inside the village, pockets of unrest boiled over with gun feuds among Croatians and Muslims.

Amid the turmoil, we delivered food to refugees, who crept toward us tentatively to avoid errant rounds. There were just so many rounds fired by so many militants. No one could ever anticipate when a ricochet might strike an innocent. Though I couldn't understand the under-the-breath utterances of terrified people as they approached, I knew they were praying. Their words were foreign to me, but their tone was universal. Praying for your life has a familiar ring that I've heard around the world.

After finishing our work, we began our descent of the mountain. The farther and faster we traveled, the more the convoy seemed to separate. I feared we might be losing the strength that comes in numbers. We seemed to be not a convoy but individual vehicles ambling along without cohesion. But the space between our vehicles soon proved to be a godsend.

We came to a T in the road where the slowing of our train of vehicles ushered their regrouping. As the gaps closed, a mortar shell landed a short distance behind one of our food trucks. Had the convoy been clustered, one of the vehicles would no doubt have been hit. Rescue workers would have been killed or injured. Instead, we pressed on, accelerating, leaving the danger far behind us.

Or so we thought.

Not much farther along, our downward trek off the mountain was again paused, this time by heavy logs dragged across the road. Drivers of each vehicle were struggling to move the obstructions when men leaped from nowhere. They were armed and determined to steal the food from a truck labeled "Feed The Children."

The thieves brandished knives and began to slice at a canvas tarpaulin. Workers and I stood by, watching food intended for hungry children vanish into the hands of greedy men. They'd sell what they didn't eat.

We were defenseless. No armed guards accompanied us on this part of our journey, and the drivers had disappeared when they were attacked.

Or so it seemed.

I'd hired the drivers to drive the trucks, not to defend them. They were contract laborers who had no emotional ties to FTC. To them, we were just some overseas charity organization administrated by people they'd never seen before, and might never see again. Nonetheless, they were apparently touched by what we were trying to do for their hungry and hurting innocent victims of war.

The drivers reappeared from under the vehicles, where, unbeknownst to me, they'd hidden homemade clubs about the size of baseball bats. They came out swinging at the knife-wielding thieves. Those who had ambushed us with weapons were, in turn, ambushed with the element of surprise.

When one would-be thief was knocked to his knees, the others were instantly deterred. Their knives would be effective only if moved inside the perimeter of a swinging bat. I got the feeling the drivers had been through this drill before, defending other cargo. I didn't ask any questions. I just thanked and thanked them for helping us preserve this cargo for those who needed it most.

The convoy resumed, eventually reentering Vitez by way of a road leading to a Catholic church that had been converted into a hospital. It was an impressive structure, if a bit foreboding, with high ceilings supported by giant stones that were hundreds of years old. The interior space was dark—windows were covered by plywood to protect against shrapnel. Much of the illumination was candlelight because electricity went off and on with the pounding of artillery.

The atmosphere of the place was much like a military field hospital. I was again reminded that suffering knows no age restrictions, as demonstrated here by old men and women moaning next to bawling infants and children.

Feed The Children had earlier set up an office not far from this makeshift medical facility. We provided food and medicine to the sick and wounded. I began to survey the situation, walking among the suffering. At times, the smell of medicine, sweat, and human waste burned my nostrils and even my tongue. It wouldn't be my first time to experience an odor of suffering so strong I could taste it.

Someone asked if I wanted to see a man who'd just been brought in, the latest casualty in the conflict. He wasn't just wounded; he was dead. A bullet that passed through his skull had claimed his life. When the blood was wiped away, the entrance and exit wounds were obvious. I wondered why I had been sought out to view the corpse. For him, it was too late to pray.

Then I learned that a sniper had shot him as he approached the steps of FTC's Vitez distribution center. He was a few feet from the front steps that he'd never climb. His quest for compassionate relief had been denied by an act of utmost hatred.

I wondered what he would have sought from us. Did he want food, medicine, or clothes? Did he simply seek prayer or consolation? Did he want those things for himself or for his loved ones?

I wondered again about the madness of war, and why the men who declare wars are never the ones who fight them. I thought about the absence of mass communication in Vitez, a remote village, and how many of the suffering might not have known a battle was under way until they were hit. I wondered if they ever heard the discharge of the bullets or grenades that struck them down.

Most of those suffering were children. I wondered if they would live through this and, if they did, how they'd feel about war when they were old enough to be soldiers.

Then I asked myself why I was wasting precious time wondering. That could come later. Meanwhile, I saw the great agony of people who needed my attention, not my idle pondering. So I began again to talk to them, assuring them that they would be all right. I held their hands, closing my eyes and raising my voice to God in their behalf. Somehow this provided blessed reassurance—intangible medicine that soothed the hearts and souls around me, as well as my own. I don't know how many I saw that first day within this church turned hospital. People pulled at me from all directions. I did what I could for each, and thanks to FTC, I was able to do a lot. And then I did what I always do when painful experiences seem overwhelming.

I just kept walking—from one victim to another. I vowed that I'd walk to all who were hurting. No matter how frightening and disheartening it became, I'd keep walking.

Eventually, I returned to the airport in an armored car provided by CNN. I made the trip with a Canadian female reporter who, for reasons I never knew, was sought by Bosnian soldiers. She had a price on her head. I remember how she counted out cash as we prepared to negotiate five checkpoints between the hotel and the airport. At each, she paid bribes to guards, and we were waved through.

DAVID CANAVESIO, the director of FTC's field videotaping, appeared from somewhere inside the church. He and I have been in and out of innumerable treacherous situations around the world. We've worked together so often we can sometimes communicate simply through eye contact.

His stare told me something was dreadfully wrong.

"You need to see this," he said.

He led me into a tiny room, the space of which was defined by hanging sheets. The dying were separated by a thin cotton veil that did little to provide visual privacy and nothing to isolate cries of pain.

Three children lay on cots. One had suffered a rifle shot between her neck and shoulder. The swelling in her upper torso magnified the heaving of her chest with each labored breath. A little boy who'd been shot in the abdomen stared blankly into space. A third child cast a glance that went through me. Her eyes were moist and deep with silent pleading. Her cherubic face shone with the fading glow of an earthbound angel. As we locked eyes, I was transfixed, hesitant to ask what could be wrong with such a radiant child.

Then someone pulled back the sheets. Her legs were missing to the middle of her thighs. The lower parts had been taken by a mortar, the upper by surgeons who struggled to stop the bleeding and save her life. The double amputation had been performed mostly by feel in candlelight, without anesthetic.

The victim's name was Marija. Her situation would eventually unfold as a story told around the world.

Just then, the pools in Marija's eyes began to overflow. As she started to cry, I tried to comfort her and was astonished at what I heard next. It was my own voice, extending a promise I didn't know how I would keep. I told her I'd find a way to see that she walked again.

This was in February 1994. Almost unconsciously, I'd started a clock with an unanticipated deadline, ticking toward the yet undetermined start of her physical rehabilitation.

Canavesio later told a reporter that my vow to Marija marked the first time he'd ever seen me make such an extensive promise without preparation. He was startled, but not as much as I. What had I done? Whatever it was, I was certain I would make good on the promise and see it through to the end.

About two weeks later, I was shaving when a CNN broadcast captured my full attention.

A girl named Marija, along with her mother and two sisters, had been removed from the church hospital in Vitez by a United Nations truck that had transported them to an airplane bound for an Italian hospital. Perhaps she might receive better medical care there. I could not be sure. And she would certainly face a language barrier in unfamiliar surroundings as a penniless refugee of war.

Meanwhile, I'd dispatched Don Richardson to a German processing center for the wounded. I'd also instructed him to include the church hospital in Vitez on his itinerary, where I'd assumed Marija would be.

Following up on my CNN surprise, I called the office of the Oklahoma governor and asked for help getting in touch with Don, who was still airborne. The governor got a call through to the German facility that Don would be visiting first. Upon arriving there, Don was given my directive to reroute to Italy. I instructed him to catch up with Marija, again promising I'd find a way to get her to Oklahoma City for medical care I could be certain of.

I wanted to know more about Marija, this child to whom I'd given this very personal promise. Through research, and eventual conversations with Marija herself, I put together the following:

On Christmas Eve 1993, fourteen-year-old Marija was digging through the rubble of what had been the basement of her house. It had been destroyed in the cross fire of Muslim, Croatian, and Serb artillery. She was searching the debris for nuts she'd hidden in preparation for the holiday. When shelling resumed, she and her father fled the ruin for a nearby bunker.

Suddenly their refuge shook violently. Marija was hurled by a blast so deafening that she couldn't hear her own screams.

When she landed, she turned to see her brother cradling their father in his arms. He watched him die. Shaken, he turned to Marija.

She felt daggers of pain in her legs. When she looked down, she discovered they were no longer there. Horrified, she yelled for her father, not realizing he could never again answer her call.

Soldiers later carried her to the church hospital, where she began a living nightmare as yet another innocent victimized by humankind's greatest act of inhumanity—war.

In the blink of an eye, it was all made very personal. War was no longer just the horror of soldiers killing soldiers. It was also the slaughter of women and children dropped by shelling while standing in line awaiting a slice of bread, the sole scrap of their last supper.

I later learned that when I first encountered Marija, she was silently praying. She wasn't asking God to give her anything. She was asking God to take her life. She didn't want to face living as a homeless, fatherless double amputee, with no chance to recover all that had been her blessings within her formerly secure and predictable world.

Traveling to Italy, Don connected with Marija in February 1994. He found her in total despair, ruminating on a past she wanted to forget but knew she never could. She recognized Don from his earlier visit to the Catholic hospital. He spoke before she could.

"I've come to take you to the United States for treatment," Don proclaimed. Marija began to weep. Her little sister crawled into a corner and sobbed.

These were not tears of joy. Marija did not want to go.

"I remember the time we had spent 90 days in a bunker with no relief from the shelling," she would eventually tell *Guideposts* magazine. "More than 300 people trapped underground with no beds or bathrooms and very little food. As terrible as it was, my family had been together. How could we (she and her mother and sisters) travel halfway around the world, leaving my brothers and other sisters behind in Bosnia?"

Don could very well relate to the "halfway around the world" part. That's how far he'd traveled, thinking that he'd be offering Marija a golden opportunity.

Through an interpreter, though, she reiterated that she didn't want to go.

Her faith in people had been destroyed by too many artillery shells she'd heard on too many nights, all fired by her countrymen. If she couldn't trust them, why should she trust an American she didn't know to take her to a place she'd never been to see a doctor she'd never met?

Don returned to Marija's bedside for four consecutive days. On the final visit she felt persuaded to take the risk, to embrace the new hope. She, her mother, and her siblings would, after all, be leaving for America with him.

Courageous Marija had taken less than a week to make a decision that would change the rest of her life.

On a layover in New York City, she was interviewed by a reporter from *Good Morning America*. She announced to him, and thus to much of America, that Feed The Children was going to restore her ability to walk. I prayed more fervently than ever that we could. I felt the eyes of the nation upon me, cautiously scrutinizing me in Marija's interest.

When Marija reached Oklahoma City, I introduced her to Dr. John Sabolich, director of the Sabolich Prosthetic & Research Center. He introduced her to the novelty of legs made of metal and plastic. Marija eyed these strange contraptions with awe. She'd never seen anything like them and therefore feared wearing them.

In hindsight, I think she might have been afraid to raise her hopes for anything that might help her walk again. What if they didn't work? Or what if she couldn't master them? Perhaps questions such as these were crossing her mind.

Marija had been transplanted to Oklahoma City from a place racked by the insanity of war. Understandably, her mind was heavy with trepidation.

Sabolich had often seen such fear in his patients. With a clever plan in mind, he asked Marija to come back in a week.

Meanwhile, he secretly arranged for two teenage girls to stroll into the waiting room at the time of Marija's return. Casually, the girls began to relate stories of dreamy nights spent dancing with their boyfriends. They noticed that Marija was holding back tears of sadness and frustration.

At that point, each raised the legs of her slacks, revealing their prosthetic limbs!

Within minutes, Dr. Sabolich was drying Marija's tears and measuring her for her own prosthetics. Two days later the legs were attached. She arose from the wheelchair, gripping a balance beam. Then, teetering slowly, she took the first step into the rest of her life.

I was recently recalling fond memories of Marija. After regaining her mobility, she went on to work for Feed The Children at our Oklahoma City office. She eventually went to college and later moved to Ohio to be near one of her two sisters who had migrated there with her husband.

I thought about the day I met Marija and my spontaneous pledge to her that she'd walk again. Had I acted out of rash impulse or determined empathy?

I know now that it was the latter.

Feed The Children is a benevolent ministry whose workers are urged to emulate the example of Jesus Christ. Jesus didn't simply observe the world of the needy. He inhabited it. He took it upon himself to enter their circle of suffering. He felt their pain before addressing their healing.

That fateful day at Marija's bedside in Bosnia, I felt her pain immediately and acutely. My impromptu promise came not from premeditation but from an empathetic intuition I've tried to prayerfully hone. God led me into that circumstance, and He led Marija and me out of it.

Arm in arm, Marija and I eventually walked the halls of FTC together. For a while we were partners in my life's quest to surmount all obstacles, to determinedly keep walking.

Chapter Sixteen

*L*IFE'S INTERRUPTIONS are God's opportunities.

I wrote a book with a similar title in 2002. It cited examples of how people set on the path of one worthy mission can be detoured by a circumstance that opens the way to another opportunity to serve.

Feed The Children's staff and I were engaged in efforts to aid war refugees in Bosnia and Croatia. Within sixteen months we transported more than seven million pounds of food, medical supplies, clothing, and blankets to the desperate and dying. We took Geraldo Rivera with us to battle zones where his crews joined ours in filming the horrific face of war—which included the faces of terrified, hungry children.

The outreach became an opportunity for me to experience the nonchalance among some who are forced to live with war.

My film crew and I were preparing to step outside our car in what had been a safe zone when we'd retired the previous night. Suddenly we noticed hand-to-hand fighting among soldiers less than two blocks away. They were shooting each other within range that was virtually point-blank. All-out war was unfolding before our eyes, like spot news coverage come to life.

We shifted inside our combat helmets and shrapnel jackets.

I wondered what our driver would do, as if he could make things right.

"Well," he said passively. "We can't take this route. Someone might shoot us. We'll have to take another one."

The man's tone was matter-of-fact and almost sleepy. He'd grown used to the idea that warfare might take his life. He wouldn't let it stress him before it did.

The crew and I didn't share his casual attitude. Someone told him to hurry, but he didn't. He instead carefully pulled the car forward and backward, as if he were trying to fit a battleship inside an intersection. Talking all the while, he never raised his voice.

Eventually we were in motion, and the echo of gunfire faded in our wake. The car didn't have a radio. If it had, the driver might have played some recreational music.

I thought of two other times on that trip when my anxiety was also at its highest.

One came when I realized that relief workers enjoyed no protection from weaponry. Snipers would shoot us just as quickly as they'd shoot enemy soldiers, and do it with scope rifles aimed from a mile away. It did no good to carry a white flag, as we'd done around battles elsewhere. Bosnian soldiers believed that white flags were the disguise of spies posing as relief workers. Those carrying the flags became targets.

My fear peaked a second time when I exercised a long-standing policy I had with Frances. We'd always agreed that she'd stay behind whenever workers and I approached hostile gunfire. I encountered such a zone on that Bosnian trip.

"We're going over here where there's fighting," I told my wife. "We're going to leave you back here because it's safer."

We returned to find Frances walking down a street near a railroad track beside a bombed-out building. She was dutifully making her part of an FTC television program.

She was focused, and hadn't realized that the fighting had moved. A few weeks later the footage was aired nationwide on the U.S. television stations that carried Feed The Children's regular programs.

Viewers watching inside their living rooms were clueless regarding the danger that Frances had faced while trying to tell the story of starving refugees of war.

Near the end of this first FTC foray into Bosnia, one of our video journalists, David Canavesio, and I spent the night in an abandoned house. David, who was then relatively new to our organization, was unaccustomed to the relentless pounding of artillery. Fearing for his life, he didn't sleep that night. I put plugs into my ears and dozed peacefully. I figured that if the dwelling fell on us during the night, we'd be in heaven before morning. It didn't fall. David and I both were whole and healthy in the morning. So I made plans for a second mission to Bosnia—to which I would eventually return by way of the Mississippi River. What's the connection? Read on and I'll reveal it.

First, I flew home to Oklahoma to fine-tune the sustained Bosnian undertaking. I saw television footage of a looming flood within the U.S. heartland. Newscasters said it might well be the worst flood of the century. They predicted the displacement of thousands.

The FTC staff soon entered a dialogue with the American Red Cross and the Federal Emergency Management Agency regarding relief and rescue.

Somebody had to get ahead of the game. This kind of quick, ad hoc response had become a priority at Feed The Children. (Someone even suggested printing "We go ahead of the game" on our stationery.) In times of natural disaster, FTC has never waited for government studies to assess the damage and itemize the needs. We respond after our own in-house assessments determine whether we should activate our resources and to what degree.

That's how we responded to the Great Flood of 1993, when the Mississippi River crested to twenty feet above flood stage for more than half of its two-thousand-mile route.

The secretary of agriculture, Mike Espy, was sent by President Bill Clinton to evaluate the stricken areas as preparation for federal disaster aid. Espy encountered massive devastation from Iowa to Louisiana—about fifteen billion dollars' worth—wreaked by this, the nation's most damaging flood since 1927. He saw or heard reports of houses completely submerged, people trapped on rooftops, victims navigating through small towns by motorboat, the absence of clean water, and a general brokenness of spirit among all affected. Wherever he went on behalf of the government, he found something else: relief trucks from Feed The Children. We ran fifty-eight semitrailers in and out of seven states for the duration of the emergency recovery period.

"I just kept seeing those big red trucks," Espy told me. Eventually he became an FTC consultant, board member, and employee. He remains an integral part of the organization to this day.

FTC's six-month effort serving victims of the Mississippi flood taught me a life-changing lesson that's twofold: First, bureaucracy cripples our nation's efforts in responding to natural disasters. The flood proved to be the most disheartening example of this I'd seen up to that time. (The response to Hurricane Katrina eventually stole away the prize for bureaucratic ineptitude.)

Second, I saw how a flood creates a special kind of psychic devastation in those whose lives it inundates. In my time, I've seen Americans lose their homes to foreclosure. I've seen twisters take houses off foundations. I've even tended the needs of victims whose homes were swept away by flooding. But in the case of most floods, the water simply invades the home, leaving everything one has known in soggy, rotting ruin. This is the psychic damage people seem to have the hardest time coping with.

When people feel overwhelmed with stress, they often seek refuge in their home. If the home simply isn't there anymore, that's a fact people can deal with: there's nothing to go home to. But when the home is still there—with water equally deep inside and outside—that's another matter. It leaves people wondering what might be salvaged. The stress continues, mounting day by day.

"I just want to go home," an elderly woman told a reporter while afloat in a motorboat in Alton, Illinois. "But home is somewhere under there." She dipped her hand in filthy water teeming with rodents and reptiles, dead and alive. Through tears, she tried to identify personal belongings floating nearby.

"I think that's mine," she said. "I think . . ."

The lingering tragedy made some people hysterical. One man, wet and delirious from exhaustion, was allegedly drunk and angry when he drove a motorboat through a levee near St. Louis, Missouri. The levee shattered. But this didn't help to drain the rising flood, as he had wished. The water level was hopelessly high on both sides of the levee. Dejected, the man tumbled out of the tiny craft into the murky runoff. When retrieved by rescuers, he mumbled incoherently.

It's been written that anything that doesn't kill you makes you stronger. This wasn't true, however, among elderly flood victims who helplessly watched their lifetime's treasures simply drift away. It must've been a young man who wrote that saying. Stamina typically diminishes with age.

Some seniors had moved their belongings into their attics just hours ahead of rising water. Days later, as water continued its ascent, they struggled with manual saws to cut holes in their roofs, hoping to retrieve their possessions and place them at the highest point. But the water never stopped climbing. Eventually the remains of their belongings floated off the shingles. Clothing, furniture, food, and photographs—everything was swallowed by the mighty Mississippi, floated downstream, washed out to sea.

Losing everything is, under any circumstance, a trauma to be reckoned with. But for flood victims like these, the aftermath seems unusually cruel. Suffer loss in a tornado or a fire, for instance, and immediately you know you have no hope of recovering what's gone. With this flood, there was the illusory hope that water would stop climbing tomorrow. But that tomorrow continued to be agonizingly postponed, day after day, from April through October.

Material loss was not the only grievous injury the flood inflicted. I ached for these noble grassroots people as they were deprived of spiritual sustenance within their own churches. Many church buildings remained mostly submerged. The only evidence of their presence was a protruding steeple.

Feed The Children set up a base station in conjunction with the Salvation Army. The SA contributed a volunteer workforce; FTC contributed food and trucks. Our combined forces served the people very well.

Ultimately, the river swelled so far beyond its banks that its surface flattened and stilled, placid as a lake. All was not as it seemed. A deadly fury lay beneath this pristine spread—as Don Richardson observed firsthand.

Two men were starting across the water in a flat-bottom boat, when they were stopped by a local character who had previously made his home on the riverbank. He was known as Catfish. He warned of powerful whirlpools and deadly undercurrents. Dismissively, the men told Catfish to mind his own business.

As the pair pressed on, the purr of their 35-horsepower outboard motor drifted across the watery horizon. Then abruptly it stopped.

From the shoreline, Catfish, Don, and other onlookers watched the boat begin to spin. The unseen churning force that had drowned the motor began sucking it downward. The passengers were powerless to escape the pull.

Swiftly, Catfish boarded his own craft and sped to rescue the pair. He delivered both back to shore, safe from harm, if not humiliation.

Disappointingly, Catfish's good deed did not go unpunished. One of the boat passengers was a game warden. Without thanking him for saving his life, he issued a ticket to Catfish for possessing an open container of alcohol. Meanwhile, a beer can rattled across the floor of the boat in which the game warden had been rescued.

While it's not entirely parallel, this instance does indicate the heartless abandonment of common sense and decency people often suffer when at the mercy of bureaucrats.

This brings to mind a seven-member family that was receiving financial aid from the government when high water forced them to relocate into a three- or four-bedroom house. A social worker visited the group and said it had one too many children for such a small dwelling. The family's financial aid was terminated. Thus, they could neither afford to stay in the temporary house nor return home.

Feed The Children found them in a parking lot next to an automobile service station where the father worked. They were trying to figure out how they were going to live in their car. Thankfully, we were able to help them for several months until they got back on their feet.

People frequently ask if I gain insights from each outreach that prepare me to address the next one more effectively. The answer is yes. In the aftermath of a relatively brief emergency, such as a fire or tornado, the plan for reparation presents itself almost instantly. But in emergencies that mount gradually, such as rising floods, human needs are harder to assess. Confusion abounds.

I'd never previously experienced confusion such as abounded in 1993—especially as reported by news media. Accurate information was maddeningly hard to come by. Trying to plan effective action based on inaccurate information proved more than a little challenging.

For example, a newscaster might say that Iowa was in good shape with regard to food and drinking water. We at FTC would then concentrate on another state, only to learn that a cluster of Iowa farm towns was helplessly sequestered without adequate sustenance. We're talking about groups of maybe a thousand people who'd gone without for two or three days. Such surprise emergencies became acute. We had to strategize how to get goods to the area's nearest dry land, determine if we'd need boats to get supplies to victims, and locate local authorities whose official quarters were most likely underwater. Landline telephones were often disrupted and, back then, cell phones were rare. Trying to respond meaningfully in this environment had us running all over the place, sometimes chasing phantoms.

Given this, we felt compelled to shift our strategy from proactive to reactive. We were definitely not used to that. Since the founding of FTC, we had approached all emergencies head-on. It felt contrary to our nature to have to hang back and wait.

We were also caught off guard by the creeping pace of this natural disaster. If you were to speak of nature in terms of human moods, a tornado is like a burst of anger; it happens, then it's done. A flood, however, is like a secretive, seething anger. It's almost diabolical in the way it sneaks up, gradually rises, and quietly overwhelms.

Even more mystifying: Who'd have thought this secretive assault was triggered by the eruption of Mount Pinatubo two years earlier—in the Philippines, half a world away? God's universe operates with many unseen connections. To anticipate what may happen, we'll do best to scientifically monitor and assess natural processes.

Mount Pinatubo's distant, fiery belch represented the largest volume output of airborne ash recorded in the twentieth century. Climatologists and meteorologists—the scientists who anticipate and predict weather patterns—had never previously dealt with such a phenomenon as it floated stealthily over the unsuspecting wheat and corn belts of the United States. This, however, is the event that precipitated the deluge of 1993, when more than four feet of water saturated parts of the Midwest, taking everyone by surprise.

"People in the Midwest are accustomed to high water in the spring from thawing snow," said one analyst. "But this flood lasted for half of a year. People couldn't understand why the water wouldn't recede. It got to a point where nobody talked about the water going down. Each morning, they got up to see how much more it had risen."

In the St. Louis vicinity, the most affected metropolitan region, thirty-six forecast points were above flood stage. Twenty flood records were broken. Fifty flood-associated deaths were reported, most attributed to drowning and suicide. Feed The Children intermittently dispatched convoys of food trucks to adjacent regions. Our mobility was constrained, as many roads remained closed.

For me as a minister, perhaps the oddest consequence of the flood was its effect on my posture in praying with people. When I respond to disasters, people often recognize me from television, and they never hesitate to ask me to pray with them. And, of course, we usually kneel.

I've knelt with people at bedsides, on the ground, inside tent hospitals, in theaters of war. The flood, however, robbed us of virtually every place we might kneel. We had to pray standing up.

Eventually the floodwaters that had begun rising before Easter withdrew entirely about a month before Thanksgiving, making it possible to assess damages and begin reparations. I began entering soggy dwellings where I often found shell-shocked-looking elderly couples staring uncomprehendingly at high-water marks on what remained of their home's interior walls. Some broke into sobs upon seeing me, asking for prayer. Again, there was no place to kneel.

Moving from house to house, I discovered yet another ugly aspect of reality in the aftermath of a flood: the slime deposits brought in from the bottom of a river. Though the floodwaters recede, the repulsive, sticky goo remains.

Slime deposits measured eighteen inches deep inside some homes lining the Mississippi River valley. Once I tried to walk in the gunk. It sucked the shoes right off my feet. It would occasionally pull hip boots down to the wearer's knees. Trying to wade through it was like trying to walk through a pool of half-set glue.

I recall one old man's attempts to shovel the muck. The wooden handle cracked in his hands. Once drying finally began, the sticky mire became hard like concrete. People eventually broke it up with sledgehammers.

I sometimes recall all this when I'm traveling by jet and hear the pilot tell passengers we're soaring over the Mississippi River. I look down at white houses dotting mineral-rich soil. I recall the floodwaters and think about people I met in that time of dire emergency.

Some rebuilt along that river, on the same land to which their ancestors returned after the Great Flood of 1927. To them, their place on the river seems assigned by God. High water can take their houses. But nothing can take their sense of home.

Chapter Seventeen

*I*N 1992 I RECEIVED A CALL from a Nashville public relations professional representing a celebrity who was interested in affiliating with Feed The Children.

I was a fan. I'd enjoyed the musician's songs on the radio. His rise to popularity had been nothing short of meteoric. It reminded me of what I'd seen as a high school student when Elvis Presley took the world by storm.

In terms of records sold, this singer became even bigger than Elvis. Eventually, he was America's best-selling solo artist of the twentieth century, according to the Recording Industry Association of America.

I'm talking about Garth Brooks.

I've worked with other luminaries. Their endorsements have served mightily to bolster FTC's inventory of goods, services, and donations. A great sacrifice of time and effort has been made by many kind and caring celebrities.

In Garth, I encountered a depth of generosity I would never have expected. His benevolence never went to his head, and neither did his fame. That's incredible for someone whose live album was the best selling in history.

He's the only artist ever to have seven albums debut at number one on both the Billboard 200 and the Billboard Top Country Albums charts. His televised concert in Central Park drew an estimated 800,000 people and achieved the highest viewing in all of cable television in 1997. And, even six years after he officially retired, he made history as Wal-Mart's top-selling music artist of all time.

I don't intend this passage as a valentine to Garth Brooks, no matter how fond my recollections. I just think I'd be remiss if I didn't share my eight years of travel and interaction with someone who has proven to be one of the most charismatic personalities of contemporary culture.

While I'm overwhelmed with Garth's accomplishments, I relate here an objective account of what I saw in my sometimes-daily contact with a man of the masses who remained right with himself. I sensed great love in his heart and peace in his mind, as demonstrated by many little things. I don't know that I've ever met a person with such amazing self-command.

For example, Garth could fall asleep at will just minutes before performing in front of sixty-five thousand people. He would then awaken from his power nap and walk from his berth to the stage, ready to give all he had. He traveled millions of miles while retaining indefatigable stamina. Where many touring performers come to rely on self-medicating, Garth never used things external. He even resisted aspirin.

I met Garth in 1992 in Edmond, Oklahoma, at the home of his mother, Colleen Brooks. We chatted about how he envisioned his participation with FTC. He soon announced the donation of one dollar from the sale of each copy of his forthcoming Christmas album, *Beyond the Season*. I'd be glad to share the amount of the accumulated donation—the largest ever received by Feed The Children—but I doubt Garth would approve. He prefers privacy regarding his contributions to FTC and other charities.

My first tour with Garth commenced when I flew to Billy Bob's, the nation's largest dance club, in Houston, Texas (where the movie *Urban Cowboy*, starring John Travolta, had been filmed). After that, I flew to California, where Garth and I, along with an entourage, boarded a commercial airliner that had been converted into MGM's private jet. Garth's record company had leased the aircraft to hustle him to interviews in seven major cities in three days. At each stop, Garth talked about the Christmas album and his upcoming involvement with FTC. The resulting press coverage proved invaluable for the charity. In the space of seventy-two hours, stories about the Garth-FTC relationship were splashed across the *New York Times*,

Los Angeles Times, Washington Post, Chicago Tribune, St. Louis Post-Dispatch, and others, as well as the wire services. Reports on radio and television blanketed the nation's airwaves.

Garth's performance tours always sold out weeks before he began them. When he did public announcements for FTC, he wasn't trying to sell tickets. He urged listeners to bring canned food to FTC trucks that would be parked outside his venue. He promised that the food would go to a local distribution center in their town.

The collections were enormous. Fans always filled from one to four semitrailers. In one city a disc jockey promised that the concertgoer who brought the most food would meet Garth in person. One determined fan cleaned out her pantry and her friends' pantries, and then spent three thousand dollars at a supermarket to win the opportunity to meet Garth while providing bounty for the needy.

I recall Garth's playing a hall in Minnesota for eight nights during the late 1990s. Before each show, fans filled the massive food truck trailers—the longest the government allows.

Before my relationship with Garth, I'd always hesitated to ask celebrities for more than they volunteered. Prominent entertainers are always being asked for something. Too many people make too many requests of their time. After careful consideration, I approached Garth with the idea of his being the "voice" of a few of FTC's national thirty-minute television programs. To accomplish this, we would shoot video backstage before his concert. I told him I'd personally guarantee that technical equipment would be set up prior to his arrival and that he could do his part in one take. I pledged that FTC would never take more than thirty minutes of his time for videotaping.

Garth consented. And I prayed that everything would move smoothly, without technical difficulties.

During one backstage shoot, Garth came from his room dressed in the clothes that he'd wear onstage. We finished the planned half-hour session in one twenty-three-minute take. From it, we garnered enough audio and video material for multiple FTC presentations.

Because of Garth's generosity, people from coast to coast would later see and hear the most popular entertainer in America make a personal appeal for food and donations for the world's starving. When finished with the videotaping, he lingered with backstage fans, posing for photographs and signing autographs for anyone who wanted. When the time for the concert came, he politely asked the gathering to excuse him. A sold-out audience was ready and waiting. He stepped nonchalantly from the backstage area into a blaze of spotlights, flashing cameras, and pyrotechnics accompanied by a deafening roar of adoring fans.

I've never met anyone who could multitask with such composure and do it all without a hitch.

Top performers draw their energy from somewhere deep inside. For athletes and entertainers, it's called heart. It's the driving force that enables them to give their all, then give some more.

I repeatedly saw that in Garth.

Most entertainers who end a two-and-a-half-hour performance around midnight understandably take time to wind down, and then sleep late the next day.

Garth went straight to his bus or to his room and went to sleep. It wasn't unusual for him to keep an early-morning appointment, such as a local drive-time radio show. Then, in the afternoon, he'd do his own sound checks, the preconcert setting of the sound equipment. (Most entertainers use a stand-in because the process is lengthy and tedious.)

I frequently saw Garth slip into virtually empty auditoriums and ease into the top row, where he listened to his band rehearse. He wanted to personally ensure that quality sound was delivered to every seat in the room. He wanted to be positive that he was playing for the person in the back as much as he was the fellow in the front.

He often disallowed the sale of seats within the first two rows. Then, just before showtime, he would have two rows of people from the very back ushered up front to fill those choice spots, much to their surprise and delight. Just another little gift from Garth.

Garth never sought press for his generosity, although he received it. Leaks of information are inevitable in such a high-profile company, traveling with a cast and crew that numbered over a hundred. I can attest, however, that Garth gave far more financial resources than the media ever knew. And even more generously, he gave of himself.

Many times, we were backstage, where dozens of fans had somehow managed access to the secured area. Each wanted an autograph and snapshot with the star. Garth graciously granted every wish and never complained about the intrusion.

Garth was preparing to go onstage one night when a security guard escorted some people accompanying a seriously ill little girl to meet him. He gave her a full half hour as the countdown to curtain time proceeded. Garth engaged the child personally and intensely, giving her all of his attention. It was obvious that he had temporarily left his world to join hers.

When curtain time came, no one had to tell him. He just knew, rising up from the youngster's side in the nick of time to walk onto the stage.

Some might think that Garth's generosity was a part of his act. It wasn't. If it had been, sooner or later I would have seen him crack under the constant pressure that was life as Garth Brooks.

In eight years I never once saw him lose his temper. I consistently saw him show compassion. He didn't seem to restrain anger any more than he forced warmth. The latter seemed to come naturally from a bottomless reservoir of goodwill. So much goodness manifested over so long a time simply couldn't be a false front.

Perhaps more than any other time, my assessment of Garth's good nature was reinforced when he played Texas Stadium for three nights during the mid-1990s. He drew a capacity crowd of 65,000 to each show; 195,000 people bought tickets, purchased approximately fifty truckloads of souvenirs—and brought their food donations for FTC—all within a furious seventy-two hours. The concerts were shot by a major television network and were edited into a two-hour prime-time special. As part of the show, Garth rode a high wire to "fly" above enthralled fans.

That wasn't just a colossal concert. It was the Super Bowl (minus the football) set to music. Almost 200,000 people eventually thundered their accolades with standing ovations that began when Garth walked onstage and continued until the last note of music sounded. Multiple encores ensued.

But one man writing for one newspaper didn't like any of it. His opinion was published and read by millions who hadn't been there.

"This is why no statues will ever be built to commemorate music critics," I thought to myself.

Before the second night's show, I sat among the band and technical people who were preparing with Garth for the concert. The review had been published perhaps twelve hours earlier. It had been read on multiple radio stations, and outraged fans had been given airtime to voice their contempt for the critic.

Nevertheless, the mood backstage was a pall. Show people who'd gone to the limit to give a triumphant performance felt personally wounded by the published review. And they were vocal about it.

Some of their colorful language reminded me of the locker room when I played collegiate basketball. Everyone had the same idea as to what the music critic could do with his writings about the concert.

I confess that I, too, ached for Garth, who never said a disparaging word. He listened silently to all the ranting. It was as if he had the weight of the world on his shoulders, as well as that of his well-intentioned people.

"Let's change the subject," he said at last. "We've got a show to do."

With that, Garth and the group got up and frenetically prepared for another night's concert. During his three-day invasion of Dallas, I never heard him say a single word about the review that had left legions of fans outraged.

Then we were off to another loving mob in another city.

IN THE MIDDLE OF A 1990S TOUR, death came for the mastermind who arranged Garth's personal appearance engagements, Joe Harris. A legendary fixture in Nashville, Joe felt genuine affection for Garth and his family. It was reciprocal.

I was asked to speak at Joe's funeral. The Oak Ridge Boys sang, and Garth did an a cappella rendition of "The River" before an overflow gathering of the most influential people in Nashville.

After talking for ten minutes about Joe, I sat down next to his pastor, who astonished me by confiding that he was having a difficult time controlling his grief. He was scheduled to deliver the main sermon.

"If I lose it when I speak, please relieve me," he whispered to me.

"You won't lose it," I said. "You're a pastor and you've delivered funerals many times. You'll be fine."

The minister spoke a few words, then fell apart.

I slowly rose, approached the pulpit, and looked into the faces of some of country music's most prolific lyricists.

" 'I will sail my vessel, 'til the river runs dry,' " Garth had sung minutes earlier, his solitary voice accompanied only by the muffled weeping of the bereaved.

I waited to hear whatever I was about to say in a totally impromptu sermon. To this day, I don't remember most of it.

I faced a roomful of celebrities whose careers had been partially choreographed by Joe. They were all suffering their own sense of personal loss and apprehension, wondering how they'd manage to go on without the man who had engineered their success so far. They were ships on the sea of uncertainty. Joe had been their captain.

"I will sail my vessel, 'til the river runs dry." Garth's singing resounded in my mind.

I remember later glancing at Garth, whose eyes were like two levees restraining a river of tears. Perhaps later the dams would break and the tears would come crashing forward. But not just now.

Garth had bravely sailed his vessel of commemoration to Joe. He had felt that song for all of us. He had touched each of us at our own point of pain. We had all been immeasurably grateful for his selection of a song that he sang in a way he never had, the right way for the time. For the moment, he and the rest of us merely floated on the consolation it offered.

I told the gathering that as surely as Joe's life had gone to eternity, theirs would go forward on earth.

After the service, attendees quietly shuffled from the sanctuary. As many were stars in their own right, they set off to sail their vessels on the currents of destiny—this time without Captain Joe. Though they had lost a friend and wise counselor, they retained their personal talents. They would go on to touch the lives of others in the heartfelt way Joe's had touched theirs, in the way Garth's song had touched us that day. And will forever.

Chapter Eighteen ～

$\mathcal{P}$EOPLE OF A CERTAIN AGE vividly remember what they were do-
ing when they heard that President Kennedy had been assassinated.
Many recall clearly the fall of Saigon and the joyless acknowledg-
ment of the war's ending that reddened faces across an embarrassed
America. And many can recollect their exact activity when they saw
President Nixon wave farewell before boarding a helicopter on the
White House lawn, setting out for California after resigning in dis-
grace.

More clearly than any of the above, I remember the heart-
stopping event of April 19, 1995. And I will forever.

Talking on the phone in my Oklahoma City office at 9:02 a.m.,
suddenly I could hear nothing but an overpowering rumble. Actually, I felt it as much as heard it. This was the bombing of the Murrah building—an act of homegrown terrorism, a blast heard around
the world.

The walls shook and parts of my ceiling fell. I couldn't imagine
what had caused this. In a vain search for answers, my mind raced
from one terrifying speculation to another. Had there been a gas line
explosion in our building? Had there been an airplane crash?

Just then, an FTC staffer bolted into the room to insist that I stay
inside. He feared for my life. All of our imaginations were running
wild for want of an explanation. Our building sits under an air traffic corridor. Had an aircraft crashed a stone's throw from my door?

One FTC staffer propped up a ladder and scurried to the roof.
He saw clouds of smoke billowing from a part of downtown Oklahoma City, approximately six miles away. Could an explosion at
that distance create such an earsplitting boom at our place?

Within twenty minutes an employee's wife called, frantically insisting that we tune in the television to Channel 9.

Onscreen we saw a cloud of that same black smoke, broadcast from a rooftop outside the city. Regular programming had been interrupted as an announcer struggled to discover and relate the facts of what had happened. Observing from his lofty perch, without betraying the slightest emotion, he reported that downtown Oklahoma City appeared to be ablaze.

Perhaps he was in shock, idly thinking out loud. The fact of the blaze was obvious to all. But what had caused it? And why?

Everyone on our staff shared an eerie feeling that this was no ordinary fire. But the outrageous reality of the situation we could never have dared to imagine.

The smoke grew even thicker. The TV camera operator zoomed the lens out, trying to capture as much of the churning black stuff as possible on the television screen.

As we watched helplessly, we began doing what most Christians do when they simply don't know what else to do. We prayed.

Our one-hundred-person home office staff assembled en masse to talk to God one-on-one. Then we appointed staffers to work the telephones. Feed The Children is known for helping those with a need wherever disaster might strike. And sure enough, people began calling in for help that very day—though they seemed to have no idea what they needed. The shock was all too new.

The picture on the TV screen began shaking, because the television camera was perched atop a running reporter's shoulder. It revealed one bloody body after another, horizontal, screaming, unconscious, or dead. The commentator said the deceased were being carried out of the Alfred P. Murrah Federal Building. One-third of the nine-story building had been blown away from beneath its foundation to its roof. Two-thirds was still eerily standing. Debris were scattered for miles.

In our naïveté, we did not yet suspect foul play. Wrapped tight in our trusting nature, we speculated that this carnage was the result of a natural-gas explosion or some such. Within minutes, though, we would know what all the world now knows—that the Oklahoma

City federal building, situated in the heart of the heartland, had been bombed.

We would never have dreamed this could happen here. We understood why terrorists seek targets in Bosnia or Jerusalem or even New York City, as they had in 1993. But Oklahoma City? Why would they bother with a place where the uncontroversial governor had just begun his hundredth predictable day in office, a metropolis where an exciting city council debate centers on funding for a sleepy canal?

This couldn't be happening here.

Eventually we would learn that someone had concocted a forty-five-hundred-pound bomb from fertilizer and fuel, loaded it into a van, and quietly attempted to park it in the underground garage of the Murrah. But the ceiling was too low. The van couldn't enter.

Subsequently the driver eased the vehicle around the corner into traffic at the front of the building. Then he inconspicuously turned off the ignition and simply walked away.

As it turns out, the bomber was carrying out a mission of revenge. His goal: to avenge the deaths of eighty Branch Davidians, killed two years earlier in a government raid on their compound in Waco, Texas. On this, the second anniversary of the raid, he would kill to compensate for killings. Such is the logic of hatred that borders on insanity.

On this day I had been scheduled to serve jury duty not two blocks from the destroyed building. I had been excused by a judge sympathetic to the unpredictability of my international ministry. Had I not been dismissed, I'd have been en route to the courthouse at the time of the explosion. I might have become a casualty.

Even as the television coverage continued, we felt drawn toward denial, insisting to ourselves that this devastation couldn't be happening so close to home. "Seeing is believing," the saying goes. This is not always true, however. Some truths prove too painful to accept.

Recovering from disbelief in my office, I was told that someone from the Olive Garden Restaurant had called requesting a van to haul food they wanted to donate to rescue workers. We received similar calls from managers at the Red Lobster and China Coast. So my people and I went to work, still having no idea of the severity of the death and destruction.

I flipped the channel, checking for other television coverage, and discovered that all three commercial network affiliates had pre-empted scheduled programming for live coverage.

I asked a staff member to call around to local van dealerships in hopes of borrowing vehicles to haul food and supplies.

I sent a staffer downtown to see where we could set up one of our eighteen-wheel, long-haul vehicles to serve as a supply center.

Soon thereafter, I got into my car and started toward downtown, carrying my cell phone. Don Richardson, my employee on the scene, stayed in frequent communication but couldn't be especially directive. Due to blinding smoke, confusion, and screaming, he, like the authorities, couldn't make sense of the scene. Streets were clogged with debris for blocks around, including automobiles that had been blown hundreds of feet.

I drove as close to the wreckage as I could. I leaped from my car, not far from flames and smoking embers. By then the local and state police had been deployed along with the National Guard. Trying to communicate, I had to scream simply to be heard above the sirens.

Finally I stood about fifty yards from the ruins. It was like a nightmare. The reality of the situation became instantly clear. It was as if a giant flaming blade had dropped from the sky to take a huge slice out of the building from roof to basement. One-third of the nine-story Murrah Federal Building simply wasn't there anymore. The remaining two-thirds stood open, a jaggedly torn testament to man's inhumanity to man.

Authorities invited me and about fifteen other relief and rescue workers to tour the smoldering rubble. I eased to the rear of the wreckage, waiting to be led through it.

Debris continued to drop around us when someone yelled, "There's another bomb!"

The group of people, including me, scattered frantically in all directions. I sprinted for two blocks, stopping only to duck behind a brick building.

It's a common pattern for terrorists to set off one bomb to draw rescue workers, then to detonate a second charge to kill those who come to help. I feared a repeat of that diabolical scheme at the Murrah building, but it was a false alarm.

Fifty-five doctors spontaneously left their offices and came to the killing field. Most of the injured escaped under their own power. All but six who were carried out were already dead.

Policemen told stories about blood running so thick that their feet stuck to the pavement.

An impromptu triage center was set up outside the building where victims were supposed to be tagged according to their medical condition—minor, moderate, critical, or dead. The makeshift facility wasn't used—all victims removed were already dead.

Earlier in my experience I'd seen war-torn cities in Bosnia. But I had never seen such destruction as I saw that day in my own hometown. Had I been blindfolded and suddenly dropped into the middle of that situation, nothing could have made me believe I was in the United States. I had previously met and felt great compassion for strangers who were victims of terrorism. That was nothing compared with the depth of emotion I felt about this. I knew many of these people personally. Many who weren't hurt themselves knew someone killed in the blast. In fact, we learned that the stepmother of one of our employees had been killed in the explosion.

Within another hour Feed The Children had set up a relief site near the fallen Murrah building. Before nightfall, almost all of our staff was either on the scene, working the telephones back at the office, or scurrying about the city doing whatever needed to be done. We had responded in minutes and remained active in the relief effort for ninety days. We served 130,000 meals to rescue workers. We gave out bandages, clean clothing, flashlights, medicine, mechanical equipment, and more.

We took in donations earmarked for Oklahoma City relief totaling $2,852,862 from regular donors, corporations, and television viewers. In addition to providing food, medicine, and clothing as we normally do, we paid for forty-nine funerals. We paid rent, mortgages, and utility bills for 118 families. We financed weeklong, intensive psychological counseling for 47 others. We sent 550 additional survivors away for a week of rest and relaxation. Feed The Children continued to help victims for years afterward, until funds were depleted.

We told rescue workers that we'd get them anything they needed. One worker requested hemorrhoid medication for himself and several colleagues who'd developed their condition from the strain of lifting debris. Another asked for new underwear. Crawling across jagged steel and concrete had shredded the pair he was wearing. We met these requests and more.

We manage our donors' money with utmost respect and responsibility. I pray daily to be a faithful steward. Our financial affairs are an open book to the Internal Revenue Service, as well as to watchdog groups and others who are—and sometimes even those who aren't—entitled to monitor our disbursement of funds, goods, and services.

Consequently, I was saddened on November 15, 1995, when USA Today reported what I had been hearing about the government-subsidized (and therefore restricted) nonprofit groups for months after the bombing. Due to various government obstructions, needy people couldn't get the money that well-meaning people had donated to help them.

The government-regulated organizations were forbidden by IRS regulations from giving directly to victims. The money had to run a gauntlet of bureaucratic approvals first, and that meant that people who needed help immediately had to wait until the government got around to it.

Even the state of Oklahoma couldn't help its own. The Oklahoma legislature had set up a special fund, the Murrah Crime Victims Compensation Fund, but money for the fund was delayed by business-as-usual politics.

Because of these and other built-in inefficiencies and ineptitudes, many injured victims were being only partially compensated for lost income from their primary employment. Those who had formerly depended on income from a second job saw no compensation for that at all.

Because some groups had restrictions, the result was funding log-jam. Mortgages were not being paid on time, and lien holders began repossessing homes. College educations were abandoned. Medical treatment was denied. And all the while, donated money sat in interest-bearing accounts and administrators were prohibited from disbursing it to the needy.

The day after the blast, a network television reporter asked how long it took us to go into action after our first committee meeting. I had to shake my head and smile. I told him that's not the way we get things done—and that's why we can get them done so quickly. We never met in committee. We just went instantly to work, like firemen do at the sound of the bell. When an emergency arises, we respond. It's that simple.

And then the reporter or someone else asked what medical supplies I'd like to see donated.

"We don't need more medical supplies," I told him, "just more body bags."

Along with everyone else, I was appalled at the most disgusting aspect of this crime. The federal building had housed a day-care center. Infants with missing body parts or killed by decapitation or fire were carried out by exhausted and weeping rescue workers, their faces awash in sweat and tears.

We had no idea how many bodies remained inside, children or adults. Many were so burned that I couldn't tell if they were male or female, black or white.

A news photographer snapped a picture of a fireman cradling a two-year-old bathed in blood. The photograph was picked up by the Associated Press, and I've seen it printed all around the globe, serving as a universal portrait of Oklahoma City's suffering.

Charred, twisted hulks of auto wreckage sat strewn about the street outside the building, still holding baby seats and toys—the precious cargo of life as people knew it before the savage attack. A man sat silently, perilously perched in a Murrah Building windowsill. He seemed hypnotized, his gaze fixed, looking out over the city. He said nothing as rescuers approached him. He failed to respond even when they shouted. Some speculated that he was in shock. His eyes remained fixed, staring straight ahead. When the rescuers finally reached him, they saw that he was dead, his face frozen in his last moment of disbelief. His legs were gone.

About five and a half hours after the blast, searchers with dogs discovered a woman trapped by fallen concrete and steel that pinned her right leg. She lay in total darkness in about eighteen inches of water. They feared that the building might collapse on her at any moment, so brave rescuers made haste to pull her out. The weight on her leg was too great. They couldn't budge her. Finally officials made the difficult decision to amputate her leg.

A doctor crawled on his stomach to her side. There was no room for him to carry surgical tools. So a human chain was formed behind him, made up of other doctors, firemen, and a licensed practical nurse. All lay flat. Together these people, working in pitch-blackness, passed surgical instruments back and forth to the doctor who was performing the operation, still lying flat on his stomach. Under those conditions, while the entire building creaked and groaned, seeming ready to collapse, he cut off the woman's leg without benefit of anesthetic. Bleeding profusely, she was pulled out, virtually drained of body fluids. But she was still alive.

After a few days rescue workers put out a request for children to come to the scene to pet the rescue dogs. The animals had become severely depressed because all the people they located in the rubble were dead. Children came and supplied ample doses of TLC. Still, it took hours to coax the distraught canines back into the wreckage.

Hours after the explosion, more grim discoveries were made in what seemed unlikely places. When rescuers entered the Water Resources Board Building, located about forty yards across the street from the Murrah Building, two bodies were found inside. A week after the explosion, police found three more bodies inside a basement tavern two blocks from the federal building. Reports of death came at us from all directions. In all, 168 people died, including 19 children. The tally of those injured reached 674. Twenty-five buildings were destroyed, three hundred more were damaged.

In a blast as potent as this, a lot of things happen that are sure to surprise you. This one ignited the gas tanks in cars as far as six blocks away, spraying even those remote areas with burning fuel and fiery shrapnel. So many tires exploded from the heat that officials at first thought ammunition was being ignited inside the Murrah building's Bureau of Alcohol, Tobacco, and Firearms.

We toiled well into that first night and pressed on into the next day, our energy and emotions nearly depleted. On April 20, Geraldo Rivera phoned me to say he was coming to do a live show from the bombing site at 3:00 p.m. His program would then air our catastrophe on network television approximately thirty hours after it happened.

It may surprise you to learn that the pettiness of human egos pollutes even such occasions as this, when overriding human need calls us all to pull together. Some competing media concerns resented the fact that Geraldo, a national personality, was assigned a vantage point about one hundred feet closer to the bombed building than theirs. Their jealousy was a factor in the restrictions imposed on Geraldo, who was told he could not bring all of the television equipment he needed. So I agreed to let him use some of Feed The Children's gear, including one of our trucks. As luck would have it, that turned out to be a good thing for us. I had no idea at the time, but that truck would soon be seen frequently on *Geraldo* and other national news reports on commercial as well as cable television networks.

Some reporters and media officials continued to complain. They thought Geraldo had a coverage advantage. While the media business is by nature competitive, such self-concern truly had no place during those terrible days in Oklahoma City. Really—can't we just put all that aside, at least at times such as this?

People were dead or dying all around. Blood flowed in the streets. And yet some reporters cared only about beating their news-gathering competition. I thought the idea of journalism was to provide the public with helpful information and present news stories clearly so that all might understand. But some of those reporters, standing amid body bags, were only interested in getting a more sensational story and getting it before anyone else. Their behavior provided a textbook example of misplaced priorities.

To use someone else's tragedy as an opportunity to advance your own personal interests seems to me an indication of a very special kind of moral sickness. One overly zealous reporter posed as a policeman to get closer to the disaster and was arrested for impersonating an officer. Another, from a tabloid television show, wore a fireman's hat and raincoat but was also discovered and expelled from the scene.

What if the injured had called out to one of these reporters? Would he have put aside self-interest and lent a hand? Or would he have turned the camera on them and added their plight to his story?

I didn't mind that Geraldo was a few feet closer to the action. Expressing my view, I said, "This man has flown in here to help. Let him set up wherever he wants. He has a national audience, and we need the help of the whole nation."

I later said the same thing about other national news personalities, such as Larry King, whose operatives were also on the scene.

Geraldo had sought my appraisal of the situation. I met with him at about 3:00 a.m., eighteen hours after the blast, twelve hours before his next live telecast. I felt a bonding with the man and sensed that his heart was in the right place. After that, we both slept for about three hours, then met at the scene early the next morning.

He asked me to participate in his broadcast. We began preparing to go on the air live in his regularly scheduled time slot. To develop his story, he interviewed survivors who sat motionless with the pictures of slain loved ones on their laps. He invited Oklahoma's lieutenant governor, Mary Fallin, to appear on the program, along with various medical and official personnel at the site.

It was hard to behold the scene and not feel overcome with anger. Many people were livid at the sight of the senseless carnage. Some, including Geraldo, lashed out verbally at the then unknown perpetrators. On live, coast-to-coast television, he twice called them "bastards."

Someone later said he thought Geraldo's remarks were inappropriate. I think that's petty criticism of a man doing noble work. I wondered how such critics could consider such a trivial matter important in the face of this truly outrageous attack.

Many national mass-media entities descended on Oklahoma City, and many asked to speak to me. I appeared on the *Today* show, National Public Radio, USA Radio Network, ABC Radio Network, *Good Morning America, America's Talking, Larry King Live, 48 Hours*, and CNN numerous times.

I feel uneasy thinking about how all this media attention boosted my national profile. I had spent my ministry developing relief efforts. And with this disaster, ironically, I had become famous for it. In the end, however, all this translated into more money donated and services provided for the needy. And that's a good thing.

There is no way to compare or rate the pain felt by those who were injured or lost loved ones forever that day in Oklahoma City. But I will say that, consistently, some of the greatest pain I saw was among people who had seen their loved ones just minutes before the blast, never to see them again.

Psychologists say that seeing the body of a loved one who has died helps those who are left behind to begin the healing process. Many anguished survivors had let their loved ones out of the car on the way to their jobs as they had routinely done so many times before.

"See you tonight," they might have said. But for them, tonight never came. In fact, some families are still waiting for the sun to set on this horror. Craving closure, they know none is likely to come. Their loved ones' remains were never discovered or identified.

I talked to one woman who, weeks after the explosion killed her toddler, still had not removed his toothbrush from its holder. His toys were still strewn about the backyard. She said that when she and her husband entered their house, their puppy would greet them, then circle their legs to look for their youngster.

Time is not likely to give such people the sense of closure they would prefer. The best they can hope for is to learn to make their own peace with the memories. For them, life changed. They needed to change the way they thought about it and lived it, or else feel forever haunted.

ON MAY 23, 1995, not long after dawn broke on a cloudless Sunday morning, demolition experts razed what was left of the Murrah building. Spectators stood silently around the perimeter, listening to the countdown. Then smoke belched from the charges set to bring the ruined structure down. The low, deafening rumble of the implosion rode down with the rubble. Echoes of uncontrollable sobbing were audible as well.

Once the dust settled, bulldozers and dump trucks pulled onto the lot to haul away the refuse. A towering building had been reduced to pieces small enough to load into trucks by hand.

As the first trucks began to pull off the lot, a few motorists fell in behind. They followed all the way to the disposal site. As the non-descript, unrecognizable chunks were discarded in various places, some of those who had followed began to sift through them. Perhaps they were searching for any small something, anything that might have belonged to their fallen loved one. Despite death, destruction, and total annihilation, they still felt a need to hold on.

A FEW DAYS BEFORE THANKSGIVING 1995, I visited what seven months before had been the site of the Murrah Federal Building. It was then a vacant lot covered with green grass and surrounded by a chain-link fence. Someone visiting Oklahoma City for the first time would have no idea that hundreds of lives once began and ended each workday there. They'd have no idea that thousands of people negotiated the building daily to pick up children from day care, apply for Social Security and Medicaid, or seek any of the other services that the federal government dispenses at the local level.

There remained no trace of what happened, except for hand-made mementos affixed to the fence and the handful of tourists who trickle through as an endless stream of mourners. The memorabilia were likely in violation of Oklahoma City ordinances that govern the posting of signs. This, however, is sacred ground. No official would have dreamed of enforcing such laws at this site.

As the sun set over Oklahoma City on the day of my visit, I could hear my own footsteps echo in the stark silence of this neighborhood that had once been the hub of a bustling downtown.

I saw a man wordlessly pointing a video camera at the vacant lot, then void of any discernible motion except for the playing of a slight breeze upon the unremarkable grass. I noticed a license tag from Michigan on a car stopped in the middle of the street. Even at evening rush hour, it blocked no traffic. The passengers could safely exit the vehicle and stand in the middle of the empty thoroughfare, transfixed by the barren lot. One seemed to be praying softly. Another wept.

Haltingly, I walked along the fence line hung with teddy bears, placards, and other homemade commemoratives. Items bore notes from every state in the nation and many foreign countries.

Many visitors silently reached out to touch the medals, photographs, trinkets, and all the rest of the tributes left along the fence. Nearby, a church had erected a small box for donations. A thin, flimsy lock secured it. To my knowledge, it has never been burglarized.

Finally, as the shadows grew their longest on that day in November, a siren pierced the silence. Police cars and fire engines once again raced through the neighborhood, as they had on that fateful morning in April. The sound seemed nightmarish and ironic at that place in time. Perhaps those sirens were on their way to a fire, a robbery, or an automobile accident. Who knows? Whatever it was, I didn't need to know, not right then.

Chapter Nineteen

*I*N 1999, Channel 5, a CBS affiliate in Nashville, Tennessee, aired a negative feature on Feed The Children that almost did us in.

Some four months in the making, the investigative report became the most devastating blow that the mass media had thrown in the ministry's twenty-year history. It proved to be a dramatic slam to FTC's reputation as a responsible steward of donated funds. In fact, it served to erode the confidence that many Nashville celebrities had in the ethics of the charity. Some entertainers who'd publicly endorsed FTC quietly withdrew involvement. Their representatives stopped taking my calls.

At the time FTC's Nashville warehouse was our only U.S. distribution center outside Oklahoma City. It was managed by someone I'd hired because of his notable work in Christian ministry.

A team of broadcast journalists secretly videotaped food and other goods being pilfered from the warehouse, carried out in boxes. Stolen items included cleaning supplies, clothes, toys, and incidentals.

The camera didn't lie. The suspects were FTC employees. They were caught red-handed stealing wares given by manufacturers or purchased with funds allotted by FTC's supporters.

"You'd be surprised by what they carried out," a WTVF reporter told viewers. "One day, it was more than a dozen box loads of brand-new clothing. What you're seeing here is just the tip of the iceberg."

I couldn't begin here to describe my dismay. Suffice it to say that I felt betrayed by the employees' actions and was tremendously distraught but determined not to be discouraged.

I learned about the sabotage through an unexpected phone call from the media. I was asked to comment. How could I? This was the first I'd heard of the matter. I believed it inappropriate to say anything until I was personally satisfied as to exactly what had transpired. The caller told me the videotape showed a few employees stealing items in packaging clearly marked "Feed The Children." I hadn't seen the tape.

I said I'd come to Nashville and agreed to comment after viewing the footage. The caller indicated that we had a pact. The terms ratified my promise to issue a public statement after seeing the clandestine video.

But that's not what happened.

The station aired the tapes before I was given a chance to view them. The broadcast seemed to indicate that my response had been "no comment." I never said "no comment."

Wouldn't it have made sense for them to first show me what they wanted me to comment on? I still hadn't personally examined anything that would qualify my responding.

I've always felt that issuing "no comment" to the press is much like "no contest" to criminal charges. The public tends to translate "no comment" as "guilty."

Nevertheless, the damaging footage was seen by millions of viewers before I finally saw it. The scenes aired were incendiary, the implications grave. With people thinking the way they normally do, the majority probably assumed that I had turned a blind eye to this misconduct. As often is the case in such matters, I was guilty until I could prove myself innocent.

My initial comment, issued in a press release, read, in part: "It has been my life's work to build this organization on the basis of integrity and I will not allow this isolated incident to malign our years of good works and interfere with our current challenges. The vast majority of our dedicated staff have high ideals and principles. Our charity policy clearly prohibits employees from taking donated items."

Feed The Children was founded on my honest and sustained efforts to address world hunger and other human needs. I was intent on speaking with equal candor in the face of this challenge. I would not remain mute about anything that might threaten the organization's outreach.

I sent a letter to FTC's contributors and offered it to the media as well. A few publishing and broadcasting outlets ran a part of the text. Most did not. I thought it ironic that so many had very quickly distributed damaging information but were reluctant to distribute my response. Did they think I'd waited too long? It was only a matter of days, during which I'd made every effort to uncover all pertinent facts. Would the media have preferred that I respond in a knee-jerk fashion, based on half-baked information?

My position was this:

> Let me assure you, Feed The Children has always operated, and will continue to operate, on the basis of high integrity and strict moral standards. In no way, under any circumstance, would we, nor have we ever authorized the isolated activity that is now under investigation in Tennessee. The executive director at our Nashville site, who resigned at my request, was acting neither in conformity with policy nor with my authority. Donated items are not "perks" to be taken by employees for personal use. Donated items are necessities to be given to families and children in need.
>
> We have completed our internal investigation and are awaiting the results from official state agencies. These results will determine appropriate action against those involved. The deeds of a few can affect the lives of many. Feed The Children will not ignore or dismiss any such actions and will pursue this matter to the fullest extent of the law. Our objective is to see that right prevails and that we continue to be good and faithful stewards of that which has been entrusted to us.

I reported that Creative Alarms, Inc., of Nashville had donated twelve surveillance cameras to our Tennessee facility as well as the cost of installation.

Apparently such devices were needed. Prior to the news investigation, I'd had no indication that theft was a problem for FTC. The cameras were set up to monitor FTC facilities twenty-four hours a day. Since their installation, they have not revealed any improper behavior.

Nashville's district attorney, Tory Johnson, upheld my claim that I was unaware of the pilferage. He, along with investigators for the Tennessee Bureau of Investigation, thoroughly interrogated the warehouse manager as well as suspected culprits.

On March 21, 2000, the *Tennessean*, Nashville's largest daily morning newspaper, reported, "Johnson said investigators found no evidence that officials at Feed The Children headquarters in Oklahoma City knew that employees here were taking goods donated for the benefit of poor children, refugees and disaster victims around the world."

Here the truth of the matter was confirmed, yet suspicion of FTC and me continued unabated. Some people are skeptical of charities and wanted to believe that I was guilty of condoning unethical activities, despite what the DA had said. Apparently they didn't want to be confused by facts.

Soon after I arrived in Nashville, I was walking beside the Oscar-nominated actress and FTC supporter Melanie Griffith. We weren't far from the FTC warehouse when a television reporter approached me from behind. He thrust a microphone around my head and in front of my face.

I hadn't yet seen him when he yelled, somewhat accusingly, it seemed to me, "How much is your salary?!"

"What?" I replied, startled.

"How much is your salary?" he shouted again.

I turned to face this stranger, who was accompanied by a cameraman. I calmly told him that the amount of my salary was posted on the Internet. I said no more. Someone later suggested I should have provided some context. My wife and I are paid less than half of what many charity directors are paid—directors whose organizations are less than half the size of FTC.

Ms. Griffith and her husband, the actor Antonio Banderas, had been working with FTC for only a short while when this assault by the zealous reporter occurred. My embarrassment at the ambush was obvious to her.

Thankfully, Ms. Griffith and her husband remained loyal to FTC. They made television appeals for us and later helped unload trucks during a mission to feed the hungry.

Not long after the 1999 exposé, I held one of several press conferences regarding the scandal. I was joined by the Grammy Award–winning country music artist Ricky Skaggs. Ricky, who'd also been an FTC activist, planted himself beside me as I faced a hostile press corps. This show of celebrity support didn't appease the reporters.

One Nashville columnist wrote a post-press-conference diatribe, stating:

> Jones didn't like being called down from the mountaintop
> to explain himself and his operations to the unwashed.
> Bill Clinton would have been proud because Jones and
> entertainer Ricky Skaggs huffed and puffed and bit their
> lips to distract the news media from the obvious. Jones
> had all the signs of a public figure with something to hide.

What was I trying to hide? Why wasn't the writer specific? I took great care to be completely candid. Sometimes the media can seem quite hostile and prejudgmental. In this particular instance it seemed I could do nothing right.

Why was I compared to President Clinton? Why was Ricky Skaggs slighted? Did they take offense at his display of allegiance to an organization he'd volunteered to support? Had that suddenly become a crime?

For the record, FTC had never paid Ricky Skaggs a dime. He had no reason to support FTC except his belief in our cause.

I have to think that FTC was singled out for coverage because its work is seen on television. The figurative target on our back was therefore larger than it was on other charities'. I later learned that another Nashville charity had been implicated regarding fifty thousand dollars' worth of missing or misappropriated funds. The amount was staggering when compared with the loss at FTC. Nonetheless, the morning newspaper ran a small story on an inside page about that scandal.

The FTC theft at the Nashville outlet involved 0.0001 percent of the total value of food and medical products that FTC had distributed that year. Yet the pilferage had been the subject of running stories that were prominently played in Nashville's newspaper and television news outlets.

I prayed intensely for God to enable the public to see my innocence. The prayers were answered affirmatively, although not as quickly as I would have liked. Many supporters turned skeptics maintained raised eyebrows as developments continued to unfold.

The original news team videotapes had revealed what seemed to be about eight individual employees stashing FTC boxes inside their cars. When a reporter asked the warehouse manager about the loss, he initially denied any knowledge of it. The Tennessee Bureau of Investigation agents subsequently found FTC boxes during raids on employees' homes. One parcel was marked as a Christmas present from an employee to himself.

The warehouse operator soon reversed his denial. He described the skimming of relief items as a perk for working at FTC.

He told WTVF that FTC employees "are told, 'This is available today.' "

This confession drew the district attorney back into the mix.

"We're trying to determine who told people what, and on what authority," Johnson told the *Tennessean*, which offered the story to wire services for worldwide distribution. Therefore, the harsh scrutiny of countless newspapers and broadcast outlets was once again focused on FTC as they distributed the DA's unsettling remark.

With every new disclosure, my spirits sank and my determination rose. I vowed to find a way to exonerate my name and that of the charity God had entrusted to Frances and me. By 1999 we were receiving $150 million a year in goods and $50 million in cash and were feeding or attending the needs of hundreds of thousands, if not millions, of people in seventy-one foreign countries while maintaining preparedness for response to natural disasters.

I adamantly refused to see the operation continually damaged because a handful of Nashville employees had stolen donated goods.

After pensive and prayerful consideration, I fired all employees at the Nashville facility, including some who hadn't been implicated by the videotapes. I was accused of unfairly punishing the innocent. I stood by my decision, having substantiated that many who hadn't participated in the pilferage nonetheless had known about it. They had not reported the thefts; therefore, I felt the whole personnel environment was at best unsavory. I didn't want to employ anyone who would remain silent about suspected criminal activity.

Legal observers warned that I might be sued for wrongful termination, as none of the employees, including the manager, had yet been convicted in connection with the ordeal.

Needing to rebuild the reputation of FTC, I felt I couldn't wait for a court to return a conviction. The wheels of justice turn very slowly. I was under the watchful eyes of many disappointed souls who had generously given of their time and resources to further the activities of FTC. Understandably, many had taken a wait-and-see attitude regarding how I'd address the corruption. Some concerned contributors were calling to ask questions. Manufacturers were reducing their product donations. And I was swimming in a rising tide of angry letters from seasoned supporters.

The situation with my handling of the employees was a sticky one. What if the suspects were eventually found innocent? How would that reflect on my judgment? Would I appear to be an impetuous taskmaster who'd acted prematurely?

The questions were never asked. No criminal charges were ever brought against the warehouse subordinates. The DA decided that perhaps they'd exercised bad judgment but had acted in good faith, taking things only after receiving permission from their supervisor.

The running scandal was approximately a year old on March 20, 2000, when the fired supervisor pleaded guilty to taking items from FTC. He also admitted that he'd "encouraged" warehouse workers to take goods, telling them that donations were a supplement to their pay.

Judge Cheryl Blackburn ordered him to pay one thousand dollars to FTC and complete ninety-six hours of public service and gave him two years' probation on a charge of theft.

In the court of law, the matter was resolved. Reaching a verdict in the court of public opinion was another matter entirely.

Indications were everywhere.

A wheelchair repair company had recently donated a hundred chairs to the Salvation Army, Easter Seals, the Veterans of Foreign

Wars, and FTC. An Oklahoma newspaper reported its owner as saying FTC was being removed from his donation list.

A Brownie troop in Lilburn, Georgia, had recently donated 460 pounds of food to FTC. Atlanta-area television stations and newspapers had reported their kindness. The eight- and nine-year-olds had bought the food with money raised from the sale of cookies.

In the wake of our scandal, the troop's leader was dismayed. Her pain was publicized. "It would bother me," she said, "to think we spent all of that time and went to so much trouble for someone who didn't need the things we donated."

The president of the West Bend Sunrise Rotary Club in Wisconsin expressed mixed feelings for FTC. He had led his organization in collecting hardware, food, household supplies, baby items, and more, with a mind to help us aid tornado victims. After the Nashville scandal, he told the press he was unsure he'd ever earmark donations for FTC again.

"I'd certainly have to look at them once or twice to see what they've done to clean up their problems," he said. "I guess I'd have second thoughts."

Thankfully, many supporters expressed their unflagging faith in FTC, saying they would continue to help the organization. In justifying their position, they cited the fact that the Nashville skimming was unusual to our global outreach. What's more, they condoned the actions FTC had taken to rectify the Nashville situation.

"Although we're disappointed by the recent incident, we're confident they [FTC] will take whatever action they need to take to make sure this doesn't happen anymore. We believe this is an isolated circumstance," said Kevin Sheehan, president of Processors Unlimited, a Dallas firm that had given 165,000 pounds of food and toiletries to FTC.

An Arkansas food distributor with a history of donating truckloads of food to FTC publicly let it be known that his firm would stand by the charity and would not penalize masses of suffering people because of the deeds of a paltry few in Tennessee.

Much of the ensuing publicity was positive. Ironically, that doesn't mean it was good for FTC. Each time well-meaning supporters addressed the controversy, even to express something positive, they revived it. I deeply appreciated all those who spoke in FTC's behalf. But for the sake of the organization, ultimately I wished everyone would simply stop talking about it. How else would this thing go away?

It wasn't going anywhere anytime soon.

SIX MONTHS AFTER THE NASHVILLE ORDEAL was legally laid to rest, Feed The Children was verbally attacked by the American Institute of Philanthropy, a national charity watchdog agency that had consistently blasted FTC's administration. A published article addressed our handling of the Nashville incident and quoted the warehouse's former manager. Why did it quote him six months after I'd accepted his forced resignation? His sentiments were old news. Why breathe new life into the situation, painful for all involved and all who beheld it? The outrageously tardy timing of the supposed revelation seemed to support my long-held suspicion regarding AIP. Apparently it had an ax to grind with FTC. It was doing its best to jump on the anti-FTC bandwagon, being among the last to board.

"If they're taking stuff home and giving their little brother a pair of shoes or some food, I don't have much to say about that. If that's wrong, fine. I don't think so, and I don't think people are going to think so," the manager had told the media the previous April. The AIP "disclosure" came in November. It's a good thing this organization doesn't cover politics. Readers might not have learned about former president Richard Nixon's resignation until six months into Gerald Ford's administration.

The AIP resorted to incendiary language, continuing its criticism of FTC. The organization gave its unqualified opinion about our management of donated funds, as well as our accounting practices in the receipt of donated goods. It gave FTC an F rating and claimed we spent only 14 percent of our cash budget on program services.

This accusation was both outrageous and incorrect, as were others hurled our way by the "institute," whose president, manager, and director were all one man. No doubt this made it easy for him to receive a majority vote when ratifying an "institute" decision.

AIP attacked FTC's relief efforts and food distribution, the ownership of our trucking company, and, of course, the Nashville blemish. The report was seen by perhaps two thousand national and international employees and volunteers, as well as millions of beneficiaries. It's mind-boggling to think all of this hoopla was inspired by the actions of a handful of FTC's Nashville employees whose full ranks could fit inside a passenger van.

The national media picked up on AIP's "findings." Once again, I had to defend FTC.

As a result, FTC's longtime nemesis was eventually forced to eat humble pie.

Consumers Digest, a buyer's guide publication, had consulted AIP's slanted findings before publishing a damaging article about FTC. I later talked to the magazine's editor in chief. Regarding our outlay of cash for program services, I explained how FTC appraises the value of in-kind gifts. I related, for example, that FTC would never spend eleven thousand dollars for a delivery of food if it could receive the food as a donation from the processor instead. I substantiated the example by citing actual instances of FTC's consistently receiving hundreds of millions of dollars' worth of food without having to purchase it outright.

The publisher was offered the opportunity to examine FTC's financial and gifts-in-kind records. Afterward, he was exceedingly apologetic about his magazine's having published a misleading rating of FTC and four other charities based on information provided by AIP. He said so in a letter, written to me in his words above his signature.

It read: "The methodology upon which we relied in our original article produced mistaken results, and I am personally embarrassed that we presented inaccurate conclusions."

His letter said *Consumers Digest* would "publish a feature-length presentation that was unprecedented in the magazine and is certainly the most comprehensive correction we have ever published."

The man kept his promise. This published correction represented a worldwide and ringing vindication of FTC: "Five charitable organizations, when reviewed using different accounting methods, do not appear to deserve the negative citations they received, and we wish to apologize to each." The list included FTC.

I thanked God for this vote of confidence. I rejoiced for the favorable repercussions as people took a second look at the organization that had been a recipient of their donations for two decades. If the battle for credibility continued to rage, it would do so without my active efforts at damage control.

I knew that no amount of positive media coverage could erase the damage caused by the Nashville debacle. I'd done my best to make sure the truth got out there, and that unbiased perspective was expressed. *Consumers Digest* had done that. It was therefore time to address new missions and cease explaining previous errant reports.

While the Nashville turmoil was raging, forty-eight people died as sixty-six tornadoes swept Oklahoma, Kansas, and Texas for three consecutive days. Damage totaled $1.5 billion. It was the most destructive spate of twisters in Oklahoma history.

Also during that time frame, an international effort to organize emergency help for Kosovo refugees had been stepped up in the wake of what seemed to be an escalation of the conflict to all-out war, as indicated by air strikes in Priština, Kosovo's capital. Artillery fire and ground fighting ravaged the city and surrounding countryside. NATO reported that tens of thousands of people had sought refuge in the woods and hills. They had no access to food or water.

FTC never ceased its outreach during the Nashville ordeal. We had been there for the victims of the tornadoes and for those in Kosovo, though I personally had given a lot of time to fighting the hostile assaults on FTC's reputation. It was time for me to turn my full attention back to developing our mission.

I felt run-down from constantly playing defense to the media's offense that had played fast and loose with the facts. They had seemed so interested in anything that might bring us down. Why did they never put a fraction of that energy into reporting the good FTC has always done, helping thousands and thousands of needy people in this nation or abroad?

I was done defending. Our good actions were known to God and the people He allowed us to serve. FTC was about more than applying Band-Aid apologies to paper cuts on the body of our ministry. The petty thefts perpetrated by nine former employees had activated the scandalmongering of hundreds of reporters and editors from coast to coast. I was finished with that.

Victims of natural disasters still needed relief. Overseas refugees desperately needed food, water, and medical attention.

My staff and I turned away from the sad situation in Tennessee. I asked everyone to renew focus on things we could change and to put behind us those that we couldn't.

That's exactly what we did.

Our work and all it entailed went forward from there just as it always had—just as it always will. Come what may, we all keep walking.

BY THE BEGINNING OF THE NEW CENTURY, Feed The Children had become a charity to which many people turned when other organizations turned them away. This was true especially overseas, where starvation and suffering seemed to present problems so pervasive they defied any workable solution. A prime example was an African refugee camp near the city of Freetown in civil-war-torn Sierra Leone.

Some Americans felt that FTC ought not to take on such a staggering foreign mission when there were so many needs to fill here in the United States. We've heard that criticism throughout our history. But we will always seek to remedy human distress wherever it's found. Pain knows no national boundaries.

By 2001 a sustained offensive initiated by West Africa's Revolutionary United Front had killed tens of thousands and displaced more than two million. A full one-third of Sierra Leone's population had abandoned their homes, running for their lives. Most sought refuge in neighboring countries.

It's easy to understand why desperate people such as these might say or do virtually anything to draw the attention of anyone who might help them. Reports of their inhumane treatment in Sierra Leone seemed increasingly outlandish. Frankly, I thought much of their testimony, which included mass starvation and the willful torture of children, simply must be exaggerated. Soon I'd realize that it wasn't.

A month's food ration in the refugee camp included a gallon bucket of wheat and two pints of vegetable oil. Family size had no bearing on the amount. Whether a family had to feed two or ten, that ration was all the refugees were given.

Eighty-seven thousand people within the camp were registered to receive the rations. An additional three thousand people, who were not registered, received nothing. They were simply left to die of starvation.

I felt a need to confirm the situation personally before appealing for help to an American television audience. Seeing was believing. Reports of the horror were not exaggerated. They were understated.

As it turned out, the one-bucket-a-month rule was just an ideal. Some families weren't getting their full bucket of wheat every thirty days. They were subsisting on a few bites a day.

The camp looked like the set of a B-grade Halloween movie. Packs of rats fed on hardened human waste as catatonic children sat like listless zombies in the midst. Insects flickered on their malnourished, sunken cheeks.

I had yet to see the worst of it.

Frances and I walked into an abandoned manufacturing plant about the size of three gymnasiums. Filthy, withered people sat motionless where rats had the run of the floor. Those who were sitting upright stared emptily into space. Those who'd fallen over stared upward.

I studied the clusters of bodies, picking out what I thought were the children. I was told I'd recognize them by one common characteristic.

They had no hands.

To prevent them from growing up to become soldiers, warring groups had cut off the children's hands above the wrists. The sight elicited astonished gasps and tears from FTC's television crew and volunteers.

Occasionally, we encountered a child who had enough strength to whisper and to raise his or her spindly arms to us. There among them I felt conspicuous and perhaps a little ashamed for being healthy and well fed.

At that time in 2001 the average life span of anyone in Sierra

Leone was thirty-nine years. Most of the younger people here, though, would never make that average. And these children without hands—how would they ever work to earn their keep if they perchance got out of this place? Were they going to farm with their feet?

The long-term outlook was bleak at best. But we chose to focus on the immediate need. Every journey begins with a first step, and providing food was the obvious first step toward breaking this cycle of suffering.

If there's one thing you learn in relief work, it's putting first things first. First we feed them and save their lives. After that, we go about the business of continuing nutrition and medicine to rebuild their strength. Later we work with them to develop skills to offset their handicaps.

Working with U.S. food processors and distributors, we started an emergency program called Feed A Child. Thus, we were able to provide lifesaving sustenance at a daily cost of just twenty-eight cents per child.

Within a week this campaign enabled FTC to begin feeding twelve thousand people in the abandoned factory as well as many of the eighty-seven thousand in the refugee camp.

For some, of course, this was too little, too late. And many of those we reached later died of disease. But they didn't starve to death. And not starving was actually quite a hopeful state of affairs in those nightmarish days in Sierra Leone.

Times like these tend to drain the will to live right out the bottom of most people's souls.

But Aruna was different.

He was a bit lucky, too. The savage militia had not touched his left hand and had only partially maimed his right one. His bad arm was gnarled and lacking about 90 percent of its use owing to nerve damage. But his good arm, like his spirit, was healthy and intact.

He'd been riding his bicycle with a friend when rebel soldiers raided his village. The friend got away. Aruna's attacker had only begun to hack when he abruptly ran off, leaving his mutilation unfinished, Aruna screaming.

We found him among the ever-growing flock of Sierra Leone's disabled children. He was sitting on a rug only slightly larger than a place mat.

I instantly rejoiced to see his good arm and wondered about the potential for surgery on the other. I turned to Don Richardson and asked him to begin investigating when, if ever, FTC might transport Aruna to America. I said nothing to Aruna at that moment. But I was determined to enlist the volunteer service of a neurosurgeon.

Soon enough we were able to bring Aruna to Oklahoma City, where a local doctor was able to increase the use of his arm to 20 percent. Aruna's physical therapy included developing the strength and utility of his left arm, which he used primarily.

Living with a guardian, he established residence in Oklahoma City and attended public school. He didn't yet speak English, and he'd had very little prior instruction, but they enrolled him in fifth grade. He turned out to be a real whiz kid and quickly caught up with his peers. At the end of the school term, Aruna could speak English, and his report card glowed with As and Bs. He was promoted to the sixth grade.

Notwithstanding his handicap, Aruna earned not only the acceptance but also the admiration of other boys his age. In basketball, football, and baseball, he couldn't keep up. But when it came to soccer, he couldn't be stopped.

Aruna was remarkably agile and light on his feet. He commanded the grade school soccer field like a promising Pelé. Local boys *always* wanted to be on the team with the African boy, the one with the bent arm. Aruna could run the gauntlet of defenders the entire length of a soccer field all by himself. Within the student body, he was famous.

When he entered his final year of elementary school, he was living at an orphanage in Dallas. He was eventually adopted by a family whose father is employed by NASA. Aruna is now being homeschooled and will finish his secondary education (the equivalent of twelfth grade) before this book goes to press.

He plans to go to college and wants to become a lawyer. Eventually, he says, he would like to return to Sierra Leone—perhaps to run for president someday—with the hope of stopping the cruel and ongoing cycle of civil war.

Aruna also says he might even work for Feed The Children, doing things that inspire us to continue helping children who face dangers and dire needs.

I guess he doesn't realize that he already has.

$\mathcal{T}$HE OLD GRANDMOTHER'S HAIR WAS GRAY, and her face was etched by hardship. She clutched what appeared to be a doll wrapped in a threadbare blanket that she'd carried for three hours beneath the sweltering African sun. The woman seemed disoriented, the result of yesterday's meager meal and today's relentless dehydration. She babbled incoherently at the doll.

Then it moved.

The baby weighed eight pounds, not an unusual size for a newborn. But, in fact, she was nine months old.

Frances would eventually receive the baby girl and learn that she had been born prematurely. After birth, the child remained malnourished, breast-feeding from her sickly, HIV-positive mother. Then her mom had died, leaving her and her eight- and ten-year-old siblings to their grandmother's care.

The grandmother teetered from exhaustion, diabetes, and the terminal affliction called life as she'd known it. The chance of living well had not merely passed her by. No chance had ever come her way. It was lost to her before she started, as she was born to misfortune and it had been her constant companion. Hopelessness was all she had known. She wanted her granddaughter to know more.

"See?" said the failing woman, weakly. "See?"

Struggling, she raised her bundle into the face of a startled onlooker who peered down into the child's barely open eyes.

"Yes," the stranger acknowledged, "your granddaughter is alive."

Later, when Frances saw the infant, she reflected on her twenty-two years of caring for the world's most disadvantaged children who'd looked to her for help. She had often stared death squarely in the face, forcing smiles of reassurance while fighting back tears. She'd never once looked away, always willing to hold a newborn's hand while holding on to hope that God might say, "Not yet," and prolong the baby's life. Sometimes He did. Other times He didn't. Why this one and not that? God only knows. Like the Bible verse says—the Lord moves in mysterious ways.

I hope the secrets He holds from us in this life will be revealed as pleasant surprises in the next.

Frances long ago grew accustomed to seeing the suffering of children. But she'll never get used to it.

She lifted the diminutive nine-month-old and gasped. The little girl's legs were mere twigs, her fingers toothpicks covered with flesh. Her eyes were sunken and rolled slightly in their sockets. Frances drew the small life closer to her, wanting to hold it to her bosom all night. She was sure the life would be gone come morning.

But the infant stubbornly held on.

The next day Frances had to leave East Africa to travel back to the United States, but not before arranging hospice care, including oxygen, intensive nutritional therapy, and a battery of medicines for the baby.

When she returned in a few months, she scanned a group of distressed children undergoing intensive care. She was looking for the "doll." But she was gone. She'd been given a name, Michelle, by health-care workers who'd overseen her near-miraculous recovery. She had stabilized and evolved into a laughing, crawling, gurgling little toddler. Michelle had weighed eight pounds at nine months. She weighed twenty-one pounds on her first birthday.

THIS MIRACLE UNFOLDED after the 2001 opening of the Frances Jones Abandoned Baby Center, or ABC, outside Nairobi, Kenya.

Since its founding, the ABC has grown steadily. By 2006, it had come to include four care cottages and a hospice building as well as an administration building, kitchen, laundry room, and food warehouse. By then, we had cared for more than 250 abandoned or orphaned babies at the center. Eventually we oversaw the adoption or reunion with a biological parent of many. We also used the center's warehouse to facilitate the feeding of lunch to ninety-two thousand schoolchildren who live in Nairobi slums.

Each ABC unit required a staff with highly specialized skills, including a pediatric physician, a medical supervisor, a nursing supervisor, a social worker, and an operations coordinator.

In America, the cost of all this would run into seven figures. In Africa, FTC builds cottages for $108,000 each and operates them on a budget of $8,000 a month.

Eight months after the opening of the Abandoned Baby Center, Frances was honored at the fifth annual gala of Leading Women Entrepreneurs of the World in Paris, France. Her achievements were celebrated in the nonprofit category. She was, in fact, the first woman ever to receive the award.

The recognition had nothing to do with personal wealth. Given that criterion, she would never have been a contender. The award pertained to Frances's success at raising money to feed children around the world.

Before the ceremony the founders had placed a call to Dorotea Liguori, an Italian jewelry and real estate magnate with an international reputation for generosity. Dorotea invited Frances and me to come to Naples to discuss what she could do for Feed The Children.

As it turned out, the invitation was a godsend.

Dorotea founded Feed The Children Italia-Onlus in 2003. Her sponsorship amounted to a substantial extension of FTC's outreach, based in Italy. Feeling honored and blessed, Frances then invited Dorotea to visit the ABC.

Now, consider this: Ms. Liguori is a pillar of high society on both the European and the North American continents. She's a model of mannered graciousness and financial acumen. And yet she agreed to accompany Frances into Kibera, the violent, desperate slum in Nairobi, Kenya. There, she witnessed horrific human suffering that her good heart felt a call to address.

Eventually, Dorotea sponsored a fund-raising event in Naples, Italy, to fund the ABC hospice. Her charity has ranged from the underwriting of building costs to the installation of a kitchen and commercial laundry to the providing of three hundred pairs of shoes and much, much more. I dare say no more because she would not appreciate my itemizing her contributions.

Suffice it to say that Dorotea has provided a shining example of personal prosperity shared joyously and unselfishly. Few people, after attaining wealth, seem to remember what life is like for people who are not financially blessed. Fewer still have heart enough to care about the future of others, especially youngsters they've never met.

Dorotea is an exception—and a great blessing to the world.

As of this writing, we're laying plans to establish a second ABC in Uganda. More highly skilled personnel, including American physicians, nurses, contractors, and professional administrators, are augmenting our ABC missions. Continuing construction and program development will outlive Frances and me.

As our long-term plans come to fruition, ABCs will be established throughout Africa, then overflow to other continents where our help is most needed. This growing chain of centers dedicated to the care and nurturing of distressed babies is the most ambitious project Feed The Children has ever undertaken.

Our master plan also calls for the eventual development of facilities in the United States where public funds are either lacking or ill-used in the care of forsaken babies.

For now, our program efforts remain focused solely on Africa, where fifteen hundred of the six thousand people who die daily from AIDS are children. Three out of four African babies born HIV-positive, such as Michelle, can be saved with proper medication and nutrition. When so treated, they become HIV-negative over time. And given proper education, they can continue to live an AIDS-free life on a continent where currently someone dies every fifteen seconds from the ruthless virus.

"But there are babies in America who need an ABC," some of my critics have contended. There certainly are. If funds allowed, FTC would be building multiple ABC outlets right now in the United States and everywhere else they're needed. We instead construct one facility at a time, as donations of money and land permit. In our experience of caring for people the world over, the need for such facilities in Africa has seemed most pressing, so that's where we decided to start.

I wish we could treat all of Africa's hungry, naked, and suffering. Throughout its history, FTC has helped millions of children and adults. But our work at the ABC is different in the scope of its outreach. Its mission is to aid babies who, in addition to starvation and thirst, face yet another peril—abandonment.

Babies are abandoned everywhere, of course, including the United States. But in Africa abandonment is an hourly tragedy, sometimes carried out by mothers in the bush who superstitiously fear that a child born with AIDS or a physical handicap is cursed. Other women aren't so superstitious but are just as desperate when forsaking their newborns. Some hysterical mothers think they love their babies too much to keep them in the conditions under which they live. They hope someone will find their deserted child and take him or her away to a better life of nurturing and plenty. These despondent women relinquish their babies to some hoped-for earthly savior, unseen and unknown. Often, that savior turns out to be the ABC.

Many babies are brought in from surrounding slums, where home is a one-room shanty smaller than a walk-in closet. The floor is dirt, the walls are cardboard. There is no plumbing. Because there is no electricity, the interior remains dark day and night. Listless people lie on top of each other inside these filthy huts they call home. And then the ABC rescues some babies who don't even have it this good. Their mothers are among the wandering homeless.

We were once asked to save two-month-old Cecilia and her one-year-old brother, Cyrus, from their "home," a tin roof over a public toilet. The children ate, slept, and were dying there, all the while inhaling acrid, toxic fumes from human waste six feet beneath them. They were being fed with whatever their HIV-positive mother could scavenge from garbage dumps, where she competed with diseased birds and rabid animals for rotten morsels. We don't know her whereabouts today.

Although we rescued both children, we were too late to save

Cyrus, who died shortly afterward. Cecilia was treated with a regimen of anti-HIV nutrients and medicines. She was declared HIV-free once the remnants of the inherited virus were banished from her system. Today, healthy Cecilia lives in the ABC. The beautiful child is being offered for adoption. And before these words are published, she will likely be placed in the security of a loving home.

Once we rescued five babies who'd been abandoned in a hospital closet. The facility had no money to care for them and had fed each a diet consisting entirely of flour mixed with water. None had ever so much as tasted milk. They'd been carried into the facility unnoticed. Whoever brought them had stealthily departed. Upon discovering the hapless babies, the hospital personnel called the ABC.

When Frances first saw the infants, they were still jammed inside a three-foot-square cubicle, where they wore nothing, not even diapers. The hospital hadn't provided them beds.

My wife oversaw their transfer to the ABC, where they were entrusted to the care of staff physicians who monitored their vital signs and began a regimen of treatment for their malnourishment. As of this writing, all five children have been thriving at the facility for a year. Their development is progressing normally. Along with Cecilia, each is awaiting adoption.

We've been called by employees of Nairobi's mass transit system who have found babies left on buses. We've heard from police who found babies in cemeteries, wooded areas, and garbage dumps. We've even rescued some found at the bottom of outdoor latrines. We once received a baby that someone literally stumbled over while walking a brushy trail. Thank God we got her before the wild animals did.

The most common reason people abandon children is not physical illness. It's social—a disease called poverty. Most manual laborers in the Nairobi area earn about a dollar a day. No man can feed his wife, children, and himself on that disgraceful income, much less provide shelter, clothing, and medicine.

Weeping parents have sometimes extended their babies to me with soiled hands, brokenhearted because they can't afford to care for an infant who's visibly sick and starving. The ABC takes in these abandoned young souls and meets all their medicinal and nutritional requirements until they're well. Then, if circumstances allow, we reunite them with their parents. Sometimes, however, we receive babies who are too far gone. They die in our care, which exacts an emotional toll on ABC workers, who unavoidably bond with every child who comes through the door.

Some parents never return. Still others come back only to say they love their needy child too much to take him or her back into the poverty they have no hope of escaping. They ask us to begin adoption proceedings.

I'm inclined to cite yet another reason our ABC outreach began in Africa. Though materially poor, the African people tend to be rich in spirit—often downright inspiring. They have an infectious zest for life. What Frances and I have drawn from that zeal gives us added will and strength to reach out everywhere. Our entire ministry benefits. In this way the impoverished people of Africa have unknowingly ministered to us.

It's been written that most Africans never leave the area in which they were born. It's true—especially in the slums where the absence of electricity prevents exposure to radio and television programming that might otherwise inform them of the wider world and better ways of life. Be that as it may, most poor Africans have heard of a faraway place called America.

Missionaries who talk about heaven often come from the United States. To the typical African mind, America is probably the place most closely resembling the heavenly realm. Many know they'll never get to the United States, but believe they will reach heaven.

Their faith comes easily, as their psyches have never been tainted with doubt. They have not been subjected to the drubbing of images that constantly barrage us here in the West, projecting danger, fear, and failure, along with outrageous excess that boggles the imagination. They are a deprived people who, being spared this onslaught of stimuli, have retained their innocence.

"Do you have slums in America?" an African child once asked an American friend of mine.

"Yes," he replied. "They're called ghettos."

"Oh," the boy continued. "Do ghettos have houses with roofs?"

"Yes," my friend answered.

"Do they really have water that runs inside but doesn't get the house wet?"

"Yes."

"Do they have power that makes them warm and cold inside?"

"Sure."

"Do they have food inside them that isn't bad [spoiled]?"

The boy was told that they do.

"Does your government provide the food?"

"Yes, it buys for the poor."

"Oh," said the boy. "How can I get poor enough to live in American ghettos?"

He envisioned life at its worst in America as a fantasyland and saw it as unattainable. He was not expressing frustration about not living in America, just an innocent wistfulness. He accepted the fact that he would never go there in the same way he accepted the fact that he would never sprout wings and fly. To him, one seemed as impossible as the other.

By and large, Africans seem genuinely moved when strangers come to address their needs. They are quick to love those who help them. Whether adult or child, they tend to take nothing for granted. Any help offered is met with humble thanks, not questions about what you'll do for them next.

The thought never occurs to Africa's children that they're separated from most of the world not only by geography but also by indifference. They express no disfavor toward those who have more. They rarely meet them. And if they do, they're likely to greet them with welcoming smiles and ceaseless curiosity. These amazing children assume that any visitor comes with goodwill equal to their own.

Give an impoverished African child a single small trinket and he and his friends will play with it for weeks. Elsewhere in the world, the same novelty might be greeted with nonchalance or even disdain if the toy is not on the mental list of that child's desires.

The prosperous child has been conditioned to want things and expect that they will be given to him. The African has been conditioned to take only what fulfills the most basic needs and to share the rest. When he's surprised by the generosity of a visiting stranger, he overflows with genuine joy and gratitude. Such human purity is precious to behold.

The sacrificial giving of missionaries has done more to create goodwill in African-U.S. relations than the deliberations of any parliament or congress ever impaneled. Throngs of African children draw their first impressions of Americans from those who come unannounced as emissaries of Christian faith. Westerners' most valuable gift is arguably their mere presence. Their help is a bonus.

To that end, I think of a beautiful story about Americans and the Masai tribe, a relatively small group who thrive on wild game. The hunters drop their prey with astounding effectiveness, hurling handmade weapons made from cured, hardened tree root. They're a people of amazing endurance and stamina. They often go for extended periods without food and water. They can travel at a trotting pace for miles without resting.

A Masai man's most valuable possession, other than his family, is a cow. Not all Masai dare to aspire to the wealth of owning one.

FTC has attended the Masai for years. The village of Enoosaen is situated near Kenya's border with Tanzania. Rift Valley runs through there. During the 1980s, FTC drilled water wells in the valley (as described in an earlier chapter of this book). The Masai travel for many miles to partake of water there. For a quarter century those wells have hydrated many Masai children who became men, several of whom eventually owned their own cows.

On June 5, 2002, in a remarkable gesture of compassion and generosity, fourteen Masai gave fourteen cows to survivors of Manhattan's horrendous 9/11 terrorist attacks. Kimeli Naiyomah, a Masai tribe member, had gone to America as a young man to study medicine. He returned to Enoosaen after the terrorist attacks on the World Trade Center. He told villagers what he'd seen.

"What happened in New York City does not really make sense to people who live in traditional huts and have never conceived of a building that touches the sky," explained Ibrahim Obajo, a freelance reporter working in Nairobi, on the Wired News Web site. "You cannot easily describe to them buildings that are so high that people die when they jump off."

The tribe saw the cruel attack as an opportunity to return kindness to America, which they saw as the source of much kindness to them. Tribesmen wanted to return the love by giving what they valued most—just like the widow in the Bible story who gives her last penny. They wanted to send their most prized possessions—living bulls and cows—to suffering New Yorkers.

Obviously, the Masai had no more concept of America's abundance than they did of its towering architecture. They simply blessed their cows, then presented them to William Brencick, then serving as deputy chief of mission of the U.S. embassy in Nairobi.

My emotions were stirred by the touching gesture, and so were those of the heartbroken New Yorkers who heard about it. What the Masai lacked in their tiny world perspective they more than made up for with their grandness of spirit. They wanted to give all they had to people they perceived to have lost all that mattered.

Someone created a Web site seeking ideas about how New Yorkers should receive fourteen cows. Of course, the price of ocean passage exceeded the value of beef on the hoof.

"The cows are the most amazing gift we received," wrote Ed McCormick, a Bronx construction worker. "Who else sent cows? We should take the cows and raise them on a nice farm upstate and then send the cow puppies back to them [the Masai] someday."

"I've been so supported by the many e-mails and calls and expressions of love from around the world," said Maureen Esposito, who lost her husband, Joe, in the terrorist attack. "It really matters that these folks sent us something so tangible. I guess cows are just better than e-mails."

Ultimately, embassy officials decided against shipping the cattle. Alternatively, they considered selling the animals in Africa, then using the proceeds to buy Masai jewelry for display in a Manhattan memorial. New Yorkers rejected the idea as disrespectful. And three years later, some of the best minds in New York City were still trying to decide how to take shipment of such a heartfelt but impractical gift. Meanwhile, the cows were fat and presumably happy, grazing in Kenya's open pastures.

The Masai, although living with hunger as their near-constant companion, refused to eat the cows they'd allocated for New Yorkers.

A plan was hatched to send the cows to the Central Park Zoo, but it was declined. And there was still no money to pay for their transport to America.

The pride of the Masai was becoming bruised. From their perspective, the Americans seemed not to want the three thousand dollars' worth of beef they had donated. To the Masai mind, this seemed quite an affront. All the while, the cattle were reproducing. By September 11, 2006, the original herd of fourteen had grown to twenty-one, as reported by the *New York Times* on the five-year anniversary of the United States' most devastating domestic terrorist incident.

Diplomats from both the United States and Kenya had long since grown frustrated with trying to settle the quandary. The Masai remained adamant that their beef should go to their generous friends in America.

In 2006 an American coalition announced officially through a diplomat that New Yorkers had respectfully declined delivery of the livestock. The statement declared that the cattle should be returned to the Masai to do with as they wished.

"What you [Americans] did to help us will not be forgotten," replied Michael E. Ranneberger, the new American ambassador to Kenya, speaking on behalf of the Masai.

Listening to this official response, the Masai applauded and laughed, dressed in monkey-skin jackets, smiles baring missing teeth.

"We did what we knew best," conceded an elder, Mzee ole Yiamboi, in a *Times* report. "The handkerchief we give to people to wipe their tears with is a cow."

The animals were then blessed with a tribal prayer. The offspring of the original fourteen were to be sold and the proceeds used to fund the education of the children of Enoosaen.

"To get the cow trust fund going, Americans are donating 14 high school scholarships," the *Times* reported.

And so the hilarious, heartwarming story came to an end. Who would ever have thought that repaying kindness could prove so tender yet so frustrating—and funny?

In the winter of 2006, an FTC worker visited Don Richardson, who'd overseen the charity's construction of the Rift Valley water wells. He asked Richardson about FTC's having provided water to the Masai.

"Is Tanzania close to the Rift Valley?" he began the conversation.

"Oh yes," Richardson replied. "It goes right through it. The Rift Valley reaches from way up north into Ethiopia, all the way through the middle of Africa."

"Did Feed The Children ever do any charitable work for members of the Masai tribe?" the FTC worker continued.

"Yes," Richardson replied. "A lot."

The ABC was ten months old when the Masai first tried to give their fourteen head of cattle to the American victims of 9/11. It was five years old before the issue was finally resolved.

During that time the ABC had rescued more than 250 babies and had given housing, food, medicine, and an education to countless children, including 75 permanent residents who were physically or mentally impaired.

In August 2006 a ceremony was held to commemorate the opening of the ABC's commercial laundry room. Days earlier, two men had stood beside a street adjacent to the ABC's grounds. They were too proud to enter the perimeter of a charity, fearing that someone might think they were accepting a handout.

Their earlobes were conspicuously stretched—the unmistakable and permanent marking of a Masai warrior.

Perhaps they'd been told that the ABC had often saved Masai babies from starvation. Maybe they'd personally partaken of the springwater flowing through the parched Rift Valley.

They could even have recognized FTC's emblem, and associated it with the logo seen in their village on recurring missions.

The Masai are seasoned nomads. There's no telling how far the men had wandered that day, searching for whatever they needed. They were clearly absent from home, and for all men absence makes the heart grow fonder.

Home and heart.

Maybe East Africa's Abandoned Baby Center somehow took them back to their own perilous childhoods. Maybe that was as close as they could get to home.

$\mathcal{M}$USIC PRODUCED BY VARIOUS MEMBERS of the Jackson family continues to enjoy immense popularity on the African continent. We were pleased to have Jermaine Jackson participate in the opening day ceremonies of the Frances Jones Abandoned Baby Center.

On returning to the United States, Jermaine asked Frances and me, along with our children, Allen and Larri Sue, to be his guests at a Madison Square Garden concert featuring his brother Michael on September 8, 2001.

On the following Tuesday morning, Allen and Larri Sue departed for La Guardia Airport en route home to Oklahoma City, by way of Dallas. Frances and I prepared for a flight to Washington, D.C.

That was the Tuesday morning of September 11, 2001. Not one of us would leave the Empire State for days.

Those were days when Frances and I, although we were busy, often resurrected fond memories of our children, some of which we hadn't indulged in years. They were days of mental inventory and soul-searching. After the terrorist attacks on the World Trade Center and the Pentagon, days passed as time seemed to stand curiously still.

I was reminded of the words spoken by President Franklin D. Roosevelt on the day after the December 7, 1941, attack on Pearl Harbor. He declared that the date would live in infamy. The words could just as well have been spoken on 9/11.

As of this writing, storytellers in film and print have continued to find inspiration in revisiting the events of World War II and the human character of the people who fought it.

So, too, has 9/11 been remembered with a panoply of movies and television documentaries, as well as enough paper media legacies to consume a sizable forest.

The esteemed broadcaster Tom Brokaw once said there are two days in American history that will probably always have television producers pondering original commemorations. One is the anniversary of President John F. Kennedy's assassination. The other is the anniversary of the murder of almost three thousand Americans on the black Tuesday of September 11, 2001.

This act of terrorism brought an early winter to the mood of Americans across the nation as we mourned the loss of loved ones and struggled to understand how we, so unsuspecting, could be hated so vehemently by people we didn't even know.

I'd seen this combination of grief, disbelief, and dark wonderment before when 168 lives were taken by terrorists in the attack on the Murrah Federal Building in Oklahoma City back in 1995. I was six miles away from that explosion. I was even closer when the World Trade Center was hit.

The event held a very special terror for me, owing to my pressing concern over the welfare of two special children.

My own.

FRANCES AND I WERE WATCHING TELEVISION when programming was interrupted. A short bulletin reported that a small aircraft had struck one of the Twin Towers. She figured the plane was probably an engine-stalled four-seater that accidentally struck and bounced off the side of the colossal building.

Then came reports of a fire inside the north tower. Frances thought this to be really curious, but small and containable. She continued easing into her busy day.

Shortly the truth of the matter began to dawn on Frances. She was watching live footage of smoke billowing from the smoldering skyscraper as the south tower was hit by a second airplane.

It wasn't small and it wasn't an accident.

Struck dumb with horror, Frances joined the nation in realizing that she was witness to an act of terrorism. The crash said aloud what, minutes earlier, people had speculated in whispers.

If we were one nation under God, we were now also under siege.

Somebody had begun a war. But who? The aggressor was unknown, invisible, even as victims were televised, choosing to leap from the fiery building rather than be burned alive.

Frances and I didn't want to look at the television set anymore, but somehow we couldn't look away.

Though mesmerized by the horror, Frances had thought to call Larri Sue and Allen, knowing they were in the last place in the world she would wish them to be at this moment—inside an airliner.

I found myself wondering if my children's plane was the same type of aircraft as the one protruding from the WTC. It was a torturous thought, but I couldn't seem to stop it, as was the case with countless other unpleasant thoughts racing through my mind. Who could know that there weren't other terrorists in other planes, set to fly them into other targets?

We'd eventually learn that at the time of our worrying, Allen and Larri Sue's plane was still on the tarmac. They were safely in their seats—she on one aisle and he on another—when a passenger rudely stepped across Allen to get to the window seat. He didn't pardon himself, and in fact said nothing when he stepped on Allen's foot.

His complexion was dark, and he appeared to be of Arab descent. He wore old, dirty clothes. He had boarded late with two other men who had walked with him single file down the center aisle. One seated himself a few rows in front of, the other a few rows behind, our son and daughter.

The man who plopped down beside Allen produced a book and began to study pages that were turned upside down. It was the Koran.

The pilot addressed the passengers over the PA system, saying that departure would be delayed. There were problems loading checked baggage.

Allen didn't buy the claim. He thought the announcement was a stall. He's a seasoned flier who's heard all of the lame excuses routinely offered by airline personnel.

But he'd *never* heard what he heard the pilot say next.

"A plane has struck the World Trade Center, and we are going to remain here at the gate for a few minutes," Allen said the pilot announced. "If you need to get off and make sure someone is okay, it's fine."

The pilot's matter-of-fact tone seemed eerie in light of the strange news.

Our son and daughter chatted about the matter and decided a Cessna must have clipped the radio antenna that stood atop one of the Twin Towers.

"Somebody was flying over, didn't see the antenna, and they are probably dead now," Allen thought to himself. "We'll be out of here in a minute."

But the announcement seemed more alarming to the three suspicious men who'd boarded after our children. The trio simultaneously bolted to their feet. They seemed quite conspicuous amid the other passengers, most of whom remained seated.

Once again, the stranger next to Allen stumbled across him— and stepped on his foot making the exit. In fact, he kicked Allen's knee. And once again, he said nothing.

He removed a bag from the overhead compartment. Then he and his companions ran off the airplane. They *ran*.

"What was all of that about?" Allen said to Larri Sue. Astonished and perplexed, she had no idea.

Larri Sue's cellular telephone signaled a call from Frances.

"Get off the airplane!" Frances commanded.

"What?" our daughter replied. "They're just now getting ready to shut the door . . ."

Allen later said his sister remained undeterred, almost nonchalant, despite the flurry of disturbing news and unorthodox behavior. She had no intention of deplaning. She handed the phone to her brother and told him to talk to Frances.

"Allen," said Frances, "we are under a terrorist attack."

"How do you know that?" Allen replied.

"A plane has hit the World Trade Center," Frances said.

"Yes, we know that," Allen answered.

"You need to get off that airplane as soon as you can," Frances persisted.

"You do whatever you want to do," Allen told Larri Sue. "I am sitting right here."

Our son activated his cell phone and called a friend in Dallas. He learned that a second plane had hit the WTC.

He hung up, turned to his sister, and predicted the plane was going nowhere.

"I think Mom was right," he said. "I don't know what we're going to do now."

The airlines decided for them.

The pilot announced that problems had continued with the main baggage compartment. Passengers were instructed to fetch carry-on luggage and disembark the plane.

Allen and Larri Sue complied, falling in line with other travelers who milled confusedly up the Jetway and into the glare of the day. As they stepped back into the airport, many turned their gaze to the floor-to-ceiling window, showcasing the marvelous skyline beyond the East River.

Their eyes were drawn magnetically to a terrible focal point—billowing smoke and a licking of flames high at the top of each of the Twin Towers.

"God made a curtain with the smoke," says a character in the Oliver Stone movie *World Trade Center*. "It shielded us from what we're not yet ready to see."

DAZED WITH SHOCK, Allen and Larri Sue flowed along with the crowd. Their pace quickened as a voice boomed over the public-address system ordering everyone out of the airport. There might be a bomb. A terrorist attack was under way.

Larri Sue wanted to retrieve her checked baggage. Allen insisted that she forget about it—the baggage was the least of their worries. They made their way safely out of the airport and stood by a guardrail, scanning the landscape.

"It was as if the world had been vaporized," Allen recollected later, regarding the absence of traffic on the roadways. He, Larri Sue, and thousands of other stranded passengers saw but a smattering of cars on a highway where lanes are normally bumper-to-bumper. Allen counted two moving vehicles. Stillness around the normally bustling La Guardia Airport was downright eerie.

"If a bomb goes off inside the airport, we're all going to die," Allen thought to himself. He'd seen firsthand the power of the blast at the Murrah Federal Building in Oklahoma City. Outside the building some people had been killed where you'd have thought they should be out of harm's way.

A friend phoned Allen to say that a third aircraft had hit the Pentagon. He didn't belabor the ramifications but suggested that Allen and Larri Sue rent a car quickly to avoid being stranded at the airport. There was sure to be a run on rentals.

The brother and sister talked it over. Larri Sue thought flights would soon resume. Allen didn't. He insisted they rent a car.

But the rental agencies were located inside the locked-down airport.

Together, my Allen and Larri Sue walked across an access road to desolate Interstate 678. They sauntered across five lanes of roadway leading into New York City, and five more leading away, without so much as a thought for oncoming traffic. There was none.

"It was almost like everyone else knew something we didn't," Allen said.

His thoughts turned to his small carry-on bag, the only personal gear he'd escaped with. He had no change of clothes or his prescription medications. He was wearing all he had: a pair of walking shorts, a T-shirt, and sandals.

Walking on, Larri Sue and Allen happened upon a rental car agency, where they procured a two-seater van, the only remaining vehicle. They drove around the perimeter of Manhattan. Authorities had the borough completely sealed.

Parents long for the closeness of their children during times of danger. Frances and I were no exception. We maintained regular telephone dialogue with them, repeatedly asking them to spend the night at our hotel. But they couldn't get to us, or we to them.

We rejoiced, though, in knowing our kids' whereabouts and that they were alive and well. We thought about the thousands of New Yorkers who had no such knowledge of their loved ones. Our prayers went out for them. Even for many unbelievers, praying came quite naturally on that horrible day. I encountered few exceptions. Regular viewers of Feed The Children's television program approached me while I was out and about. A few asked me to pray with them, some without introducing themselves.

The long, agonizing day wore on. Then came another, and another. Each day seemed like a month of Sundays as Frances and I were separated from our children by miles none of us could travel and a sense of lonely foreboding none of us could escape.

In a phone conversation on the third or fourth day after the attack, Allen mentioned the incident with the rude Arab-looking man on the plane before his flight was canceled. Frances urged him to call the FBI hotline. He did so immediately, telling the story to an operator who promised to relay the account to official personnel. Allen would then receive a callback if the bureau thought the matter worth pursuing.

He received the call within the hour.

An agent listened to Allen's recollection. He then asked for the flight number and other specific details regarding the flight. He was looking for any information that might allow him to approximate the location of other seats, and the identities of those who occupied them, based on passenger manifests.

Allen described the three men's exit by saying they bolted as if the aircraft were on fire.

Thereafter, Larri Sue and Allen returned to La Guardia each day in hopes of catching a standby flight home. Each day they were turned away because departures either had not been rescheduled or were already full. There was simply no predicting when they might make it back to Oklahoma City. They could do nothing but keep showing up and hoping.

After five days they got lucky. To their great astonishment, they were issued boarding passes to Dallas and for a connecting flight to Oklahoma City.

Before boarding, however, they had to run the gauntlet of security checks. They underwent prolonged searches and other delays inherent to the process, inching along in congested lines. For days, they'd focused on getting home. That day, all their concentration was focused on just getting to the gate. Perhaps that's why they didn't stop to call anyone to say they were at last set to travel.

Once safely back in Oklahoma City, Allen retrieved his car from the parking lot at Will Rogers Airport and drove home. Pulling in to his driveway, he glanced into his rearview mirror to see that another car had pulled in behind him, partially blocking the street. Two men got out of the car and approached his.

Both men reached inside their suit jackets and withdrew badges identifying them as FBI agents.

The New York bureau had somehow found out that Allen was taking a flight back to Oklahoma City by way of Dallas. The Oklahoma City bureau was then notified of Allen's scheduled arrival. He didn't realize that agents were apparently casing him at the airport and tailing him all the way home. Had they secretly arranged for him to get on the flight in the first place? Everything about their showing up there was a made-for-TV mystery.

There, in his driveway, they politely and matter-of-factly grilled him about everything he'd told the New York agent. The Oklahoma City agents had other questions as well. They asked for a precise physical description and what the suspicious travelers had worn.

In Allen's surplus of idle time over the previous days, he'd had ample opportunity to ponder 9/11's airborne assaults on New York and Washington.

He wondered if the canceled flight that he and Larri Sue had been scheduled to fly was actually a part of the terrorists' diabolical plan that had been fatefully foiled. After all, the three Arab-looking men had left immediately when the announcement came that the WTC had been hit. Had their flight been part of a backup strategy? Was it part of an aborted plan to strike another landmark?

Did anyone know? Would anyone ever know?

Without hesitating or going inside after being away for nine days, Allen answered all questions while standing in the driveway. In the course of the conversation, he discovered that he and one of the agents shared a mutual acquaintance—the agent was married to one of Allen's college classmates. Establishing that one personal connection helped to cut his sense of tension a bit. It's no fun being grilled by the FBI under any circumstance.

Before the lawmen left, Allen posed a question of his own.

"Can you tell me if my sister and I were ever in some kind of harm's way?" he asked the authorities.

"We can't tell you that," one of the agents responded tersely and perhaps a bit too quickly, looking Allen squarely and earnestly in the eye.

Allen glanced at the second agent, the one with whom he'd established the personal connection. The man made fleeting eye contact, then abruptly glanced downward.

Apparently, the agents weren't at liberty to say a word. But Allen felt their gestures had answered his question quite well.

NEITHER ALLEN NOR ANY MEMBER OF OUR FAMILY ever heard from the FBI again regarding the situation on the plane that day. We don't know if the suspicious men were checked out and passed muster, or if they were investigated at all. If any of the three was ever arrested, it wasn't publicized—at least not in connection with 9/11.

My son and daughter were never injured, never threatened, never feared for their lives. When I began compiling this book, I had no thought of including a chapter about their unnerving experience.

My gratitude for their safety compelled me to write about it. My senses raged with alarm at the mere thought that they might have been harmed or lost. My heart raced with a very direct, connected sense of compassion for the parents, children, and siblings of the innocents who perished on that cloudless September morning.

Volumes have been written about the financial cost of pursuing our attackers, a pursuit that, some experts concur, led to U.S. participation in the Middle East war that continues to rage as of this writing. We citizens are forever given updates regarding presidential requests for more money and troop strength. During 2006, a midterm election year, we were subjected to candidates' endless speculation about the consequences of depleting our military arsenals and manpower. Some doomsday exponents were predicting Armageddon. There's probably some merit to their thinking.

My anxiety over what might have happened to our children inspired a sense of empathy I could never have shared without at least the degree of direct involvement Frances and I experienced. It's not that we can fully identify with what it's like to know you've lost your innocent loved ones to outrageous hatred and violence and that you'll never see them again in this life. But we came close enough to the edge of that abyss of horror that we were able to see halfway down.

For some, the unfathomable loss is as fresh as this morning's spate of crying, as spontaneous as feeling ambushed by a song they hear on the radio that reminds them of the one who's no longer there in their life to share it with them. Changing the dial won't change the emotion. The damage is done.

My point is this: Consider their anguish. Take pains to empathize. Too many Americans are forgetting to remember those who've suffered the grievous losses of 9/11.

I expect that getting over it is going to be beyond the emotional capacity that many can muster. I think of my late mother, a devout Christian who went to her grave upset with God because He let my brother, Mike, die of natural causes at age thirty-nine. She simply never got over it. She told me as much, and I told mourners when I delivered her eulogy.

Mike's death came early but not abruptly. It wasn't a big surprise, like those on 9/11. Yet it caused my mother, a lay minister, to question God's judgment—or at least His fairness.

That's why I feel shocked and saddened to hear people ask, "When are they going to get over it and get on with their lives?" Wow. Talk about not getting it. I pray for the pain of those who suffered loss, and for the impatience of those who didn't.

I think about stalwart men such as Jimmy Boyle, former two-term president of New York's Uniformed Firefighters Association Local 94, whose son Michael—also a fireman—lost his life in responding to the inferno at the World Trade Center.

Michael had been off duty for sixteen minutes on September 11, 2001, when the call came about a blaze inside the WTC. Other men in his firehouse were just beginning their shifts, relieving the team of firefighters on his shift. Mike didn't have to join them on the call.

He was acting essentially as a volunteer, helping an evacuee out of Tower One, when the building fell on top of him. He had been on a waiting list for seven years before being offered a chance to join the fire department. He had spent six dedicated years on the job. Then came the emergency on 9/11, when his life was ended in seconds.

His remains were uncovered four and a half months later when searchers pulled them out from under a tangle of steel fifty-seven feet below street level. The crumbling tonnage had crushed Mike's body down, down, down, to a distance equivalent to almost four times the length of a fireman's pike pole. Bones and human ashes, mixed with debris, were found inside the lining of the coat he'd been wearing. He'd been partially cremated.

The elder Boyle, as former union boss, felt duty-bound to act as host to memorial services commemorating many fallen fire-fighters throughout 2002. Each was a painful reminder of his own fallen son.

I also think of Ken Haskell, a former New York City police officer who became a fireman because he believed he would get more opportunities to help people.

"Each time a fireman leaves the firehouse he's off to help someone," Haskell said.

Like Michael Boyle, Ken was off duty when disaster struck on 9/11. Thinking he might find his brothers, Timmy and Tommy, who were also firemen, he responded to the call and headed straight for Ground Zero.

He recovered arms, legs, and other body parts when he arrived at the scene. Intent on rescuing any living person he could find, Ken started to dig, with a shovel and gloved hands, repeatedly changing gloves that burned or shredded in the process.

Fourteen hours later, at 1:00 a.m., he took a rest, physically spent and emotionally depleted. But he was back at Ground Zero by sunrise to resume his obsessive quest.

He recovered the gear of firemen he'd known. However, he found no trace of Timmy or Tommy.

Another fireman found Timmy.

Wrenched with anger and grief, Ken searched his mind for something to be thankful for. Timmy's body remained in one piece. He could at least be thankful for that.

He could not extend thanks regarding Tommy's remains, no trace of which was ever found.

Tommy had been working on a lower floor of the WTC. The force of its collapse must have crushed him into a grave that will forever be hidden within the crater that was eventually sealed with concrete.

Altogether, only twenty people were pulled out alive from the ruin of the World Trade Center. For rescuers, Feed The Children provided gloves to protect tender flesh and diamond-blade saws to cut through debris. I'm thankful that we could be a part of their efforts.

I'll forever give thanks for the twenty who were saved, and for the relief of their loved ones who were spared the pain that thousands of others, who were not so fortunate, suffered. These thousands continue their own individual vigils of sorrow. As grief is always a deeply personal journey, one must endure it alone, no matter how many others may also be hurting.

For all of these folks, I continue to pray. Sometimes I suddenly become aware that I've been praying for them unconsciously, they are so often in my thoughts. Many things prompt these thoughts, such as hearing the national anthem, turning the calendar to September, or the unexpected visit of Allen or Larri Sue.

Chapter Twenty-two

*E*VERY DISASTER HAS ITS OWN PERSONALITY, a realization that un-folded daily in the aftermath of September 11, 2001.

Air traffic was grounded, and the authorities weren't letting any-one enter or leave New York City. I was stranded—and grateful for it. Otherwise, I couldn't have overseen our landmark relief effort, the likes of which had never been undertaken in the history of Feed The Children.

How was this effort different? I quickly realized that the primary needs were not necessarily those of the survivors. Most of them had food and shelter. FTC's efforts would instead be focused on rescue workers, the selfless men and women working around the clock to find and save the few who survived the fall of the World Trade Cen-ter and to uncover the bodies of those who didn't. The number of these searchers added up to a small army. Circumstances had hurled me into their ranks.

I also became fully aware of the benefits of having worked FTC's previous New York outreaches. I personally knew some of the offi-cers at the police station around the corner from my hotel. Many had provided security at our food drops. My relationship with po-lice and other officials proved to be more valuable than ever.

I walked from my hotel into the frenzy within the station house and encountered Captain Frank Bogucki, an officer who had really come through for me in the past. He had no time for small talk, so I got straight down to business.

I told him FTC had a warehouse filled with emergency supplies in North Brunswick, New Jersey.

"If you can arrange clearance, Feed The Children can be attend-ing people at Ground Zero in a matter of hours," I said.

Bogucki eyed me skeptically.

I intensified my appeal, ensuring him that I didn't need to wait for committee approval to authorize relief services. The need was immediate, and we were ready to step in and make a difference—as we had in the aftermath of the terrorist attack on the Murrah building in Oklahoma City.

He was sold.

I'd made my pitch, shouting over screeching sirens and bustling bedlam. Bogucki had listened with one ear, keeping the other tuned in to the information squawking loudly over a dispatcher's radio. He stepped out for a moment, asking me to wait while he made a telephone call. To whom I have no idea.

When he came back, the captain instructed me to have my trucks at the designated exit within a few hours. Again he sought assurance that FTC could do all I'd said it could. I affirmed my commitment, and I left there with great resolve. Bogucki was taking me at my word that FTC could provide for the needs of thousands of rescuers. I was not going to let him down.

Two empty FTC semitrailer trucks were parked about thirty-six miles away. I needed to have them loaded with pallets of supplies and delivering in Manhattan within four hours.

The first plane had hit at 8:45 a.m. At 9:21 a.m., the Port Authority of New York and New Jersey ordered all bridges and tunnels in the New York area closed. At 10:05 a.m., the south tower of the WTC collapsed. At 10:13 a.m., forty-seven thousand people were evacuated from the United Nations building. At 10:28 a.m., the WTC's north tower fell, releasing an impenetrable curtain of smoke and airborne debris. At 11:02 a.m., Mayor Rudolph Giuliani ordered the evacuation of all roadways south of Canal Street.

Because the roads had been closed for security reasons, I would need a police escort to get downtown. Officers who were desperately needed at Ground Zero would instead be awaiting FTC's trucks on the shoulder of an interstate at Exit 27. The trucks simply had to get there on time if I wanted to maintain credibility with that hour's most overworked police department in the world.

Around 1:45 p.m., FTC's pair of eighteen-wheelers pulled up to Ground Zero. Their trailers, in twelve-foot-tall letters, were emblazoned with the words "Feed The Children." A few astonished workers applauded.

By 2:00 p.m., just five hours and fifteen minutes after the first plane hit, FTC's provisions were being issued to firemen and other rescuers. Over the next twenty-four hours we dispensed an entire truckload of water (about twenty-five thousand one-liter bottles). We emptied another truck filled with power bars, snack items, and the like.

The next day police again assisted us in pulling our empty trucks out from the site and ushering two full ones in. Again, the new arrivals delivered water as well as ready-to-eat food, soft drinks, grade-A bulk food, shovels, sacks, rakes, flashlights, work gloves, and more. On the third day we brought in more of the same, plus more substantial meals.

The following weeks would reveal that almost three thousand lives had been claimed by the World Trade Center disaster. This being the area of greatest damage done by the 9/11 terrorist attacks, our relief efforts had served the needs there instantaneously. We also dispatched other trucks from Oklahoma City to Washington, D.C., where they arrived only days after the attack on the Pentagon.

Being a private outreach devoted to public service, FTC is free to jump in and serve when needs arise.

On day four, the Federal Emergency Management Agency began serving laborers at Ground Zero. At that time FTC relinquished its efforts of direct supply and began working hand in hand with the government.

But FEMA's supply office was set up about four miles from the disaster area. We pressed our trucks into service as shuttles, running supplies from the FEMA post to Ground Zero. Rescuers gave us lists of things they needed, FEMA filled them, and we hauled the cargo back to the site.

Functioning in this way, we found that we, too, needed a depot near the work sites. Out of the blue, a woman called one of our offices to say she owned a garage on Spring Street, about fourteen blocks from Ground Zero. She offered FTC free use of the space. We accepted and continued to use the facility free of charge for about six months.

The disaster of the World Trade Center created needs no one would ever have thought to anticipate. For instance, rescuers found themselves needing to replace their conventional footwear with steel-toed boots because the soles quickly wore out when pressed against concrete and iron. By coordinating our trucks with FEMA and the Spring Street garage, FTC became a veritable shoe store where volunteers could fit themselves.

Working nonstop, tired and distracted, rescue workers didn't always remember to note everything they needed on the supply lists we were committed to fulfill.

I told the people on 9/11 the same thing I'd told rescuers at the Murrah bombing: "Just tell me what you need when you think of it. If I don't have it in our warehouse, I'll find it and have it here within twenty-four hours."

Some of the bewildered laborers looked at me as if I'd inhaled too many toxic fumes. Many still didn't comprehend my promise to meet their every need. They had no experience in dealing with the aftermath of terrorism, as I had. When they failed to come up with ambitious requests, I tendered a few suggestions.

"Have you ever used diamond-blade saws?" I asked a few of the firemen and ironworkers. Many had heard of the blades' effectiveness but had never actually seen them cut through inches of solid steel without dulling. They were overjoyed because a donor gave diamond-blade saws to cut through steel at Ground Zero.

I'd previously interacted with the manufacturer and distributor. He called, and rescuers had the incredible saws the very next day. Once again, a previous relationship had proven valuable.

By that time FTC's ad hoc distribution center was dispensing supplies with considerable precision and efficiency. Having established momentum, we were just getting started. Our efforts continued smoothly for the next five months.

We didn't leave New York City until March 2002. I'd arrived there on September 7, 2001, for a food drop in Harlem, then stayed to attend the Michael Jackson concert.

When our mission was finished, records indicated we'd emptied 117 trucks containing 2.67 million pounds of food and other essential material support, all delivered with love in our hearts, which recipients seemed to recognize and appreciate.

Thus, for the second time in my life, I'd been able to activate emergency services to a disaster-stricken city where I just happened to be at the time. But I don't think my presence was merely coincidental.

FEED THE CHILDREN NEVER FEATURED our relief efforts for 9/11 in one of our television broadcasts, and many viewers asked why. I hope by now the explanation is obvious. An abrupt disaster, such as a terrorist attack, throws us instantly into action. We obsess over the immediate needs. I feel we can't afford the time to think about television production as we might with slower-developing or ongoing human problems that call for sustained relief efforts. I simply told viewers that we were on the scene in New York City. Many didn't need to see what we were doing. They knew about our policy of providing immediate relief and sustained follow-up. They simply trusted that we were busy doing all we could after having seen us daily on CNN's live telecasts from Oklahoma City's Murrah bombing in 1995.

The events of 9/11 left many personal tragedies in their wake. Family, friends, clergymen, professional counselors, and others tended to the bereavement of thousands. Throughout the final months of 2001 and into 2002, President George Bush himself addressed numerous memorial services that kept the fallen and their survivors in the national consciousness. I was thankful for the outpouring of goodwill toward the grieving, and prayed shortly after 9/11 that God would guide me in determining what direction my ministry should take.

I considered this prayer answered after I was told about a family who'd come to our garage on Spring Street.

A woman explained that she and her husband had been laid off from their jobs waiting tables at a restaurant. The two who'd served food to thousands suddenly had no food to serve themselves and their children. We gave them a prepackaged box containing a week's supply of groceries for four.

Later that day, others came who'd also been dismissed from service-industry jobs. Word of mouth spread about FTC's willingness to help those whose livelihoods were casualties of 9/11. The unemployed converged from all five boroughs. Without prompting, some felt it incumbent to present their old employee identification cards. They wanted us to know they'd been willing wage earners who were ready to work again.

About that time, I read that an estimated forty thousand people would lose hotel and restaurant jobs due to a decline in tourism. Travelers were apprehensive about visiting the Big Apple, fearful of more attacks. Major hotels were defiling their stately exteriors with gaudy signs advertising significantly reduced rates. The Chamber of Commerce had also launched an aggressive campaign to rebuild tourism. As Thanksgiving Day approached, David Letterman and other nationally known New Yorkers issued coast-to-coast appeals for people to return to their city.

But conditions didn't improve right away. Fearmongering hysteria continued in the form of terrorist rumors and anthrax scares. The powdered poison had been received via mail at two television networks. People reacted by sequestering themselves in their homes and essentially boycotting restaurants. After everything else it had endured, New York City was firmly in the grasp of economic decline.

Many who'd been let go from their low-paying service-sector jobs had no financial nest egg to fall back on. A substantial portion of New York City's labor force was left essentially destitute. They discovered that hunger is an equal-opportunity problem. Suddenly it raged quite inclusively across racial, social, and economic boundaries.

In the wake of it all, we opened an additional food and hygiene outlet in Queens, where the hotel and restaurant employees' union and health center were located. We conducted major food drops there and in Washington, D.C., with follow-up distribution every three to four weeks. Altogether, we supplied forty thousand unemployed New Yorkers, their spouses, and children, as well as thirty thousand families in Washington, D.C. This outreach became the longest-running domestic food drop effort in FTC history, up to that time.

Steve Whetstone, the FTC staffer who coordinated these distributions, said he was constantly hugged and kissed by grateful recipients.

"So many times we were told that we weren't just giving them food, we were giving them hope," Whetstone said. "It was nice because the media was so focused on the number of bodies at Ground Zero that everybody seemed to forget about these people who were now totally unemployed. They were so thankful."

Someone suggested that some beneficiaries of our unusual distribution effort to the unemployed weren't former service-sector personnel at all. They were accused of receiving food they didn't deserve.

Deserve? Anyone who stands in line for hours in bone-chilling cold certainly must be hungry. If they're hungry, they're hurting. That's deserving enough for me.

Whetstone has numerous photographs depicting lines of as many as three thousand people. Some of those in the lines were mothers pushing carriages they had covered with plastic to shield their infants from blinding snow or torrential rain. They couldn't leave their infants at home—they had no money for babysitters. They still had no money when they left our distribution point, but at least they had food.

Many in line qualified for unemployment benefits. Some actually received them, but not in a timely manner due to slower mail service after the anthrax scare. Meanwhile, we saw to it that they were well supplied with essentials.

In addition to distributing from our own pool of donated resources, FTC ended up supplying goods for the City of New York and some of the nation's most respected charities, including the Salvation Army and the Red Cross. They called when their transportation systems became overloaded, so we donated the use of our trucks.

FTC also helped to address one ironic aspect of the 9/11 relief effort that no one would have anticipated.

Many of the nation's smaller charities that stock local food pantries all over America were left wanting for donations after the terrorist attacks. Their contributions dwindled as regular donors opted to send funds to big charities with hands-on outreaches at Ground Zero. When they couldn't feed the needy who regularly relied on them, they called Feed The Children.

FTC maintains six warehouses, totaling more than one million square feet, situated on both coasts and in four inland states. We can deliver anywhere in the nation within twelve hours. Thus, we were able to help every organization that asked for our assistance.

I described this unusual situation to our television audience, and viewers responded with increased contributions. Food processors came with larger and more frequent donations. It was like opening a floodgate that poured forth the generosity of good-hearted, concerned Americans.

Given the national scope of our improvised work, I'd be hardpressed to say just how many hundreds of thousands of people we served in the months after the tragedy of 9/11. I do know that no request for help was denied.

AT CHRISTMASTIME, New York City was still vexed with economic stagnation that belied the usually festive holiday season. With regard to tourism, Manhattan was virtually a ghost town. Hotels that normally rented rooms for $269.95 a night lowered rates to $69.95. A psychological pall had fallen over the place. Everybody felt it—demoralized New Yorkers as well as the handful of tourists who did venture out.

It was the first Yuletide for thousands of people grieving lost loved ones—some of whose remains had yet to be found.

The usually teeming city was a grim shadow of itself. Pedestrians had lost the spring in their steps. If there was a bright side, it was that traffic flowed more smoothly owing to the dwindling number of cars on the streets. Out-of-state tags were few and far between. The accustomed holiday aroma of street vendors roasting chestnuts was masked by the unnatural stench of still-smoldering ruins.

Meanwhile, our Spring Street center for rescue workers continued operating in high gear. Our visitors, mostly firemen, continued their search for yet another body. Grimly they pressed on, looking for what they didn't actually want to find.

Some did so obsessively, working a forty-eight-hour shift, and then voluntarily spending the next forty-eight hours going on with the search. What drove them to do this? Perhaps it was a compulsive sense of duty. Perhaps it was a relentless desire to bring the matter to closure. Perhaps it was emotional meltdown.

Perhaps it was all of the above.

The most frequent lament among firefighters, rescuers, and cleanup personnel pertained to the towering pile of wreckage. Hundreds of men worked on it around the clock. Tons and tons of debris were removed daily. Yet for the weary laborers at Ground Zero, it seemed as though the looming stack didn't diminish.

"Gee whiz, we are not making a dent in that mess," a fireman said one night.

FTC workers began to sense a deepening melancholy among civil servants who toiled in the dreary midwinter cold, their only warmth rising from the glowing embers of the fallen towers beneath them.

Then, one December morning, our Spring Street outlet was blessed by a ray of warm sunshine from San Angelo, Texas—a package of Christmas gift boxes that merchants had prepared for firemen still searching for the slain.

The contents consisted of essentials, such as soap, shampoo, toothpaste, snacks, and reading material. The gifts weren't anything special. But the exhausted firemen didn't have to be told it's the thought that counts. They were touched beyond words because the gifts confirmed that people somewhere, even in faraway Texas, were holding them in their thoughts, appreciating their dedication.

With grimy faces caked so heavily that it was hard to determine their ethnicity, they opened their boxes with quivering hands and shed tears, revealing tender humanity.

I like to think that, month after grueling month, FTC offered not only sustenance but also encouragement to the firemen, rescue workers, and civilian hungry who frequented our Spring Street mission. Granted, we did nothing to ease their workload. But I'm sat-isfied that we made a difference in their lives.

This is the constant blessing for FTC workers—making a quiet difference in the lives of others when that quiet difference is most needed and appreciated. Making a small, temporary difference in the lives of the needy makes a huge and lasting difference in our own.

Chapter Twenty-three

*I*T WAS ONE OF FEED THE CHILDREN'S most highly watched programs, thanks to its topical subject and mysterious opening, spoken extemporaneously as I trekked through some of the most disheartening destruction I'd ever seen. No one, including me, wanted to face the grim reality. Yet what we saw was so horrifically entrancing we could not look away.

"No, I'm not in Iraq," I told the audience. I walked determinedly toward the camera's lens against a background of total ruin.

"I'm not in the southeast Asian tsunami," I continued. "Just hours ago, where I'm walking now was one of the most beautiful spots in the United States," I said. "Now it's been reduced to rubble. Please don't turn the channel."

People remained riveted to Feed The Children's ensuing coverage of Hurricane Katrina. It was, in fact, the United States' third-strongest tropical storm on record, flattening homes, businesses, hospitals, and schools along the Gulf Coast for hundreds of miles—ninety thousand square miles, according to the federal disaster declaration.

Deaths attributed to the tempest totaled 1,836. Damage was eventually appraised at $81.2 billion, making this the most expensive natural disaster in our nation's 229-year history.

The scourge had raged for about twelve hours. Within twenty-four, Feed The Children was active on the scene. We tendered relief and lasting efforts that began as soon as the National Guard admitted us. We remained intensely focused and engaged for a full six months and continue with follow-up to this day.

As of April 24, 2007, we had distributed 623 truckloads of food and supplies weighing in at 14,283,000 pounds, with an appraised value of thirty-four million dollars. This relief effort stands as the most expensive and exhaustive FTC has ever undertaken in North America. I have no idea when lives will be rebuilt enough for us to consider the job done.

AS KATRINA DEPARTED THE SUNSHINE STATE, moving westward across the gulf into Mississippi and Louisiana, I monitored the hurricane's progress via TV reports at the home of a friend in Jacksonville. His living room became my command post.

I maintained intermittent dialogue with Steve Whetstone, co-director of our 9/11 efforts. He, in turn, contacted the offices of the governors of Louisiana and Mississippi and the National Guard in both states.

I also called Jack Rickett, leader of a thirty-seven-member team of FTC volunteers based in Glasgow, Kentucky. The group remains on constant standby and can mobilize to emergency action within two hours. All members maintain their own provisions, including food, water, work clothes, a sleeping bag, and incidentals. Thus, they can work tirelessly and self-sufficiently for days.

I asked Rickett, an industrialist with his own fleet of long-haul trucks, to use his own rigs to pick up goods at FTC's Nashville warehouse, which is located just ninety-six miles from Glasgow. We met the next day in Jackson, Mississippi, where I arrived directing a fleet of twenty-five FTC eighteen-wheelers, all filled with relief and emergency cargo from our flagship warehouse in Oklahoma City.

Altogether, we lined up about forty trucks near the Mississippi capital before Governor Haley Barbour. Then we formed a single-file convoy to begin our trip to Hattiesburg, Gulfport, and eventually Biloxi, which were to be our first of four stops on this impromptu southern outreach.

The motorcade flowed with the precision of a Swiss watch, as Barbour had arranged for a highway patrol escort past interstate entrance and exit ramps that were closed in favor of FTC's passage. Minutes before we pulled out of Jackson, the governor addressed a press conference where he expressed his appreciation for Feed The

Children without restraint. Someone later joked that his praise sounded as if he were FTC's public relations spokesperson. Someone else suggested that I hire him to be just that.

On our press southward, Feed The Children's trucks, each carrying three hundred gallons of fuel, passed station after station where cars had run out of gasoline while waiting to buy more. It was common to see cars pushing other cars to gas islands where they found only empty pumps. We saw what probably amounted to hundreds of vehicles abandoned around stations marked with signs that read "No Gas."

Rickett and crew entered Mississippi from the northeast, where high winds had blown away highway signs and directional markers. They cautiously negotiated roadways where there were no remaining indicators of their direction or whereabouts, not even commercial billboards. The debris was so thick in some places that it was hard to tell where the highway ran. Everything that had been upright was gone.

Rickett's eyes scanned the jumbled horizon, then rose heavenward—perhaps in prayer. In that moment he happened to notice his vehicle's OnStar button. It was as if his prayer was answered. He activated the OnStar satellite service and got an operator in a city far away from the destruction.

He explained to the disembodied voice of OnStar that he was in the hurricane-ravaged South, where conditions were far worse than news coverage had indicated. He said he was with Feed The Children and was trying to provide immediate relief to those who were displaced in Mississippi—people who were among the poorest in all the United States.

The OnStar operator became a deputy member of the relief team, pinpointing the convoy's location and directing its progress via satellite.

Thus, as Rickett and company approached highway junctions along the way to Jackson, the OnStar operator would advise him which way to turn. Rickett usually couldn't see the concrete beneath him. He felt as if he were flying blind, directed by the instruments that OnStar provided. Rickett trusted his unseen helper. Together, they steered tons of steel and relief supplies off one road onto another, with the rest of the convoy following suit.

Even as they were being properly guided, the conditions created a constant state of tension for the drivers. Not far off any surface lay Mississippi's soggy bottomland. Straddling the sides of some roads were deep ditches, brimming with runoff from the storm, hidden beneath the sea of debris. Following someone else's directions required a lot of faith and trust.

But that's the way they proceeded—by faith—until God and OnStar ushered them all into Jackson, then led them on to the first leg of the rescue tour.

Some people might consider Mississippi's August swelter difficult to survive under even ideal conditions. Throughout the hurricane-affected region, three-digit heat and humidity topping 90 percent are the norm. Without electricity to power air-conditioning and refrigeration, all perishables began rotting from the day the hurricane hit. An acrid stench hung in the heavy gulf air, so thick it was all but visible. And there were so many flies we were reminded of the Old Testament plague in which swarms of locusts blot out the sun and cover the earth.

Feed The Children's rescuers also included fourteen members of the National Basketball Players Association, as well as four members of the Women's National Basketball Association.

Those athletes weren't formally trained in rescue, but they did have natural inclinations toward caring. I'd previously worked with players on planned missions, such as food drops. We had usually gathered in New York City, Las Vegas, Los Angeles, or wherever an NBA or WNBA game was scheduled. Their coming instantly to a disaster-stricken area was psychologically reassuring to harried victims. The players responded from all over the nation, flying into Jackson, Mississippi, where no rooms were available. They instead stayed in Vicksburg before boarding a bus with the FTC group to attend survivors across Katrina's ruthless path.

The New Orleans/Oklahoma City Hornets also responded when FTC went to New Orleans. The team had earlier been a New Orleans franchise and wanted to help its hometown.

This was not vacationland. Many motels were closed or had been blown away. Meanwhile, Feed The Children's Glasgow volunteers worked all day and slept on open ground at night. They took turns standing guard, protecting co-laborers and the relief supplies from looters who were drawn to the conspicuous Feed The Children trucks.

Many locals stumbled around as if they were drunk. I guess they were, in a way. They were punch-drunk, as if surprised by a left hook that had knocked them to the mat. Then, dizzy and staggering, they had picked themselves up, wondering what it was that had hit them.

For days, most just wandered around in a continuing stupor of shock and disbelief, recoiling at the destruction they saw around them.

For survivors, this was the beginning of the second storm. The first had been the hurricane. The second was the whirling mix of confusion, anger, grief, and terror within. Most of these people had lived in one place all their lives. They had known every rock in the road, every plank of wood with which their communities had been built. Now nothing looked familiar.

Searching piles of debris mixed with mud, people looked inside children's clothes for name tags. If they found identification, it usually belonged to a youngster they didn't know. Clothing, furniture, and household items had washed in from other coastal towns located miles away.

Concrete slabs were the only visible evidence left of some homes. Victims could be heard violently arguing over whose home had sat on which foundation. No fences, trees, or other distinguishing markers remained that might help them tell one lot from another. The anonymous slabs were floating on a uniform sea of goo.

"See this? *This* is where I lived!" I heard them exclaim as they referred to differentiating features that existed mostly in their own desperate imaginations.

The victims' psychological needs were clearly every bit as pronounced as their need for food, shelter, and dry clothing. Feed The Children set out to serve at every level of need.

We delivered truckload after truckload of nonperishable foods as well as millions of gallons of drinking water. Because we reached the scenes of destruction so quickly, we were able to introduce a sense of much-needed stability to the areas we served. People probably didn't expect such a bountiful inventory of food, along with blankets, medicine, personal items, and paper products. They certainly didn't expect hot meals. We fed ten thousand people nutritionally balanced servings three times a day in parts of Louisiana and Mississippi. FTC kitchens remained open for almost five months. Though we couldn't fill the hole in people's souls where their sense of home used to be, they certainly were happy to have the sustenance and the small comforts we were able to offer.

Former U.S. secretary of agriculture Mike Espy, a consultant to Feed The Children, surveyed the damage wrought by Katrina before succinctly summarizing the storm's effects at the human level. "She [Katrina] didn't discriminate by wealth or by class or by age," he said. "She destroyed everybody."

Many victims seemed desperate for human contact. Some who recognized me from television pulled on me urgently. Meanwhile, Jack Rickett's thirty-seven volunteers from Kentucky charmed the fearful crowds like politicians working a room, offering hugs to anyone who wanted. They hugged a lot of people.

While this tactile approach offered a measure of comfort, I believe it also prevented some riots from breaking out. Anger boiled just beneath the surface in a lot of people. Some could barely contain the hysteria they felt over their losses. Sometimes they lost control and shoving ensued. Thankfully, certain members of our Glasgow volunteer team were weight lifters and bodybuilders. They didn't hesitate to walk into any fracas, telling people there had been enough pain, that they had to work together to restore each other.

The psychology may seem trite, but it worked. When panicked, people want to hear anything truthful, no matter how simple. They like for someone to take control and lead. Rickett and his team filled the role. Sometimes they even distracted survivors with simple sleight-of-hand tricks. The antics provided soothing balm to broken souls.

Still, the crowd remained as volatile as nitroglycerin—a thing to be handled carefully. Looting was rampant elsewhere in the disaster zones, where people flagrantly brandished stolen wares. One exasperated grocer in New Orleans simply yielded to the pillage, opening up his store with goods for the taking. He hoped insurance would cover his loss. People just came in, grabbed what they wanted, and carted their loot out the front door.

Thankfully no one, no matter how crazed by the circumstances, ever pilfered from Feed The Children.

We immediately sought out areas hardest hit by Katrina in order to deliver relief supplies, not to create shows for the television ministry. We televise the plight we discover to enlist additional support. For years I've made a policy of returning to disaster scenes after television cameras were turned off. I've often asked God to direct me to a particularly desperate person. Once this person was shown to me, I'd reach out to him or her in a personal way. No one ever knew except the beneficiary and me.

I tried this after Katrina, but there were just too many people who continued to need dedicated personal attention. My emotions short-circuited. I felt fried.

In times past, my reaching out one-on-one had provided the most fulfilling experiences of my ministry. But Katrina wasn't about self-fulfillment. I felt selfish for seeking it.

So I took cameramen with me into the waterlogged wastes of post-hurricane Mississippi and Louisiana. Misery greeted the camera everywhere we turned it. Day after day, there was lingering misery as far as the eye could see.

I RETURNED IN SEPTEMBER with a television crew, stumbling through fallen cypress trees, to a house where only one wall remained standing. It was well after midnight. A panorama of starlight and a pale yellow moon gleamed where the roof used to be. A half dozen people sat around outside, perched on fallen trees.

For them, the hurricane had come and gone days ago; they had sought no relief. Maybe they were suffering from shock. Maybe they'd

been able to salvage enough nonperishable food and simply preferred to keep to themselves. Throughout the region I found many
people who were too overwhelmed and disoriented to put things
together—or perhaps just too depressed to care about anything anymore. I sensed that if some of them could have suddenly died without having to commit suicide, they would have gladly done that.
Their despondency was so deep that it seemed their eyes had turned
backward to where they could no longer see a trace of sunlight or
hope for a new day.

Those folks we discovered perched on fallen trees around their
fallen home felt some odd comfort of safety there, I guess. But I certainly couldn't guess why. After the storm passed, they'd existed for
days without electricity, natural gas, running water, or sanitation.

In the middle of their fallen house sat a toilet that was full and
wouldn't flush. The debris-strewn yard outside had become their
bathroom. Stench, flies, and bacteria permeated the humid air. The
area was, no doubt, disease-ridden and unfit for human habitation,
yet this small cluster of storm-tossed souls was terrified at the notion
of leaving.

"Lightning never strikes twice in the same place," an addled old-
timer told one of our people. "I'm praying it's that way with hurricanes. I'm staying right here."

Over and over we discovered people who shared this unreason-
able fear, this intense wish to cling to what they had known even
though ruin was all that remained.

We broadcast the plight of one family who'd climbed to their
roof as four-foot waves battered their home. Had they stayed in the
house, they'd have surely drowned. Here again, though, the folks
just did not want to leave it.

Another family, the Hallies, had been forced to tread water for
hours, bobbing in the rushing sea of floodwater after their home of
thirty-seven years was washed away. Praying for the water to recede
enough for their feet to touch ground, they departed only when
they saw that there was literally nothing left for which to stay.

We discovered one man holding a shattered picture frame containing a photograph of his wife, baby, and himself. Wife and baby

were gone—casualties of the deluge. He moistened his thumb with his tears to loosen mud on the picture's broken glass. Then he steadied his hand to hold the photo out for our camera.

This tiny gesture bespoke pain of epic proportions.

NEWS CREWS WERE SWARMING EVERYWHERE on each of my visits back to Mississippi and Louisiana to monitor our follow-up work. Like many relief workers, I found myself watching television to try to get some perspective on the confusion all around me.

I saw panic in the people of New Orleans when they were told that many members of the New Orleans Police Department had walked out on their jobs. From a human standpoint, the officers' action was understandable. They were physically, mentally, and emotionally spent from trying simultaneously to fight runaway looting and to aid flood victims.

Feed The Children inherited the daunting task of trying to feed the twenty thousand who sought refuge at the New Orleans convention center, where they found only filth and pandemonium.

In trying to deliver supplies to the convention center, the government unwittingly created a riot on the second day after the hurricane. A helicopter dropped boxes that split, scattering provisions of food and water everywhere. People pushed, shoved, and fought over the spoils.

In connection with this abysmal situation, the media presented a story about a woman, her husband, and her pets who had been trapped inside their home for two days. Rising water had forced them upstairs into a small cubicle, where they lay in their own waste.

Hearing the helicopter as it flew toward the convention center, the man and woman set their clothes on fire, hoping the pilot might notice the flames. But the helicopter just kept flying. With that, the woman told her husband she'd abandoned faith in anyone or anything. She felt as if God had let the hurricane happen and that mankind simply wouldn't help.

The couple eventually removed a door and used it to escape from the house, floating across standing water that was twelve feet deep. They set out for the convention center on foot, walking for two days through water polluted by gasoline, oil, and floating bodies. They encountered countless snakes.

Once they finally reached the convention center, they refused to enter. They'd heard reports of dead bodies inside. Instead, they staked out a spot on the lawn, "living" there for five more days. Helicopters came and dropped more food—which ignited more fights.

In the midst of the bedlam, Feed The Children responded with thousands of gallons of bottled water and food, drawing on resources we had placed earlier at local food pantries with which we enjoyed an ongoing relationship. Of course, we couldn't feed everyone inside the convention center and Superdome. We didn't try. The focus of our Louisiana relief efforts was mainly on the outlying areas. But we helped everywhere and in every way we could, moving tons of food through our regular outlets.

Feed The Children may not have been able to provide total calm after the storm, but, as they say, every little bit helps. We definitely provided solutions where at first there were only very, very ugly problems. Our function is a bit like that of an emergency room— we perform the equivalent of relief-supply triage. First we attempt to address the life-or-death threats, and then we see to the rest.

Once the dire emergencies were tended to, our rehabilitative efforts fell into a functional groove. The kinks that inevitably crimp any relief work pipeline had been smoothed. Both relief supplies and goodwill were flowing.

Then a stranger approached me, saying he didn't want to be the bearer of bad news.

I eyed him up and down, dumbfounded. "After everything we've been through here, what could possibly be bad news?" I inquired, almost tauntingly.

"A hurricane is approaching the coast of Texas," he replied matter-of-factly. "Winds are predicted to reach 180 miles per hour. They're calling her Rita—Hurricane Rita."

THE MOMENTUM WE'D ACHIEVED in the current disaster was transferred to the next, as if Katrina had been a dress rehearsal for our response to Rita. Feed The Children's weary relief workers rose to the challenge—again.

There's no point in describing specifics of the damages or our responses to them. They were similar to Katrina. (Although, thank God, the number of fatalities was markedly less—even if no less cause for grief and sorrow.)

I'd like to say the events were the same, that only the faces had changed. But that wasn't entirely the case.

In the course of the storm and resultant displacement, thousands of people sought refuge in the Houston Astrodome as well as Joel Osteen's sixteen-thousand-seat Lakewood Church. Ironically, many of these had been victims of Katrina who fled Louisiana and Mississippi only to run directly into the violent grip of Rita on the Texas Gulf Coast. Feed The Children anticipated and monitored their migration. We had trucks waiting in Houston before they arrived.

With this, we suddenly found ourselves nurturing evacuees from Florida to Texas—fully half of the southern border of these United States.

I heard a lot of weary people say they felt like transients, with every destination being just a deeper level of hell. One poor guy told me he'd always believed that history repeated itself and that Louisiana and Houston must be replays of the Bible's Flood.

"Where's Noah?" he asked in jest. "Ain't somebody got an ark?" Desperation underlay his humor, of course. I realized that as soon as he began to cry.

I've often observed that each disaster seems to manifest its own unique temperament. Coming one right after the other, Katrina and Rita were a bit like terrible twins. Many people had fled Katrina in Mississippi and Louisiana only to meet Rita in Texas. This double-whammy experience sent victims fleeing far and wide—walking, hitchhiking, boarding buses, carpooling—going anywhere they thought they might be safe from another deluge.

These people were overwhelmed, hurt, bewildered, and largely at a loss for how to get on with their lives. On top of that, they were hungry and lacking in basic necessities. Feed The Children was determined to make sure these people didn't go without. But first we had to find them.

FTC workers began calling our regular food conduits around North America to determine which had received people from storm-stricken areas. We found them as far north as the Great Lakes, as far south as Mexico.

We contacted various state offices of the Federal Emergency Management Agency and pinpointed people who were redeeming their government-issued vouchers for rent. We knew those same folks would need material support, at least until they found jobs.

Our search also focused on travel-trailer camps, where we found many, many people who had previously worked with FTC. We enlisted their help again. Many trucks filled with relief supplies were dispatched straight from FTC donors to locations where the displaced were gathered.

It's no secret that many people—and not just evacuees—have been upset with FEMA over the fact that hundreds of manufactured homes intended for use by hurricane survivors remain empty almost two years after Katrina, at the time of this writing. Meanwhile, many victims of the storm are still in need of housing.

This has made for quite an ugly controversy, featured in headline stories of newspapers from coast to coast as well as numerous television newsmagazines. I'm not going to address that issue here, except to point out that FEMA workers have merely adhered to the federally mandated guidelines that govern their operation. They are legally obligated to follow certain rules, no matter what the circumstance. The workers who must follow the rules aren't the same people who make them. Had FEMA personnel not followed the rules, they'd have broken the law and been punished accordingly. That's bureaucracy for you.

I confess I could never do what they do. They must wait on permission from the government before they act, and I simply couldn't. Emergencies don't wait for permission to develop. How can effective responses? I'm too impatient for that. What's more, I don't think it's wise—especially in the face of overwhelming needs.

I'm not suggesting that responses to emergencies should be exe-

cuted in a reactive, half-cocked manner. What's offered must be offered responsibly. I'm just saying there are many situations in which
detailed regulation offers more hurt than help. Some responses call
for decisions to be made and for help to be offered at the speed of
light.

When I encounter a homeless family who's lost everything to the
ravages of a natural disaster, I can quickly determine if they need a
place to stay. If I were in charge of FEMA and its trailers, I'd instantly
match the available homes with the homeless. After that I'd be
fired—maybe prosecuted.

In the midst of the Katrina and Rita debacles, the television journalist Geraldo Rivera actually called on President George Bush to
name me director of FEMA. He was serious, I think. I've never asked
him. I'm afraid he might tell me he wasn't! Nevertheless, the president didn't offer me the job, so I didn't have to decline.

Instead, I went right on administrating Feed The Children—a
private charity that is, thank God, accountable to those who support it and no one else.

During Katrina and Rita, Feed The Children met the needs of
many people who were successfully placed in trailer camps, such as
one in Baker, Louisiana, where we delivered twelve truckloads of
food. For some perspective on how much food this represents, suffice it to say that each forty-eight-foot trailer filled from top to bottom is virtually a supermarket on wheels.

The recipients of these goods were making do in temporary
housing. We tried to help them create a sense of home, complete
with underwear, socks, televisions, toys, and sundry items of personal comfort—not the least of which was an ample supply of food.

Some among this twice-displaced group suffered yet a third body
blow of bad luck. They sought jobs in towns where unemployment
was high, the economy weak. Many reported being given food and
even money by well-wishers who then asked them to move on to another town. They were warned not to compete for jobs with the
longtime local residents.

I think of Dedrick and Melanie, a couple whom Katrina and
Rita had driven out of both Louisiana and Texas prior to their set-

tling in Memphis, Tennessee. Their Memphis neighbors greeted them not with open arms but with guarded suspicion. They were viewed as tragic transients who would likely bring nothing to the community but an increase in the crime rate. Nothing could have been further from the truth.

Christmastime came, and the couple continued to endure antagonism from Memphis locals who insisted that they leave. When Dedrick and Melanie refused, their apartment door was kicked down, and their meager belongings were stolen. When they still refused to leave, Dedrick was shot.

Thankfully, he survived. Believing it better to leave than to push their luck any further, Dedrick and Melanie returned to Louisiana with no home, no prospects, and no reason to hope that things would ever get any better.

That's when Feed The Children discovered their predicament and stepped in to help. We subsidized their relocation with rent money, food, and necessities. With renewed strength, Dedrick and Melanie worked hard to get back on their feet. At the time of this writing, both are gainfully employed.

Feed The Children is unique among charities in its ability to respond to emergencies immediately and directly and in its freedom to improvise, creating solutions tailored to real-world needs rather than trying to fit problems into existing policies that bureaucrats create. This has been the charity's practice since its founding. Our people have had a lot of experience, and we're very good at it. Working this way hasn't eliminated imperfections, but it certainly has minimized them.

After Katrina, journalists had a field day attacking a New Orleans chapter of the Red Cross. They clearly had no idea what the dedicated Red Cross workers were up against. They, too, were victims of the storm. Almost half of them had lost their own homes. Two staffers lost family members.

No charity, public or private, is fully equipped to respond to nature's full-tilt fury like that seen during hurricanes Katrina and Rita. Destruction of that magnitude is impossible to anticipate. In these particular cases, it was all but impossible to imagine. Nothing in any living person's experience could have helped him or her know exactly what kinds of and how much relief supplies to keep at the ready and how to distribute them on such a mass scale.

All any charity can do is monitor its inventory and stay prepared to dispense what it has on hand. At best, such preparedness will enable it to serve some of the people some of the time. At worst, the next emergency might blindside the charity with human needs it never anticipated.

After that, all any charity can do is regroup, quietly bracing for nature's next cataclysm, knowing it can't predict when it will transpire, only that it surely will.

Chapter Twenty-four

*M*ORE THAN THIRTY-SEVEN THOUSAND PATIENTS are treated annually at Houston's 178-bed Children's Memorial Hermann Hospital. At 6:30 a.m. on June 1, 2006, amid the usual morning marathon of confident doctors in hospital scrubs leaning over frightened children in pastel pajamas, Daniel Wachira awaited his first surgery of many to come. Scurrying figures in surgical masks and plastic hairnets hustled about him rattling carts of prescription drugs, hypodermic syringes, plasma, and other intensive care materials.

They wheeled him into a ten-by-ten-foot preoperative room, and the four-year-old nodded off under the influence of a strawberry-flavored oral sedative. Stronger anesthetics that would alleviate the pain and trauma of his upcoming eleven hours of massively invasive surgery awaited him. Two of the nation's most esteemed reconstructive surgeons were at Daniel's side. They didn't stand; they knelt, praying for God's hand to guide their own, asking aloud for God's guidance of their skills.

The praying doctors eventually spoke more rapidly, intensifying their pleas for heavenly help to correct the horrible disfigurement inflicted on Daniel by a hungry dog minutes after the child's birth. Daniel had been orphaned inside an African slum on a garbage dump, a filthy, rancid, and insect-infested repository for a half ton of unwanted refuse and one unwanted baby.

When he was a newborn, his first visitor was a viciously carnivorous mammal. Like the child, the animal was fighting for survival. The dog's nutrition that day was baby Daniel's ear, part of his foot, and half of his face. Even at this horrendous scene, Daniel had experienced his first miracle. The fact that the ravenous mongrel had not been attracted to the bloody tissue of his umbilical cord was in-conceivable.

"If the dog had pulled that cord, he would have pulled Daniel away and eaten him alive," my wife, Frances, deduced. "But he didn't, and that began a series of wonders in his life."

The newborn screeched in pain. Daniel's hysteria jolted a passerby who didn't pass by. Hence, another miracle. Daniel's piercing cries had penetrated her heart. She summoned police, who took him to a hospital, where he st ayed for the next eight months in a small bassinet with several other babies. His extremities had started to grow into soft semicircles inside the contoured crib. Daniel, already missing part of his face, was indignity waiting to happen.

His arrival at the Frances Jones Abandoned Baby Center, sponsored since its 2001 founding by Feed The Children, was his next miracle. His path to restoration was now before him.

Frances worked on Daniel's behalf for the next eighteen months to assemble the plan for his facial reconstruction. Her journey ended at the Houston hospital, two continents away from Nairobi, Kenya, where Daniel was born.

During preoperative procedures, little Daniel moved only slightly after ingesting the synthetic strawberry solution. He wearily nodded yes when asked if he liked the drink. He tried to sip again, but was too sleepy to swallow, even through a straw. Soon he was completely out, and gone was his memory of that relaxing elixir and the way he once looked.

Before he went under, his last glance into a mirror reflected for the final time the image of a face minus a left cheek beneath a sagging eye atop a missing ear above an absentee lip. Scarred skin, not fatty tissue, was all that covered a quarter of his frontal cranium.

Before entering his medicinal trance, Daniel babbled delightful nonsense that surgeons and onlookers won't remember. However, no one will forget Daniel's words uttered days earlier in childish desperation.

"My face is broken," he told Dr. Sean Boutros, the team-leading surgeon. "My face is broken. Will you fix it?"

Daniel, and perhaps others inside the waiting facility, didn't hear Boutros's soft vow as he departed for the operating room.

"Here we go, Daniel," the doctor almost whispered. "We're going to fix your face."

FOR FRANCES, the wait didn't begin; it continued in the same stop-and-go staccato that was her tempo during her previous year and a half with Daniel. Occasionally, he's left her side. Never has he left her prayers.

She steadied Daniel most of the night before the first of four operations. Arising at 4:30 a.m. on the day of the initial procedure, she waited for Daniel until he was brought from the operating room near midnight. She slept in a chair beside his bed, which was draped with medical tubes running in and out of their subtly breathing patient. Daniel was not aware that his "Mama Frances" was present. He saw her only in wistful dreams.

Daniel's recovery room temperature was eighty-five degrees, an intentionally warm setting that accelerates healing after skin grafting. The temperature was especially taxing on Frances, whose lupus is exacerbated by heat. She never complained because she's made that way. Fatigue also weakens the victims of lupus. She became too tired to talk, except when it came to words about Daniel. Even the sound of the medical equipment monitoring his motionless body inspired her.

"There's a Doppler machine, a sound-sensitive gauge that's used every fifteen minutes to measure the blood flow to his skin grafts," Frances explained. "It's electronic, and it purrs so softly that it sounds like the wind."

"Like the rushing wind described in Acts?" someone asked.

"No," Frances said. "The sound is softer, sweeter, like the flutter of tiny angel wings.

"There's something special about Daniel."

I'd heard her say that before, but never with the fervor she had during the first hour of Daniel's postoperative care.

"Larry once said having him inside your house is like having the presence of Jesus," a visitor pointed out, fearing that the analogy was melodramatic.

Frances, however, instantly concurred. She was qualified to know, given all the years she's spent talking to children, and to Jesus Himself.

Someone noted that even Jesus' first resting place, a manger, was more dignified than Daniel's. The Christ child was surrounded with domestic animals that perhaps disquieted him. The animals stirred and made noise. Not one tried to eat him.

The baby Jesus had lain in unknown danger from one of Herod's soldiers; Daniel had lain in harm's way from a cold-blooded animal. Both infants were sought for killing. Both survived.

For years Frances has employed the same driver to take her through the blighted parts of Nairobi. Together, they've encountered the city's decaying and filthy underbelly. Yet the driver wouldn't take Frances to the part of the city where Daniel was found when she wanted to see it for herself.

"It's just too rough," he told her. "You and I won't be safe there."

Given the precautions necessary for adults, I could only imagine how dangerous it was for a naked and partially eaten baby amid the ruthless men who sell young children, as well as the hungry animals who eat them. Daniel began life as a helpless and luring centerpiece for predators, man or beast.

"Do you really think Daniel is special?" Frances was asked again.

Her response was an impromptu litany of praise for the little guy.

Frances told anyone who'd listen that Daniel is the third child she's brought to the United States during our twenty-eight years of treating and feeding untold millions, and the *only* one who ever lived with us.

"Why would I, a sixty-four-year-old woman, bring home a four-year-old to live with us?" she asked herself. "That in itself is a miracle, and it came from something special about this boy. He's like Jesus in so many ways, and the best any of us can do is to strive to be like Jesus. This child does that and doesn't know it."

Dr. Todd Price, who recruited the two-member team of surgeons, later agreed that there's "something special about Daniel." He was the third person of the day to stress that fact without solicitation. Those words don't come lightly from a doctor who annually negotiates overseas missions in which he personally immunizes children against disease. He's treated impoverished and malnourished youngsters as they waited in lines for as far as he could see.

He sees patients at least five days a week, but saw none on the afternoon of Daniel's surgery. He canceled appointments to stand by the doctors who stood over the thirty-eight-pound boy.

"I don't know why I came today except that I couldn't stay away," Price told Frances and me.

The night before, Price named Daniel the guest of honor at a dinner attended by Price's wife and his two children, Frances, a friend, and me. Daniel's always unpredictable behavior made the doctor proud. Frances had asked the child to say grace, thinking he'd respond with a youngster's predictable prayer. Daniel didn't know the food would be his last full meal before surgery. Frances and company didn't know that Daniel would pray not only for the food but for everyone at the table. Individually and by name.

Daniel's arms, once bent in deformity, now stretched and systematically pointed one by one to each of the seven people surrounding him. A youngster whose education barely included preschool prayed personal prayers for five adults holding as many college degrees. Two have Ph.D.'s. The one who prayed this night had graduated from nothing except infancy and the school of survival.

Daniel knew exactly what he was doing, as evidenced by his familiarity with everyone at the table. Amazingly, he'd met one of them only once, a week earlier, during a few minutes spent on the Eastern Seaboard fifteen hundred miles away.

"How many four-year-olds have a memory like that?" Frances asked. "How many can remember seven people after a week of meeting maybe a hundred others?" No one answered. Each was silenced by marvel at the youngster's recall and consideration.

"Most children this age are focused only on themselves," Frances said. "I've never seen a child so thoughtful. God has a place for this boy that defies my understanding."

Frances pointed out another delightful eccentricity that others have affirmed. If Daniel accidentally bumps someone's hand, he notices. The other person can't help but notice when he instantly snatches his or her palm, massages it, and apologizes for his intrusion. Frances recalled Daniel's ritual inside our home, where he places his clothes in order and matches his shoes in a line, pair by pair. He enacts the same scenario on the footwear belonging to Frances and me. At the fifty-four-bed ABC, Daniel was seen going from bed to bed as soon as he learned to walk. He chattered comforting words as he hugged the other children to console them.

Frances's assessments of the child prodigy prompted no arguments, not from Price, whose medicine has given children life, and not from me, whose prayers have been their eulogies. She instead received unified and positive answers to rhetorical questions concerning Daniel, the regular recipient of miracles.

Someone said Daniel has the frame of one whose growth is stunted but whose mind is expanded. Additional anecdotes confirmed that, and they kept coming.

There was Daniel's first visit to New York City, where he couldn't see the tops of buildings inside low-lying clouds.

"I can't see the top," said Daniel. He obviously knew nothing about cloud cover, so he simply spoke the obvious.

"I don't know what to think," he said, awaiting an adult's explanation. The grown-up also didn't know what to think, dumbfounded by the boy's penchant for obvious logic.

Little boys like cars. Few have seen limousines, and of those who have, fewer have noticed their exaggerated size. Daniel did.

A stretch car stopped in front of Daniel as he monitored Manhattan traffic.

"That's long," he said about the vehicle. "Is that all one car?"

The query, like the others, was rational. The logic from a prekindergartner? Exceptional.

Perhaps the most telling incident about the awareness and personal security of a disfigured youngster came during a national telecast. Two months before his first surgery, Daniel was held in the arms of Pastor Joel Osteen before sixteen thousand people. The lad was unaccustomed to mammoth gatherings and should have been intimidated at being the focus of such a group.

Osteen gently coaxed the little guy toward oratory. Everyone in the audience and on the platform simply thought Daniel was shy. He wasn't; he was calculating. He'd coyly observed that the person whose voice carried across the crowd always held a microphone. Daniel determined that to be heard, he needed to speak into the shiny thing that no one let him hold.

Daniel continued to remain silent. The audience grew still, and I now realize that he intentionally let them. He suddenly snatched the microphone from Osteen, one of the most high-profile preachers in North America. The startled minister and his onstage cadre instantly laughed aloud as Daniel grabbed the instrument. The crowd followed suit, roaring its loving approval of a tot's bravery mistakenly thought to be fear.

Daniel wasn't finished. He let the uproar subside, and the crowd waited in suspense to see what, if anything, he'd do next. Would he laugh or cry? Neither.

"My name is Daniel," he said. "I am four years old. I am from Kenya, and Jesus loves me."

Then he suddenly began to sing "Jesus Loves Me."

An arena that had earlier been filled with amplified instruments and raised voices again fell silent, stilled by the echo of a child's delicate soprano. When Daniel sang his last note, the room was mute with awe. Then it suddenly erupted into thunderous applause.

"The audience had been 'Danielized,' " I later said, jokingly. My assessment was amusing not because it was funny but because it was so accurate.

The bombing of the Murrah Federal Building in 1995 and the mass-media coverage of Feed The Children's 120 days of rescue translated into the overdue "exposure" of our charity to the world. The coverage of Daniel's miraculous rescue at birth became the ministry's most striking single event to put a face on what we do.

God happened to use an imperfect face.

That face has nonetheless been seen on countless local and network television shows. It has graced major newspapers from Los Angeles to Florida, and notices in policy-shaping periodicals, including *Newsweek*. Daniel's life is a herald for humanity, as reported in the foreign press, where his likeness adorned front pages throughout Europe. Feed The Children's work at the tsunami, at Hurricane Katrina, at New York City's slaughter on 9/11, at the Murrah bombing, in Bosnia, and in Third World countries has not generated compassionate interest like that shown for a solitary child who emerged from the bowels of desperation found in the darkest side of Africa.

The world is searching for a hero. Some people already see that hero in a youngster who somehow arose from lying at death's door to gain the attention of the whole world.

Daniel rose to a level reserved for someone who's launched by God. His life is still rising, his story still spreading, his spirit still deepening. God only knows how this saga began, how it will end, and, more important, how many lives it will touch on its glorious way.

DANIEL'S STORY has put another face on our outreach. That face belongs to the millions of unseen people who underwrite what we do. In the months preceding Daniel's reconstructive surgery, I realized that the donors who send the funds to help Daniel are modern-day Samaritans, and there's one who's a Samaritan's Samaritan.

Hers is another invisible face of the ministry. I speak of the Samaritan who took the time to respond to Daniel's dying cries, and took additional time to attend to his need.

When Jesus told the story of the Good Samaritan, he spoke of someone beaten and left in a ditch, dire circumstances similar to Daniel's.

A priest and a Levite preceded Jesus' Samaritan. They passed by the man in distress before the Samaritan came by. I wonder how many people eased by Daniel.

His story reminded me of a reporter's man-on-the-street interview.

"What are the two most pressing problems in America?" he asked.

"I don't know, and I don't care," the subject responded.

"You're absolutely right!" the journalist replied.

Feed The Children is a nonprofit, private charity supported by people who know and care.

Daniel has become the most recognizable of all the ministry's beneficiaries. An unidentified African woman, Daniel's rescuer, was an unknown soldier in our war on suffering. Her rank was higher than a seasoned general's. She was a Samaritan, if only for an instant. The ramifications will be seen throughout Daniel's life. And that life will touch other lives that will touch other lives. That's how it goes with God, who selects imperfect people to change an imperfect world for the better, and forever.

FRIDAY, June 2, 2006, was a springlike overture to the kind of summer that Houstonians dread, when, no matter how high the temperature, the humidity is almost always higher. The day began with gentle rainfall, and by afternoon Houston was a soft sauna amid skyscrapers that blocked a hint of breeze from the Gulf of Mexico.

Inside the hospital pressroom, the bright lights of television cameras elevated temperatures. A few journalists shed their coats and loosened their ties, despite air-conditioning.

The men at the speakers' table didn't notice the interior climate. Each was accustomed to the heat of surgical illumination. Two of the three had stood for almost half of the previous day under electrical searing while meticulously repairing the face that Daniel had insisted was broken.

Boutros and Dr. Michael J. Miller were introduced to the press corps by Price, whose learned colleagues compassionately participated in the historic undertaking because they were asked, and were asked only once.

Boutros and Miller at first struggled to reduce their scientific parlance to a layman's vernacular. A reporter winced when Boutros used terms such as "distraction osteogenesis," knowing the press at large wouldn't understand, and therefore couldn't communicate with readers en masse.

Yet the physicians soon fell into individual monologues that fluently explained marvels that evolved into miracles through medicine. Frances and I, for weeks, had been enlightened about Daniel's surgery more than any other nonmedical people in the gathering. We were nonetheless transfixed, hearing some things for the first time.

"When I first saw Daniel," said Boutros, "it turns out that it was a little bit more of a surgery than I initially thought. He would require a much larger procedure."

"When Daniel was attacked by a dog," Boutros continued, "the dog managed to eat all of the cheek tissue, about 40 percent of his lip tissue and eyelid tissue. All of this tissue is replaced by a skin graft, which was taken over by a scar. As a result, his entire face became distorted with this scar, and it prevented the bone from growing properly. As a result, his face was twisted and deformed."

Miller explained that the operation had been twofold: the repair of bone, or Daniel's lower mandible, and the replacement of skin tissue.

His jaw would be stretched by screws inserted in parts of its bone. They'd be turned one rotation three times a day for almost a week, ensuring the lengthening of that part of his skeleton.

Frances would be taught how to manipulate the screws. The rotation was crucial, as turning the screws too much would shatter Daniel's lower face. That was additional pressure she didn't need.

The scar tissue on Daniel's face had been removed, the doctors explained, and was replaced with skin removed from one-quarter of his back.

My thoughts raced to the part of Daniel that I knew best, the walking sunshine who'd undergone surgical Olympics, trauma that could have undone someone much larger and less tough. A few stories above us, Daniel still slept, unaware that he was the priority of the best and brightest medical minds, as well as journalists nation-wide.

The meeting lasted thirty minutes. The caregiving marathon had culminated in its thirtieth hour.

Frances returned to the hotel to freshen up, and then stationed herself on a cot, where she was awakened every hour as Daniel's intensive care was monitored. I thought about her lupus, agitated by fatigue and heat, and how rest eluded her inside a sweltering room. Its thermostat remained locked at eighty-five degrees.

Still, she wouldn't leave Daniel.

On June 4, I departed Houston for Feed The Children's Oklahoma City headquarters, then flew the next day to Chicago and points east. I rejoined my administration of daily feeding 1.5 million children.

Daniel took a turn for the worse . . . twice.

His body's acceptance of the skin graft was dependent on increased oxygen, and tubes carrying life support had been inserted into his nostrils. As the anesthetic began to wear off, he stirred, unknowingly flailing his arms. He almost ripped the tubes from his "new" nose. His surgery was four days old.

Despite arm restraints, seventy-two hours later Daniel succeeded in freeing himself from the oxygen by taking his nose to his hands and jerking out the tubes. He lay unattended for three minutes, during which he didn't breathe.

When Frances called me, I could hear the subdued terror in her voice. She'd been told there was a possibility, however remote, of Daniel's having suffered severe complications through oxygen deprivation.

Her bedside vigil intensified, as she executed her nonstop watch virtually without food or rest. On June 7, Daniel was again sleeping soundly when the life-threatening scenario repeated itself. He again jerked away the oxygen tubes, conduits to his lungs.

My wife and I believe every part of the Bible, including passages that are reassuring and those that are unsettling. One can't spiritually subsist with half a faith. If we believe in the forces of all that is good, the spirit of God, we must also believe in the forces of all that is evil, the spirit of Satan. That's the most basic of biblical themes, those commonly accepted by all Christian faiths and denominations.

Frances and I have felt the presence of God and its sweet goodness during our missions and personal lives. We join untold millions who regularly undergo that joyful bliss. We've also, however, felt the forces of evil in some of the godless places where Satan has ravaged the minds and bodies of those who don't know God. Those people, many of whom we feed, don't realize there's an invisible enemy who'll undermine their lives, just as there's a God who'll sustain them.

No one can fight an enemy without first identifying him. Frances has time-proven discernment in recognizing the spirit of destruction. Some call Satan the devil. That's not to say he wears a red suit and carries a pitchfork. The devil is a force, a loathing and a life-stealing spirit.

"The devil is trying to take Daniel," Frances told a friend during a telephone call from the hospital. "The devil is trying to take Daniel. I won't let him."

And so my wife, who had sometimes physically carried Daniel on parts of his trip from Africa to America, carried him again in relentless prayer. With a hand on Daniel and another on a telephone, she solicited the unified prayers of scattered friends of Feed The Children. Our employees gathered to pray, combating the satanic assault on Daniel and his life-support system. Under Frances's direction, many workers sent e-mails to prayer partners around the globe.

In a dark and hot Houston pediatric intensive care unit, accompanied only by a deep-sleeping child and her spirit of prayer, my wife fought exhaustion and lupus while staging her personal offense against that which Satan would undermine. As of this writing, she and the God she serves are winning.

She called me countless times on day nine of Daniel's fragile recovery. Her voice was weak as a result of that grueling mixture of stress, exhaustion, and trauma. I'd seen Frances walk through the world's most deprived ghettos. I've watched her stoop under sniper's fire and work around the clock to get food and medicine to those who needed it, whether in front of battle or behind its lines.

I prayed that my wife would once again get through any opposition to sustain the life of a child who'd arrested the hearts of the world. Only God knew if she and Daniel would go through Satan's opposition. He and Frances each knew that no matter what, she'd go on until she or Daniel died, or until victory prevailed.

Chapter Twenty-five

*H*ARLEM HAS TWO CULTURES.

One is made up of the night people who currently indulge in crack cocaine, who replaced those who indulged in powdered cocaine, who replaced those who indulged in bathtub gin—the history of such local vices dating back to the Great Depression. The other culture is made up of the day people—the solid citizens, many of whom are working single mothers who regularly see too little money with too much month remaining.

At 5:00 a.m. on December 21, 2006, beleaguered people from both factions filed into multiple lines for Feed The Children's last food drop of the year. We had joined forces with the National Basketball Players Association, Harlem's Abyssinian Baptist Church, and random volunteers to feed approximately forty thousand people for about a week. It was the largest distribution effort in the organization's history.

The outdoor temperature, an unseasonably warm thirty-eight degrees, rose to a daytime high of fifty-four. A contagious spirit of goodwill filled the air with warmth that was beyond measure.

Some of the needy stood in line for five hours before the distribution of boxed meals began at 8:00 a.m. Then they stood a while longer, waiting their turn to receive a ninety-two-pound package that included nutrition, hygiene, beverage products, and *surprises*.

Many recipients didn't arrive until after they got off work, forming new lines that snaked around corners from 135th to 139th streets along Seventh Avenue. The last parcels were passed out at 10:00 p.m., almost fourteen hours after the distribution had begun.

By then, many recipients were waiting with their backs braced against the icy midwinter wind. The darkness of the moonless night engulfed them all, sporadically penetrated by the glow of televisions tuned to local network affiliates covering the landmark charity event.

This Harlem food drop was my twenty-third in eighteen years. Everything was distributed from thirty of FTC's eighteen-wheel long-haul trucks, which collectively carried 900,000 pounds of nonperishables, administrated by four hundred volunteers from multiple churches, social agencies, and FTC.

And when the last truck pulled off the site, it was followed by the glistening eyes of hungry people who would, despite our efforts, too soon be hungry again.

So many people, so much ongoing need. The sad truth is that FTC can't feed all of the people all of the time. We have never had the wherewithal to do so, and I'm fairly certain we never will. Given the abundance in the world, and if the world was more fair, we shouldn't have to.

"This is called 'The Miracle on 138th Street,' " said a Harlem official at a press conference that same day. "It shouldn't take a miracle for us to feed our people."

I knew what she meant.

The Christmas season had been laced with television programs addressing the issue of benevolence. Statistics were trotted out—especially the one claiming that about 10 percent of the world's population controls 90 percent of the world's resources. One network profiled the philanthropic habits of the high-profile billionaires. Across the United States, the majority of such people gave only a fraction of their incomes to the less fortunate. One national personality, whose net worth had been ten billion dollars, saw it plunge to two billion dollars. He said he was no longer making donations to the needy. He said he had tried it and found it to be unsatisfying.

Some in the food line that day were oblivious to this TV exposé on the giving habits of the rich and famous—and for a good reason. They didn't own a television.

Trump Tower on Fifth Avenue is only about seventy blocks from the Wagner Houses in East Harlem, but it might as well be in another universe. It is, perhaps, in a way. "They epitomize the highest and lowest earning census tracts in Manhattan, where the disparity between rich and poor is now greater than in any other county in the country," wrote Sam Roberts in a September 4, 2005, story in the *New York Times*.

On the day of our Christmas season outreach, the average annual household income in midtown Manhattan was $875,267, compared with $41,966 in Harlem. We were feeding some five-member families whose wage earners brought in less than $25,000 annually—if they were working. Others drew financial aid from the state. Still others had no legal income.

FTC wasn't there to overhaul Harlem's economic structure. We made no pretense of being able to provide for much more than the people's most fundamental needs—and those only temporarily.

While New York City may be the world's financial capital, more than one million people go to bed hungry there each night, according to the New York City Coalition Against Hunger. We were helpless to modify this basic statistic in a lasting manner.

Another chilling statistic states that 62 percent of children in Harlem are under the care of their grandparents. Their parents simply departed, having lost the war on poverty, drugs, and unemployment or gone AWOL from the constant battle for dignity and sustenance that is the nature of daily experience in parts of Harlem.

Even a charity with the explosive growth of FTC can muster no more than a breeze against a hurricane of recurring hunger, including that in Harlem, one neighborhood in one borough in one city in one nation. Nevertheless, on that one day and for those hours, we were able to take people's minds away from their empty pantries by providing them with preparations enough for meals before, during, and after Christmas Day.

Perhaps they spent the holiday worrying about how they'd pay the January rent. If so, at least they didn't do it on an empty stomach.

For me, it was a time of giving thanks for another year's work with FTC. We were, after all, the conduit through which the kindness of donors had reached forth to the desperate.

I reflected on the charity's first mission, the one in Haiti before the organization even had a name. Frances and I utilized the proceeds from donors we'd never met. We entrusted grain to people we'd never seen to feed people who wondered if they'd ever see another meal. It seemed not all that long ago. But with this mission, four days before Christmas 2006, we had almost as many volunteers as we had beneficiaries in that charter mission.

During that 1979 undertaking, our efforts and organization were unknown. Twenty-eight years later, some of the nation's most famous people were joining us to provide daily sustenance to 1.5 million on a global scale.

For our Harlem event, about thirty members of the mass media participated in a press conference featuring Senator Hillary Rodham Clinton as well as star players of the NBA, including Kareem Abdul-Jabbar, a former Los Angeles Laker and Hall of Famer returned to his native New York City. He was flanked by Kobe Bryant, the new millennium's answer to Michael Jordan.

I thanked God for the endorsement of these celebrities, many of whom are seen on our national telecasts. Again I thought about that initial outreach, when Frances and I had co-labored with virtually no one except an obscure but kindhearted Haitian preacher.

I looked at the platoons of policemen who guarded our precious food cargo, ensuring order among those eager to receive it. Many officers came on assignment by the City of New York. Others were donating a day off to provide their uniformed presence.

I reflected on former food drops when FTC wasn't provided with security by the local police force. In 1993, for example, I went to South Chicago for a drop inside a blighted neighborhood, where I came toe-to-toe with chalk outlines on asphalt where two people had been murdered. The crime scene lay on a lot adjacent to where we parked our Feed The Children truck.

I was afraid that response to FTC's first-ever Chicago food drop would be dampened by promixity to the crime. I was wrong. People came to the food drop directly from church, placed their Bibles atop stacks of donated food, and headed home. For some, the food we provided was the real-life fulfillment of the biblical story about manna from heaven.

I remember feeling uneasy and hoping to distribute all the food before nightfall, lest the gunfire be renewed.

During the "Miracle on 138th Street," I relished the support of so many police and remembered again the times when law enforcement had not so readily embraced FTC as it does today.

As recently as five years earlier, FTC staged a food drop in Cincinnati in the wake of civil riots. One of our trucks was parked beside a homeless shelter, and about two hundred people formed a line to begin receiving our offerings.

Abruptly, about fifty people came from nowhere, forcing themselves ahead of those who were already there waiting. A fiery argument ensued, and a small squad of well-intentioned police officers struggled to push them back. Still, the intruders broke through.

The wives of Jack Rickett, leader of FTC's volunteers, and Carson Palmer, quarterback of the Cincinnati Bengals, were caught between the angry mob and the side of the truck. FTC workers inside the cab hung out its window and attempted to pull the women to safety. Shaelyn Palmer's legs were pinned between the pressing throng and the side of the truck. For an instant she seemed in danger of being pulled to the ground, beneath the feet of angry agitators. Volunteers were screaming for the crowd to settle down, but to no avail.

One policeman suddenly brandished mace, spraying it into the air but intentionally avoiding hitting anyone. Finally the aggressors dispersed toward the end of the line, where they belonged.

Cincinnati was still in the grip of the anger that had originally given rise to the riots. For some reason, the excitement surrounding FTC's visit almost revived that madness. But the food drop proceeded without further incident.

At the Harlem drop, I found myself thankful for FTC's most valuable intangible asset: credibility.

After little more than a quarter century of delivering on our promises, and despite many efforts to discredit us, FTC has earned a solid reputation for dependability. Desperately hungry or victimized people know they can count on us.

As I walked the food lines in Harlem, people told me and my associates that they were cold, hungry, and frustrated. Restlessness was brewing. Understandably so, as people feared there might be no food left when they at last reached the distribution point. They'd stood in that line for a very long time, and they were hungry before they got there.

"There are so many of us," I heard so many say. "Are you sure you won't run out of food, or that someone else won't get my share?"

"You have a ticket," I calmly reassured them. "You'll get all of your food. Trust me."

And they did. People in Harlem trusted me, a stranger to them, because they had heard from people they respected—people to whom FTC had proven its mettle in previous food drops—that I was trustworthy.

I gazed out across the sea of FTC volunteers. Some lived as far as a thousand miles away, yet they participated regularly in FTC's missions. I'd seen them before, but we'd never met. They were there to help—not to seek recognition for helping.

I remembered some from FTC's relief efforts after Hurricane Katrina, when we had dispatched twenty-five trucks, each carrying seventy thousand dollars' worth of food, to four distribution points in Louisiana and Mississippi. They'd been right there with us, feeding victims by day and sleeping nights in open fields beside the people whose needs they had come to attend.

The Harlem food drop was 2006's final reminder about the goodness within the hearts of everyday people—not only in giving, but also in receiving. I was often approached by people who told me they'd seen me on FTC's televised food drops, but witnessing a live drop affected them in a way they hadn't expected. They felt overwhelmed with gratitude, not just for themselves, but also for their neighbors. Where Feed The Children had previously been just a television program, seeing it all happen made it real.

"You really do care about us," a woman said.

"People don't care how much you know until they know you care," I thought, repeating the old saying silently to myself.

Some passersby who needed no food were nonetheless drawn to the huge FTC logo on our trucks. They introduced themselves, presenting cards that identified them as FTC donors. They said they felt as if they were a part of the goings-on. They were.

I recalled the first time FTC joined forces with the National Basketball Players Association five years earlier. It had been here at this place, at the same time of year. We fed only half as many people in twice as much time, during a blizzard. We've since done countless drops in major cities from coast to coast, including Los Angeles, Oakland, and New Orleans.

My nostalgic thoughts drifted to Billy Hunter, then executive director of the players association, and to negotiating our plans for that premiere collaboration. I envisioned a drop scheduled several months in the futrue. He wanted to do it in three weeks. I thought he expected to feed a few people at a small homeless shelter.

He wanted to feed five thousand people.

At that time Feed The Children had never done a scheduled drop that large.

"If you're as good as you say you are, you can do it," Hunter told me. "I'm from the Show Me State of Missouri. Now, show me how we're going to do this. Make a believer out of me, then we'll go forward."

We began counting down from twenty-one days.

First impressions really are the most lasting. I was determined to administrate this food drop without a glitch, hoping the players association would thereafter partner with FTC regularly. We amassed the food; the players association subsidized the fuel for the trucks and committed many celebrity athletes for live appearance. The clock was ticking on a world-changing experiment.

FTC employees and volunteers were prayerful and sure we could pull it off. Some Harlem residents apparently weren't as confident.

The City of New York posted notice not to park on 138th Street on the date of the drop, as space was needed for the lines of eighteen-wheel trucks. People ignored the city's mandate, and cars were snowbound where the trucks were supposed to park.

City officials ordered the cars to be towed. Harlem residents who had been merely hungry were now also outraged.

The players association had bonded with FTC in order to continue their compassionate help for needy people. It could be argued that the forced towing of vehicles provoked negative publicity. Many television viewers and newspaper readers agreed.

The 8:00 a.m. distribution drew a crowd that assembled at 5:00 a.m. Snowfall alternated with freezing rain. A stiff wind created a chill factor in the teens. People loaded carts with food, then couldn't push them through accumulating snow.

The weather worsened. Volunteer workers constantly wiped snow off the food drop boxes. Beverages froze inside the containers. Finally the last package was placed into weather-stiffened palms. At last the drop was finished.

On this maiden mission, FTC and the players association had given five thousand people enough food for twenty thousand. FTC had passed its audition with Hunter and the athletes. Two months later we staged the mission again in Los Angeles, under markedly different conditions. Our partnership continued through the 2006 drop and will continue here and abroad. As long as a hand extends in hunger, we will reach to fill it.

DARKNESS RENDERED the last recipients virtually invisible as I departed Harlem in 2006. The lines were still almost a block long, being constantly replenished by streams of tired people who'd ridden subways after a hard day's work to await their turn for food.

Many of those waiting nudged closely to the walls of bordering buildings, camouflaging themselves against the aged bricks whose texture was as battered as their lives. From the street, human outlines were a blur.

I could nonetheless picture the people in my mind's eye. I knew they had dirt, calluses, and time on their hands, all warmed inside pockets that were as empty as their stomachs. Thanks to FTC and those who support it, at least their stomachs would be filled before nightfall's gray eased to ebony.

My car turned the corner into holiday traffic, caught at a standstill. We inched forward only intermittently. To my right, I saw the weary stacked in the food line that barely moved. Nevertheless, they were making slow progress. They were moving forward. They would keep walking.

And so will I.

ON MARCH 8, 2007, I embarked on the year's first regularly scheduled overseas tour, a biannual trip to the Dagoretti Children's Center and the Frances Jones Abandoned Baby Center near Nairobi,
Kenya. I wanted to check up on the operations of both facilities and
monitor the distribution of food to the ninety-two thousand children we'd taken on responsibility for feeding during a July 2006
visit.

The trip was unusually packed with planned activities. It also
held some surprise calamities and became yet another chapter in the
story of my life about expecting the unexpected.

My television crew had gone ahead of me on an earlier flight.
They checked ten bags carrying expensive technical equipment that
couldn't be replaced—at least not in Africa. Six of the ten went
missing. So on our first day of production, the crew worked without 60 percent of their gear. Somehow they were able to get the
footage we needed. But they would not have been able to do so on
the second day if their lost baggage hadn't eventually shown up. Our
crisis was resolved, the tension defused, and production resumed.

I often say that every disaster has its own personality. Actually,
the same is true of our planned feeding missions. When we return
to a distribution site we've established previously, it always feels like
we've never been there before. There's one thing we can always
count on: surprises. Some of these surprises limit or even undermine
the mission.

Helpers mysteriously fall ill from bacteria against which they've
previously been inoculated. A visa that's always allowed passage is
suddenly revoked by a government without explanation. A meeting

is scheduled with an orphanage official who wants to establish a program to feed a predetermined number of enrollees. Once in the meeting, he asks for twice as much food, and we begin scrambling to procure it.

Similar setbacks affected our African mission of 2007.

The crew and I set out for the half-mile walk into Dandora, a slum, intent on documenting the extreme deprivation to be found there. Of all the missions we've served in Kenya, I'd never been into that part of the country—and I wasn't prepared for the obstacle course we had to run to get there. No wonder these people were deprived. Few would take the pains to try to reach them.

I wasn't ready for the perilous route, but neither was I ready to turn back. I'd come ten thousand miles. My goal was to offer remedy to the desperation of those at the end of this treacherous mountain path.

Carefully placing each step, the crew and I eased forward.

The slope was steep, the rocks many, the path winding. One crew member stumbled but instantly yelled that he was fine. Good thing. This was no place to suffer a broken bone.

To illustrate the hazards, the cameraman captured the surroundings and the treacherous pathway on film. Stumbling, I turned to the camera three times, telling viewers, "We're almost there." One shot included my own feet slipping into an open sewer. My shoes remained sullied with human waste for the remainder of the project.

Whenever I struggle to get into a place, I wonder about the difficulty of getting out. I wonder if it might be my final journey into the depths of hunger, the one during which the hostile environment—or even a crazed victim of poverty—might prevent my return. Such thoughts are usually fleeting. I don't allow them much time in my mind. No one who does what I do can afford to.

I felt a need to go to Dandora because I knew I'd find what I almost always find in situations of such geographic and social isolation—a desperate need for food and provisions, and the follow-up commitment to send it regularly. Dandora was no exception.

I'd never seen that particular part of the world, but in a sense I'd been there before. The desperation I found there I've seen everywhere in my missionary travels. Hunger and deprivation know no boundaries. I certainly see no end to this being the case.

We remained in the region for approximately ten days. Scurrying to fulfill spontaneous and constant requests for food, we found ourselves running late in our television production schedule. Over and above our mission to document human suffering, our primary mission remains, of course, to serve needs where and when we find them.

Our television appeals are mini profiles of particularly needy persons or families, followed by a financial request for these victims and others like them. I often videotape two or three appeals in a day, and have done as many as a half dozen. On the last day of our first 2007 trip to Kenya, I did thirteen appeals in less than twelve hours. Though I have writers who often help me with such things, I wrote each of these personally. In some of the shoots we got what we needed in one take. Others required three or four. Our schedule had to allow traveling time between many places. Sometimes the crew and I trekked along barely passable paths; at times we bounced along barely negotiable roads.

Running behind schedule, we had to shoot like there was no tomorrow—because in this case there wasn't one. My flight home was scheduled to depart at 12:20 a.m. I needed at least two hours to get to my hotel. Forty-five minutes to pack and shower. A half hour for the ride to the airport. And time to be sufficiently early for my eight-hour flight to Zurich, Switzerland. A schedule this tight is rough on anyone, especially under the conditions one experiences in Africa. Making it all work was mentally numbing.

Nevertheless, I made it to the Nairobi airport in time.

I felt ready to collapse with exhaustion when I arrived in Zurich at 6:00 a.m.—which was 8:00 a.m. Nairobi time, where my body clock was stalled. I dozed wherever I happened to sit. Four hours later, when boarding began for the twelve-hour flight to Dallas, I fell into my seat.

We couldn't take off. The aircraft's computer had malfunctioned. For three hours I sat inside a disabled plane, where approximately two hundred other passengers and I awaited the arrival of an airplane part that came from Paris, but not until the next day.

The airline canceled the flight, as there were no others going to the United States for the rest of the day.

So I got off the plane and started booking my passage to Dallas for the next day. Once I arrived in Dallas, I would not be assured of a connecting flight, as I'd missed the one I'd been scheduled for. At this point there was no way for me to know whether that next day's connections might already be sold out.

Downstairs at the Zurich baggage claim, I scrambled for my things and boarded a bus bound for a hotel. Once there, other passengers and I were told that the bus would pick us up for our return to the airport at 5:45 a.m. I feared oversleeping. I had an alarm clock and hoped exhaustion would not prevent my hearing its ring. Sleep deprivation, crossing a time zone, jet lag, and the stress of running behind schedule during my ten days on the Dandora mission were all taking their toll.

I did, however, manage to awake. In predawn darkness I found my way to the bus and back to the airport. I was still so tired that I barely knew what day it was.

I flew twelve hours from Zurich to Dallas, arriving safely and on time. Other passengers on my flight were hustling to catch connecting flights on this busy Sunday afternoon. The airport teemed with travelers trying to get home from weekend excursions. I arrived at 7:30 p.m. on Sunday—which, to me, felt like 3:30 Monday morning, Nairobi time, since that's where my jet-lagged metabolism remained locked.

I felt depleted beyond description as I prepared to resume my hometown schedule. I found that it, too, was rife with surprises. While I was away, an old friend had died. I agreed to preach his funeral in El Reno, twenty miles from my office. The service was attended by three hundred people, who used an open microphone to reminisce about their experiences with the departed.

The 3:00 p.m. funeral, burial, and time with old friends lasted for four hours.

By 9:00 p.m., I was asleep in my own bed. Finally, without having to think, plan, or travel, I knew exactly where I was.

I RECOUNT ALL OF THE ABOVE simply to say this: this trip's helter-skelter ordeals were not entirely unusual for today's overseas travel. Many times my journeys come off without a hitch. Nonetheless, I have to travel aboard three, sometimes four aircraft to get from Oklahoma City to Africa. Calculate the round-trip math and you realize I depend on eight airplanes and their untold thousands of parts, eight flight crews, eight uncertain weather forecasts, eight handlings of my bags—thus virtually millions of possibilities for things to go wrong.

Citing economic reasons, airlines have been slower to update the aircraft they dispatch for overseas flights since September 11, 2001. The planes seem less reliable. The flights are fewer, so they are virtually always full. These factors have, in many cases, reduced the passenger experience from one of enjoyment to one of endurance. If you add to this the delays and cancellations, the net effect is stress that brings on exhaustion.

I love my work. I hate modern air travel. I must do what I hate to fulfill what I love. I meet many travelers who say they envy what I do. Why? I can't remember the last one who said he enjoyed traveling overseas these days.

Two thousand and eight will mark my twenty-ninth year of trotting the globe in behalf of FTC.

Sometimes, when I'm too fatigued to even read, my mind races back to previous mission trips. I think about the bullets that have missed me, the floods that haven't drowned me, the military aggression that has spared me, and God's grace that has *always* supported me.

As the saying goes, "God isn't always on time but He's never late." In due time, He has always come through over the course of my pursuing what I believe to be His calling for my life for almost three decades.

My mind races to particulars, such as the time African police detained Don Richardson and his wife, Gwen, for discrepancies regarding their visas. They were placed in a cell near other prisoners who didn't talk to them. (Most didn't speak English.) Their cell prominently featured one toilet in the middle of the open room.

Thankfully, they were able to maintain contact with FTC's home office. Someone from headquarters eventually got a call through to me. I gave the person a message, and my words were relayed to an English-speaking African jailer who, in turn, passed them on to Don.

The predicament was resolved, and the mission went forward.

I remember on another occasion being the last person in our group to depart Afghanistan. While alone there, I severely burned myself.

I'd been glad to get one of the few hotel rooms in Herat, located just twenty-five miles from the Iran border. The weather was cold—below freezing. A kerosene heater provided warmth. The supply of kerosene tended to run out daily around 4:00 a.m.

Thinking I might somehow modify the heater to make the fuel last longer, I reached around it and, in darkness, accidentally touched my bare arm on its hot surface. My burning skin stuck to the pipe. As I frantically withdrew my arm, some skin remained on the stove.

I left for America at sunrise, without seeking medical attention. I was later diagnosed with third-degree burns and wear the scar to this day.

My mind also wanders back to inconveniences and hassles that fatigue made seem stressful, such as the time my flight was canceled and I was forced by circumstance to stay at a hotel where twenty guests shared one bathroom.

And yet the more I reminisce about the perils of my past travels, the more I want to continue them.

Why, in light of all the troubles I've related here?

I know what it feels like to go hungry. And of all my unpleasant life experiences, I dislike this most of all.

No matter how pronounced my weariness, one of my most consistently taxing ordeals is to go without food. Hurrying from one flight to another; arriving at hotels where the kitchens are closed for the night; an airline's running out of prepared meals on my flight—all of these are reasons I've gone for hours, passing through time zone after time zone, without having a bite to eat.

My good fortune is that, at some point in each journey, food always becomes available. Among the people I minister to, a satisfying meal—or even essential nourishment—is *never* guaranteed.

Most never leave their tiny spot on this earth during their entire lifetimes. They don't know there's a big world out here. And even if they did, their existence is so primitive they'd be hard-pressed to take advantage of opportunities to improve their standard of living. They would never know where they're going to get the next meal were it not for Feed The Children.

I've seen their hunger. They're forced to feel it.

I often postpone sleep in order to accomplish various things. They often go without it as the throbbing pain of hunger keeps them from getting any rest. Many never fall asleep. They simply pass out.

People sometimes ask why we at FTC don't entrust food distribution to overseas workers. I don't know why they presume we don't. In this book I've shown that we do. We do often travel ourselves to check up on how things are going and to help those who want to eventually produce their own food supply. We prime the pumps of ongoing nutrition.

Sometimes my mind races to places I've been and will likely never go to again, unless there's another disaster such as the 2004 Asian tsunami that took me to Gano, a tiny fishing community outside Banda Aceh. Most of its fishermen were out to sea when the tsunami hit. They were never seen again. Women and children were left to restore their village. When the FTC team arrived, the survivors were living under tarps propped up by driftwood. We gave them ten tons of rice, but they wanted something else: two fishing boats.

They claimed that if we would furnish these boats, they could catch and sell enough fish to buy two more in a month. Admiring their spirit, I authorized the purchase of two craft. Within three months, these women in a village of eight hundred had bought four more. They carried on their lives with great determination.

Sometime during 2007 or early 2008, I have plans to take Feed The Children into Darfur, arguably the most beleaguered part of Africa. Other charities have been there and have done remarkable things to address the desperate situation. Those benevolent organizations and the people they serve will welcome the support of FTC.

We also intend to keep expanding the television outreach, seen now in all fifty states. This book you're now reading is my eleventh, the most comprehensive digest of my life and ministry so far. And I intend to write more books. In fact, I plan to expand my ministry across multiple channels.

Whenever I get on a roll of recalling the people and places that are the fabric of my life, I invariably return to whatever may be my most recent undertaking. As of this writing, that would be our trip into Dandora. We fed the people, promised to return, and made arrangements to continue providing food and medicine in our absence.

I held a gaunt, seriously malnourished child in my arms on that first day after my treacherous climb up the path into Dandora. As I fed the emaciated little girl, her dull, sunken eyes somehow sparkled as she swallowed the first tiny bite. She sat on my lap that ached from my climb and moistened my legs with urination. The excitement of receiving food was simply too much for her to contain. She didn't understand English, so I was unable to tell her I'd come to help. But I didn't have to. Food speaks very clearly and eloquently in the silent language of love and gratitude that starving people share the world over.

Arising to leave, I looked around at the tiny faces. A few children sensed my imminent departure and began to cry. A translator assured them everything would be fine.

Their forlorn faces made me grateful that I'd negotiated the twisting path to Dandora. Once again, I was glad I'd kept walking, and glad that I always will along the unforgiving path of the world's desperately deprived. My associates and I will continue to attend their sicknesses, clothe their nakedness, and shelter them from merciless elements. But first, we'll feed them.

Then we'll press forward, motivated by legions of children who are pitiably waiting for someone from somewhere to feed them, one child at a time.

As long as they wait for me, I'll get to them, no matter how the land falls and even if I have to walk.

FEED THE
CHILDREN

®

Dear Reader,

I trust that reading this book has encouraged you to join us in ending one of the biggest problems facing mankind today . . . childhood hunger.

Feed The Children began by asking the simple question "Why should children be starving to death while we have surplus wheat in America?" Feed The Children has reached out and helped children and families in 118 countries and all 50 states.

You can help us write the next chapter of Feed The Children's story by sending a donation or by volunteering.

In addition to medical services, Feed The Children annually provides millions of pounds of food, medicine, medical equipment, educational books, clothing, shoes, and many other needed items to children who live in extreme poverty. We have a fleet of 55-plus semitrucks ready to pick up the above items and ship them all over the world to children in need.

When disaster strikes, we hope you'll join us as we help provide needed supplies such as:

- Ready-to-eat foods
- Baby items
- Personal hygiene items
- Nonprescription drugs
- Cleaning supplies

If you can donate your time, please consider volunteering for one of the many programs Feed The Children provides:

- The **Frances Jones Abandoned Baby Center (ABC)** is located in Dagoretti, just outside of Nairobi, Kenya, and offers a medical center, playrooms, and care cottages to help babies recover, grow, and thrive.
- **Builders for Children** is a unique program designed to provide hands-on opportunities for people to use their gifts and talents in short-term construction projects in developing nations.
- The **Medical Missions Team** travels to third world and developing countries to provide hands-on medical care to people who would otherwise have no hope of receiving medical treatment.

Your tax-deductible donations may be sent to:

Feed The Children
P.O. Box 78
Oklahoma City, OK 73101-0036

Or you may call our main office at (800) 627-4556. Our office hours are Monday through Friday, 8 a.m.–5 p.m. (CST).

For more information about our programs, visit out Web site at www.feedthechildren.org.

Our e-mail address is ftc@feedthechildren.org.

All royalties from this book go to support the work of Feed The Children.

For the children,

Larry Jones